Alternative Education
for Parents and Teachers

LARRY A. MILLER, M.ED.

Copyright © 2013 Larry Miller, M.Ed.

All rights reserved.

ISBN: 978-1492215226

DEDICATION

I dedicate this book to my Mother, Judith Ann Miller, and my brother, Jonathan Marc Miller. They should both rest in peace, and I hope they both have an Aliyah (elevation), in Heaven, from whatever merit this book may bring. They have both been tremendous inspirations to me as a person and a writer. I always say I wouldn't be half the person I was if it wasn't for my twin brother Jon, and I wouldn't even exist if it wasn't for my Mom. So I would have been a "negative" person if it wasn't for them. They have been the spark and motivation for me to be the person I am. Thank you!

CONTENTS

	Acknowledgments	vi
	Preface	vii
	Introduction	x
1	Offer Choices, Alternatives; Be Flexible	1
2	Use Whatever You Can	10
3	Use Rewards and Consequences	19
4	Be Positive	27
5	It Is Acceptable to Make Mistakes	37
6	Persist	42
7	Prepare for the Worst; Expect the Best	56
8	Structure It	81
9	Be Cool	126
10	Use The Shell; Act Well	133
11	Keep It Fresh	146
12	Be Bold; Be Brave	158
13	Use Humor When Possible	191
14	Be Firm; Draw Boundaries	196
15	Speak Simply	211
16	Model	216
17	Be Patient	225
18	Choose Your Battles	228
19	Use Projects and Journals	232
20	Sharpen Your Senses	267
	Appendices A-I	273

LARRY A. MILLER

ACKNOWLEDGMENTS

I would like to thank my father, Marvin Miller, who edited this book. He is a pillar of love, inspiration, motivation, and determination. He built the foundation for our home which allowed me to explore, learn, and grow.

I would like to thank my brother, Alan Miller, who helped me keep the joy in learning and is a model of living the dream. His positivity, enthusiasm, and sense of humor are unparalleled. He is such an outstanding brother.

I would like to thank all of my family; they have been supportive, positive, and encouraging of me in the pursuit of truth, becoming a better educator, and publishing this book. Their assistance and care have been fantastic.

I would like to thank Rabbi Baruch Goodman, who I met at Rutgers in college and who reconnected me to my roots. He gives me inspiration, guidance, and help in navigating this world. His happiness is beautiful.

I would like to thank The Rebbe, of Sainted Memory, all of my Rabbis and teachers. They helped me become who I am, shaped and guided my mind and personality, and served as mentors and models. I am so grateful.

I would like to thank the principals, teachers, staff, schools, and boards with whom I worked. They guided me, trained me, and gave me an environment in which to learn, grow, and create. Of course a big thank you to the kids!

To my future wife, Rochel, I can't wait to marry you. I love you to no end!

Above all I thank G-d, who gave me the will and ability to write this book, and empowered me to reach the point of publishing it. I feel blessed, humble and grateful to be able to share this. Thank You for everything.

LARRY A. MILLER

PREFACE

The seeds for my beginning this book were planted in 2004: I was teaching a mainstream elementary class in Jefferson, Oregon, a small farm town an hour south of Portland. It was a grade six multi-subject class, and as I had my students write journals daily to start off the class, I thought I should write in a journal as well, to model this behavior. In my journal time, I would write several parts: I would "free write" random ideas or thoughts; I would write about activities or pertinent plans or thoughts for the day; and I would write down ideas, activities, and concepts that I was already using and which were successful, with the hope that one day, I could translate these writings into a book. It wasn't a realistic, concrete, focused plan of any sort at that point, but I knew that I was doing original things in my classroom and I knew that a lot of the things I was doing were working; I also knew that I wasn't going to remember them by the time I got around to writing the book, if ever, so I decided to write them down in order to be able to revisit them if I managed to get around to writing this alleged book.

The next phase of this project came in 2005, when I had moved to Coos Bay, Oregon, and was teaching in the Harding Learning Center, which is the alternative education building for the town. Again, I was doing all kinds of innovative things in the classroom, some of which I had learned some in my Master's Degree Education program at Rutgers. I modified some of these activities, lessons, and procedures, and added new ones, to the point that I was using different teaching strategies, and I thought they were worth encapsulating. I knew I had to write, but, at this point in my life, I was also at a personal crossroads. Besides my teaching career, I led a very interesting and exciting life as a deejay, for weddings, events, and sweet sixteen types of parties, as well as bars and rave-type situations.

In this same vein, I had always led an interesting life, and it had gotten more so when I arrived in Oregon in 1999. In fact, my life through that point had been pretty wild, exciting, and unbelievable; the way I thought of it was that I could not believe I was pulling it all off: I seemed to be taking such big risks and managing well. I thought this aspect of my life and experience was worthy of writing also, besides the education part. I had trouble deciding what to write about: on one hand, I sought to write a book based on my teaching experiences and practices, which I figured to be a relatively unique and interesting teaching experience, as the reader will soon learn. On the other hand, I wanted to write a novel about my wild and crazy experiences on the Oregon frontier, so to speak, and possibly pose it as fiction to avoid conviction! I even had the idea to write the book from both ends, possibly with the book turned upside down at the back, with one end describing the good teaching practices and methods I had learned, implemented, and created, and with the other end documenting the other side of my life that was going on while all of this exciting education was blossoming and taking place, which, in hindsight, would have done well to be in the upside down part of the book, since that's how the life was!

In the end, I realized that, even if it was a great seller, the fiction novel about my wild years really wouldn't have a positive impact on society as a whole. I shelved the idea and wrote the concept into a song with this part of my life entitled "Porch Stories", because they are stories which, G-d willing, I'll be sharing with my family and friends later on down the road. As my song says, "When it's time to retire I'll be rocking the porch, spending time singing rhymes with my kin on the porch: I know, porch stories, for sure." Now if this book sells, G-d willing, and if it makes sense and cents, I might be convinced to lay down those lines in a second book, which tells all the nitty-gritty that went on behind the scenes while I was learning to teach. In the meanwhile, my audience will have to settle with some educating on how to educate. This seems, to me, to be a better contribution to the world at large, and, while I have a good few years experiencing the most the world has to offer, I'm not so much into the wild craziness anymore; I've turned a different direction. Teaching is something that has been with me, and stayed with me, and something in which I have experience since I was fourteen years old. That was when I took a job at Rolling Hills Day Camp in Freehold, New Jersey, teaching children from three to twelve years old how to swim, (it was a lifeguard/swim instructor position). So by the time this book gets published, I might be able to say I have had over 25 years teaching experience. That's why this seems a better choice than the wild ride story, though that one might hold your attention a little bit more tightly!

That was back in 2005 when I really started writing, and by the time I left Oregon in 2008, I think I had 50 pages written. Now I have completed it, and finally got around to writing the introduction to this piece of work, and to tell my audience why I wrote it; why I think it's worth reading. Why is it worth reading, you ask? For starters, I have education experience at the bottom and the top, at the left and at the right, on the edge, and at the corners, and all around. When I started kindergarten I was pulled out for speech therapy because I couldn't say my "R's" or "L's"; look at the author's name: try to say it without saying those letters. By third grade, my twin brother, who should Rest in Peace, was in all the high classes and I was in the middle classes, and I wanted so badly to be in those high classes. By the time I was a junior or senior in high school, and I just kept chugging along, I had no idea that students were ranked against each other, until someone told me I was ranked really high. I found out I was second in a class of 350; I graduated salutatorian and gave a speech to thousands at our graduation.

As an educator, I taught in alternative education classes of 15-20 students where half of the students had special education requirements, (and I had only one aide in the classroom), and in alternative education classes where none of the students had special education needs; in classes where I taught all subjects, in classes where I taught one subject; I restructured an entire public alternative education academy (Destinations Academy); I taught in Oregon and New Jersey, in both public and private settings; I taught in a homogeneous farm town of 3000, a medium mixed town of 15,000, and in a suburb of Newark, New Jersey, with the most diverse population I have yet to see in a school; I taught in standard education classrooms (multi-subject self-contained), and in alternative education classrooms; I taught grades four through twelve with almost every mix of grades imaginable, and worked with and educated all the remaining grades in a host of settings. That experience includes one "middle school" alternative education class with students from grades five to ten in one little windowless room (the 300 pound, 6'5" tenth grader was in there because he had issues with the high school alternative classroom setup). In all those classes and settings these methods, strategies, activities, and ideas, worked and worked well, but not without tweaking. I don't like to toot my own horn, but maybe someone might ask whom I am to write such a book; and since you're reading this you probably bought the book, and I thank you for that; now you have something to tell your friends. Enjoy!

LARRY A. MILLER

INTRODUCTION

The goals of this book are multi-fold: to educate teachers and parents on how to improve teaching and parenting. I don't guarantee that you will need, use, or not recognize all methods; but I am pretty sure that everyone will find something in this book they can walk away with and apply in their own life, and I hope there are more bonuses than that. This is aimed at regular people, and is not meant to be an academic work. Therefore, my goals are not to add to the liturgy of writings on education in the collegiate environment, to be read and reviewed by academics the world over. I aim to give a practical guide with useful tips and information that can be easily utilized and applied to make a person a better teacher and a better parent; so I hope everyone finds something in this book that works for him or her.

Further, one of the primary goals of this work is to outline some of the more successful methods of alternative education I have found and applied. While this is not meant to be an academic treatise, as I mentioned, I am not at all opposed to academics finding these methods, ideas, and practices, and researching them further to test their efficacy and application. The further the knowledge can spread, the better, by whatever means do it faster. While my original goals were more in line with the intent of reaching academia, I now recognize that my real point in this book, and in education, and my main goal in life, is to make this world a better place, and I truly hope this work can be an aid to that end.

In that regard, I aim to share these methods with teachers in an attempt to integrate these practices into the mainstream classroom, as I have found that most of these methods and strategies, *differentiated* in their nature, (modified to differing ability students, each on their personal level), work very well in the mainstream, and any classroom for that matter, and tend to turn the most difficult students into leaders. Finally and possibly most importantly amongst my goals, I seek to build a good bridge between parents and teachers in an attempt to help parents understand the methods that teachers use to "parent" thirty students per classroom every class period; and for teachers to recognize the parenting they are doing. Since the book is aimed at parents and teachers, and will hopefully be read by teachers, it wouldn't seem condescending of teachers to encourage parents to read it, as opposed to telling a parent to read a book about parenting. That would be insulting even if true.

Parents might reply in defense of their positions to the previous paragraph by pointing out that parents have kids full time. They might say teachers get to go home from their kids at 3:00 PM, but many teachers have their own children at home; and the best teaching methods and practices work for parents as well as teachers. So there is no reason for parents not to have access to this wonderful bank of teaching tools and tricks that get teachers through those moments, those classes, and those days. The main point is that these methods that work in an alternative education classroom, with the most difficult students, and they happen to be successful across the board, with all kinds of students and children, and people in general, if you want to help them grow; the methods are universally successful.

The most common question I get when I tell people that I teach Alternative Education, is (as you can probably guess), "What is Alternative Education?" There are many answers, and there are many different types of Alternative Education, and varying definitions, the details and arguments of which I will leave to the academics to discuss. As I have learned in my varied experience as an Alternative Education Teacher, Alternative Education involves teaching, guiding, and leading students who have been removed from, or left, the mainstream, voluntarily or otherwise, for motivational, behavioral, academic, emotional, or social reasons. It can be for a temporary or permanent basis, and though there is often a higher concentration of special needs students, there need not be any at all. The term used these days for these types of students is "disaffected", which seems to imply they are not affected by education in the same manner as regular students, and includes a loss of motivation for learning in a standard classroom environment. As a result, they are moved or they move to an alternative setting, which is different from the regular and mainstream classroom in various ways which follow in brief.

To begin with, the setting of an alternative classroom is a smaller student to teacher ratio. I have never had more than 18 students in an alternative classroom, and I have had as few as one, and there is often a mix of age and grade groups within the same classroom. The population often changes throughout the year, and there is almost always much more flexibility, control, and autonomy for the teacher to differentiate instruction and find alternative ways to motivate students to learn. Of great importance to alternative education students is the bond they form with the teacher; it is much more of a parent-child relationship than in a standard classroom, as, often, many of the students come from broken homes or difficult home settings. They find it difficult to cope with the world and school, and manage more to do that through and with the teacher and the program; it supports them in a family-like way. We use all kinds of non-traditional methods for instruction that link education to the real world, so students see a purpose in education and can learn to like school, and they are able to relate the education to real life experiences in their own lives, and find meaning. That meaning fosters connection, and the connection is what brings them to enjoy learning and education, and that is the main goal of alternative education.

So how do we reach these students? It is having a solid and consistent, fair and balanced philosophy and approach that are most necessary in reaching them and connecting to them; it is having the flexibility to keep an open and clear mind so that you can be objective about what is taking place. It is about 220 pages and it won't even tell all. I included a Philosophy of Education at the end of this work, (Appendix A), which details my basic philosophy in this regard, if you want to know, academically where I'm coming from. One of the key concepts mentioned in this book is about being in control, and there's a lot to be in control of, but most importantly, it is about being able to control your emotions and the way you display them. There is not one clear answer to being a good or great teacher or parent. It is an ongoing process, and you should never rest on your laurels and think how great you are. If you know there is always room for improvement, you will find ways to improve, and your students and children will model this after you and improve themselves as well. You should always be checking, revising, and improving yourself and your setting; that will show you to be a good model to those you wish to influence. Modeling is the best method and it is the first one listed in my Philosophy of Education. Practice what you preach. There's no right or success in education with "do as I say, not as I do".

So grab a spoon and dig in, these are the goods on good and solid teaching.

LARRY A. MILLER

1
OFFER CHOICES, ALTERNATIVES; BE FLEXIBLE

In order to make choices a person must know what the choices are. To that end, the reader probably requires some background in what really goes on in this kind of education. One of the most essential principles for directing learning and connecting with children is choice. Nobody wants to feel cornered or forced into something, and people generally have more connection and involvement with an activity or a process if they get to make a choice about it; they have ownership and responsibility. The choice empowers them, which is important for our students. Let your students be choosers and let them be leaders; empower students, children, and people. That means a whole lot of tolerance and understanding, and mainly flexibility; and flexibility is often one of my answers in interviews when asked of my best qualities. You need to be flexible if you are going to offer choices. The old days, like it or not, of giving out one assignment to everyone and forcing students to do that one assignment, are gone, and we need to empower students to be decision makers and to handle responsibility and authority. Not that we should let them run the class unsupervised, and not to seem like I'm going against my own principle of establishing boundaries and being firm, but we need to give students the sense of control and power that they already are used to, for the most part, before they get into school. Without going into a grand discussion on the benefits and costs of technology, it is a reality, and students have more access to more information than ever in history, and we need to teach them to use that power well.

In Destinations Academy in Coos Bay, Oregon, I was constantly modifying assignments and work to fit student needs. In fact the flexibility and authority I had in assigning credits was unmatched by any other teaching job I ever had before then or since then. This was, on one hand, a bit overwhelming; on the other hand it really allowed me to get students to work in whatever way or method they excelled, with a variety of incentive and structured systems. I also had to find the right balance between direct instruction, and hand outs and assignments, because too much of either will have a negative effect on students. With our population, there is only so much instruction that they can handle in a week before they get overwhelmed, and the wrong amount of work given will result in its not getting done well, or not getting done at all. I also had to modify assignments and the way they were managed in terms of deadlines and structure. I found a nice combination that worked well, and assured fairness and balance. For some assignments, I said there was an absolute deadline of a specific date. This method worked best when we did a science unit, and especially when we started having science tests. The test was the final deadline for any of those science assignments to be turned in because, after the test, the unit was done, and for the next two or three weeks, we would be going into math units, (we rotated between math and science throughout the term, which was how students got credits in both subjects from one teacher). For science we used "Geo-kit units", which come from National Geographic, which have videos, transparencies, handouts, group activities, internet activities, extra credit work, research work, etc.: you could teach a whole term of science from one geo-kit).

Most of the time in this program, the pattern I used for collecting work and deadlines, was what developed partly based on the grading methodology of the program and partly based on the quality of student work. Destinations Academy did not give letter or number grades, only pass/fail. So in the first term I just put a check on my Excel grid, which was my online grade book, when students turned in assignments. At the beginning of the year, much of the work was of the same caliber, which was not exactly prize worthy. Towards the end of the term I started noticing differences in the quality of work turned in and so I began assigning number grades to the work handed in. In Destinations you needed 80% to pass, so the minimum number I gave was 80, if it was worth less than that, I returned the assignment to the student, and told them they had to correct it because it was incomplete.

One of the keys to notice, which is important with students, children, and anyone you are trying to help improve themselves, is this: Continue raising the bar. There is a fine line between the time to congratulate and the time to increase expectations. When you look at the starting point of what is acceptable from students or children who are not performing well, it may seem below standard, but you have to realize that is where they are at this moment, and that is their ability and skill level. You have to begin teaching them from that point, and gradually work upward. As long as you know and believe and see or imagine the goal in the distance, and realize what you are working towards and for, it is OK to start the bar low. If the bar is too high in the beginning or at any point, while some students have the persistence and determination to follow through and never give up, some students don't have that skill set, and will give up if you put the bar so high they cannot reach it. Work from their level upward.

As grades rose and grades started being given to assignments, the possibility for extra credit arose. Students were now able to earn more than the one credit of math and the one credit of science they had previously earned. The way to earn this extra credit was through solid work. The flip side of this process was that they had better motivation to get assignments in on time, because I started telling them that was the only way to get extra credit. Yes, as silly as it sounds, these students needed motivation to do things timely. The truth of the matter is that, occasionally students did turn in work that was so great, that despite its lateness, I still gave them extra credit. But I did not tell them this (I just gave them the credit in my grade book), and the amount of extra credit they earned was never what it would have been if the assignment had been handed in on time. This system worked well and fairly. There were assignments turned in that were done so well, that I gave them double value, and there were times I would allow students to get out of doing assignments based on work they had done that was done excellently. The "get out of assignment deal" was a favorite because everyone had something they did not want to do, and they relished their free pass time, and as much as I never wanted to let them out of an assignment, because all the work seemed important to me, I had to honor the system.

This has been probably been enough of grading for the parents reading this wondering how they will use this with their children. We assess because it lets the students know where they're at, and parents wouldn't do badly to use some light assessment system with their children, despite the fact that it is probably the most boring part of teaching, it could be the most exciting. It's just often confusing when you get close to the edge of a grade, when students are between two grades, how and where to round. No matter how clear your line is there is always a case right on the edge of it, and the clearer your line, the harder that case is to decide. But to get back to fascinating topic of testing… As far as I knew there had been no testing in Destinations when I got there; there often is not testing in alternative education in general; I had used it only later in the year in those classes, and in this case I instituted testing carefully. Most of school frightens these students, and people in general are afraid of tests, and since I spent most of my work gaining trust and helping to build confidence and self-esteem, testing needed to come later once students were comfortable learning and trying new things and being successful.

It wasn't until late second term that I even mentioned the word "test" and it had the consequences of minute hysteria and panic that I thought it would. I quelled the fear by promising students there was nothing they would lose from taking the test; if they didn't do well they could take it again and again until they did well, and that they could get extra credit and even get out of an assignment if they did very well. This was where choice and control came into play, and giving the students ownership and buy-in so they felt they had a realistic chance of success. Thus they accepted this on themselves and believed. We reviewed for the test carefully, (I tested science, but never tested math, which I tested by Math Jeopardy, which we did every Friday for a long time). The review consisted of our going over notes on the board and discussing the most important facts to learn; which facts would definitely be on the test; which had a good chance of being on the test, and so on. Students took the test and did surprisingly well; most passed; the few who didn't pass had rarely been to class, and only one had to retake it more than once. It was a long test, 50 questions, multiple choice and fill-in-the-blank.

The fun part of the test for me was writing the questions. Part of the review for the tests was an assignment where students had to write ten questions for the test, and if they wrote a bunch of open-ended questions, which are generally easier and faster to write, then that was what I was going to use on the actual test. They wrote some really great questions. The best part of this whole process was that we were able to have tests again after the first one, once we had initiated success, which is the most important part of education, if you want to repeat a pattern. Help the child succeed so they want to do it again, then raise and re-raise the bar. When we did take tests again, like everything else, I was able to raise the bar a little higher as to what was required and what was expected. It's important to have high expectations without a doubt, but most of these students have lost so much confidence, that they don't see themselves as being able to do anything, so they will give up at the first chance of failure. It is very important to build confidence and success continually on the way to raising expectations and raising the bar. That is how limits expand.

To give some contrast in different types of alternative education programs, in my last alternative education position before my current position with West Orange Board of Education, I was employed by a public school commission in Westfield, New Jersey, which is an umbrella organization with many programs under it. It has, for example, several alternative high schools, which are a tougher population than what I was used to in Oregon, especially since many of these students in the New Jersey program were on some kind of probation program or even incarcerated. The program that I was hired under, however, was the Nonpublic Services Program. The federal regulations governing that program guarantee that students with learning disabilities who attend private schools will receive assistance from the government. In the past, and at the school which I serviced, a Catholic high school, the separation between religion and state led to the placement of trailers at the sites of the schools where the classes would be held. Over the years as stringencies lessened, some teachers moved their classrooms into the buildings themselves and left their trailers behind, stranded on the cinder blocks they were propped up on, and held class in the school. Such was the case with me in my first year. That story is a little funny.

When I first stepped into my trailer which was my new classroom for this Westfield position in August of 2008, I got an empty feeling. It seemed so small and dark and blah. I couldn't see how somebody could teach a class in there. It was a trailer! After all, in my last position out in Oregon, when they moved me upstairs to Destinations Academy, I was given a triple classroom to share with another teacher, along with a meeting room that could hold forty people, and another classroom under our jurisdiction for the Teen Parent Program. Those classes were huge with tons of space for storage; all the jobs I had before that always had ample storage room and tons of student space, more or less. There was no way I was going to fit all my stuff in this little trailer and how could someone even work in a trailer? Not to mention the fact that the teacher before me piled 40 years' worth of outdated teaching supplies haphazardly into the little cabinets that were there leaving a worthy mess to be filtered and cleaned.

But I am flexible; after cleaning out and reorganizing that mess I started to get a liking for the place. I decided to actually filter through my own teaching stuff and bring in only relevant materials; I didn't have to leave too much in my basement at home, and I really started to enjoy working in my new little classroom down by the creek. There were two sides to my cozy trailer with a "wall" in between. There was a thermostat with air conditioner and heat and I could choose my temperature any time of the day. It was actually pretty sweet! Plus the previous teacher left her hot pot and cookie plate and tradition of serving cookies and cocoa, since students had to make the "long" trek out of the school to get to the trailer, and in the winter, in New Jersey, it gets pretty cold. I thought it a good idea to continue the tradition which made things extra sweet, figuratively and literally. After one of the first days of school, before I met any students, I had been in the school building talking to all kinds of people, and I remember stepping out, thinking, "I can't wait to get into the trailer." I mean, really, when you think about it, it's a teacher's dream: your own building, with no one inside except you and the students; no administration; and your boss a few miles away. I got to like it a lot! I would go into the school building for tea in the AM, check in at the office, and eat lunch in the staff room; the rest of the day in my world.

Now for the kids when I worked at this position: they were so sweet!! They rarely took a cookie until I insisted that they could take them, even though the cookies were sitting there right there in front of them. They had manners!! Sure most of the students had learning disabilities and some had issues; there were some with emotional problems. Amazingly the ones with the psychotic problems rarely acted up. I mean they acted up, but, not compared to what I was used to out in Oregon where I had some real troublemakers. Maybe these students in the Catholic school had learned from doctors or parents how to skim by. Or maybe they knew that if they messed up they would be pulled out of sweet private schools by their parents or by the school who didn't really need to take their money. It still amazed me to hear guidance counselors and administration talking about a student, saying, "This might not be the place for him if he doesn't shape up and that we might have to send him somewhere else". It is a foreign philosophy to me. I couldn't get over it; I was used to public schools who had to take anyone and everyone, and didn't have the luxury of choosing not to take or keep a student. I didn't really want to accept this philosophy of easily dismissing students, so I looked at this time as a temporary position with many other learning opportunities, where I was reacquainting with the New Jersey education system and more specifically with the special education system and honing my teaching skills.

So we took a slight detour from the main topic of the chapter which is choice, but background in education is essential, as much as can be given in a few pages at least. So one of the best ways to connect to these alternative education students is to empower them and give them ownership of the work in which they are involved. Students often leave the regular education system because they feel no connection to it; they feel the work is thrust upon them and they are to complete the tasks, much like an assembly line; however in the student's case, there is no relevant finished product or goal the student can foster an interest in. The argument can be made for the benefit of students' learning to task completion, as it relates to the working world where people are given jobs to do that may or may not have meaning. Some people need to strengthen the desire to learn in order to even be able to enter such a work world at a later point in life. For whatever reason these students never developed the desire to learn, or lost it somewhere along the way; and it is our job as educators to re-instill this desire, if we have any hope of these students becoming successful and productive members of society.

Destinations Academy provided a great example of student having many options to earn credits, which translates as having choices, options, and control, which was one of its greatest asset. Here is the breakdown of how students were able to earn seven credits by coming to Destinations, and staying on track to graduate timely. They got one credit in the morning meeting for journal writing, daily. They got one credit in my math class and one credit in my science class. They would get another credit in their English class, (and students in the Special Reading Program could earn two credits). That's four credits, plus another credit from a life skills class; one credit from watching CNN, answering a set of questions, and free reading for ten minutes; and finally one credit they would do on their own, (out of a textbook of their choice, answering the questions and chapter tests from that book), in the hour and a half they had every day after the afternoon meeting. Amazing as I saw it: it seems a simple formula, but it was not easy for students to attain. Students didn't always get the class credits with teachers' classes they took; in the beginning I was the only teacher who would give partial credit. In other words, if, by the end of the term, I had given out fifty math assignments, and a student only had twenty five, I would give them a half credit in math. The same applied for my science class. I did this actually to quarter credits as well, so that I could give students the most credit based on what they had earned.

The other two main teachers, however, preferred a more mainstream approach to grading, where it was either pass or fail, at least they employed this system in the beginning. I knew that these students needed more than just grades, they needed self-confidence, and to feel they could accomplish something, if we were going to get them back on track again. I also knew that this mainstream method would be a one-way ticket back to the failed Destinations of years past. There would come a certain point where students realized they could not get the credit for that term, and then what point would there be to their attendance in that class? And where would they go when they realized there was no purpose to being there? Also I believe that work completed should be rewarded, especially in an alternative education environment where students lack the basic skills to think long term, schedule, and plan. I knew there was no way the Academy could function well on an all-or-nothing pass/fail system.

Besides these choices and options, there were extra opportunities for students to earn various credits. Every day for the morning break, I took a group of students, (whoever wanted to go), for a stroll around the block; there wasn't too much ground we could cover in eight minutes, but it was better than being cooped up inside. They could earn a quarter of a credit per term for doing that. Once the program was solidly under way, students began to ask about having a gym class. I had nixed it based on its previously disorganized state from the previous year's Destinations program, but by that point in the year, they had proven themselves to me in their behavior, and I was ready to give gym an organized try. We actually started two gym activities. One was the afternoon gym three times a week. I took the boys, our trusty assistant took the girls. The boys generally played basketball and the girls did aerobics. At the end of the period we met up on the mats and closed out with a yoga class which I instructed; I was still the hippie.

On one of the three gym days in the week, we all got together and played some group game. One of the days we were playing kickball, which had been a favorite of all, present company not excluded: it is a game that everyone can play and generally feel good about. We were having a great game and both the assistant and I were playing, on opposing teams. When she was running around the bases, someone pegged her and she fell, and it was funny, and people started laughing. When I saw she wasn't getting up, I went over to her to check how she was. She had fallen wrong and was in pain. I told the students to stop playing, sort of take a knee, like they do in football, while we figured out her status. It was one of the lowest points of my teaching career, I think, when they kept playing other games, like throwing a basketball against the wall from a distance; it was hard to get them to stop while I was trying to take care of her. I was very upset that they would take someone's injury so lightly, and not care enough to stop playing for ten minutes. It turned out it was a serious injury, and she had torn her meniscus, and had to have surgery, and was on crutches for months. I canceled gym indefinitely. Students were very unhappy about this, to say the least, but I explained that if I couldn't count on them to take a break when someone was hurt, we couldn't play. They countered with the fact that I kept playing after she had fallen, but I pointed out that as soon as I realized she was hurt, I stopped running and playing and got serious. That was when I tried to get them to stop playing, and they hadn't gotten that point; sometimes you have to teach things the strong way when they don't get it the soft way.

The other gym activity we offered to keep the choices varied was the weightlifting class, which ultimately got sabotaged by a former student of mine, who at this point was attending CE2, another program in the Harding Learning Center where all these alternative programs for Coos Bay, Oregon were housed. Students had been asking me about getting weights for the building or going to the weight room, so I contacted Marshfield High School, which was the main high school in Coos Bay, went through the twisting channels to get access to their weight room, and finally permission slips and a key. Things were going pretty well with our weightlifting program. We had about five students who were coming regularly to lift weights and we went in the morning. When the CE2 students heard that we were going to the gym, they asked if one of their students could come along. This was a student I had previously who had been removed from my class the year before, when I taught AIMS/IPASS (to be explained later). He was removed because he was repeatedly harassing a girl there, who he'd been harassing since they were children. He had a little anger problem and one day, he got so angry at me that he yelled something very loud in the hallway that was right on the borderline of a threat. But his final stroke that got him booted from IPASS was beating the pulp out of a student outside of school to the point that the other child had to go to the hospital, and I understand that the beating was done in a way where other students were surrounding the two boys and not allowing the loser to exit the fight, forcing him to fight.

Now that I was in Destinations, and that boy was in CE2, we had been going to the high school gym for a couple of weeks, and that boy had come once. I don't know what made me allow him to come; I guess I hoped he had improved since going into CE2 and figured maybe he grew up. Go figure. The kids knew we went as a group and stayed as a group when on Marshfield grounds, and were on super tight behavior since we were guests at Marshfield High School. I wanted to make sure that our group behaved in an excellent manner. When we went there this particular day, the first doors we normally used were locked, so we needed to go around the side of the building. This boy kept knocking on the side door after we had left the original doors, and got a student to let him in to the building; he went in separately from us and for a little while, I did not know where he was, which did not sit with me well. When we found him I took all the students immediately back down to the Harding Learning Center and that was the end of weightlifting for that boy. We continued a few more times and then it petered out. It was good while it lasted, and I think it built some confidence in the boys; they earned credits too.

2
USE WHATEVER YOU CAN

Using whatever is available doesn't have to be an in-the-moment kind of situation or decision. You have to use whatever you can and whatever you have that motivates the children to do what you want them to do. For me, no matter how hard I try to hide who I am, my history and the like, students and children want to know all about their teacher; they want to know about your personal life and your non-teacher side. I remember clearly in high school asking our math teacher all about his side job as a bartender and being completely enthralled by the fact that he had another life outside of school, and it seems nothing has changed, other than the fact that students want to know at younger and younger ages about more and more. I was surprised that my fifth grade Hebrew School students, after some discussion about Torah (the Bible) that involved a married couple having children, wanted to know about whether I was married and whether I had a girlfriend or not. To this day, I am still curious and excited when I learn something new about my parents or grandparents. Just today I was fascinated and excited to find out from my father that my mother, (May she rest in peace), loved all kinds of seafood; I had no idea!

When I came into the middle school in Jefferson, Oregon, for my first year as a mainstream teacher, I don't remember how my principal found out that I wrote rap songs, but she did, and she asked me to write a rap song about a new program. We were instituting a recognition trip, which had three qualifications: students had to have no "C's" or below on their report cards; no unexcused absences; and no office referrals, (and only two citations, minor disciplines), in order to go on the recognition trip. I had never written an education song before, and at this point in my song writing career, I had two or three songs written at most, but I set out to the task. It came out pretty well, (Appendix E). I hope it's well received. On that note, when I performed, I was pretty nervous, about as nervous as I had ever been. They assembled the entire school, which was about 400 students, plus teachers, grades five to eight, to tell them about this program, and my performance was the main show. They put the words up on a giant screen, and they had the drum section of the band keeping a beat, while I had all of the students in the gym clap the beat to get them involved. When I finished, they went wild, and later in the day, students actually asked me to sign autographs, which I was happy to oblige. It's not easy to perform in front of middle school students; they are less reserved than anyone about giving their honest opinion on whether they like something or someone or not, regardless of any feelings that might be hurt in the process, and I was opening myself up here. But I used what I had available to me and it paid off!

Warning: get used to radical transitions while reading this book. It happens like that in the classroom and it happens in life. I remember 9/11 as clear as day. I was living in Corvallis, Oregon, and a friend of mine called me at 7:00 in the morning freaking out about us going to war and New York City being attacked and she was saying it was World War 3. The following year in school we had to teach a bit about that horror and I remember that the school had a moment of silence in recognition of the tragedy that had happened the year before. I realized while we were having that moment of silence, how quiet and peaceful it was, and how the kids seemed to really be relaxed, and I thought to myself, wondering why we only did this in recognition of tragedy or sadness, and that it would be a good idea to do it more regularly, as it seemed to be a good thing for the class and for people individually. I told the students about my lines of thinking, and made them a standing offer that if any of them wanted to have a moment of silence at any time, all they would have to do was give a certain sign, (we were using hand signs for all different needs at that point, like going to the bathroom, or getting a drink, etc.). We ended up using a few of those moments of silence every month; the kids liked them; I didn't even ask for them myself, and it turned out to be a great tool created literally from the ashes of tragedy. Use what you have and use what you can, and never stop innovating with the tools, skills and materials available.

When I first started teaching in Jefferson, Oregon, in 2000, I really had no idea what I was doing, even though I substitute taught a couple of times before then; that only gives some basic tools and tricks that may only work on a daily basis and not in the long run. I thought it very important to connect with the students when I started, and I was still in my old frame of mind where I wanted to connect to them in a cool way, and wanted to be the cool teacher. I wanted to be the exception to the rule of teachers who seemed above or distant from their classes; so I allowed the students to call me by my first name. I should have caught a hint at how excited they were to call me "Larry" when they first said it, but I thought it was a sign that I was doing things right, and it was proof of their excitement. I had a feeling shortly after that it might not have been the best choice, and then my boss, the supervisor of the program, told me it was probably a better idea if I had them call me "Mr. Miller"; I readily agreed. To this day, when students graduate high school, I allow them to call me "Larry", but none of them take advantage of it; they say it doesn't feel right; and I can relate, I will still always call my former teachers "Mr." and "Mrs." I tried a tool and applied it, used what was available which I thought would motivated students, and though it didn't work, I learned a lesson, applied it to my own learning, and moved on.

One of the things I tried at Jefferson was writing prompts. I assume it was something I learned in my education program but I'm not positive. I didn't want to use boring writing prompts, so I made some up, and then I used examples of stories that had happened in my life. Some of the earliest ones I remember were along the lines of "My favorite subject in school is…" I remember a nice student I had in that first year, a sixth grader, who was the only real injury I had in my classroom. He was playing outside during break and came in and had cut his knee to the bone, literally; nothing was broken, but there was a lot of blood. He was the nicest kid, and when I first tried to get him to write, he wouldn't write anything, he said he couldn't think of anything to write, and even when I gave him that prompt, he said he hated everything in school, so he couldn't write about it; but when I asked him, "OK, which subject do you hate the least?", he was finally able to put pen to paper and get some thoughts out. I used what was there.

The other prompts were a lot more interesting and came right out of my life. The kids knew I was a deejay, and at that time, when my school day went from 12:00 PM to 9:00 PM, I was able to deejay in bars at night. After working at one bar one night, when I got home, I noticed that my CD's were not there, and I got furious, and wasn't sure what to do. I couldn't go back to the bar and start accusing people of stealing my CD's, when I had no proof that anyone had taken them and no reason to suspect anyone. I just knew they had been in my car, and then they were gone. I turned it into an assignment: leaving out the fact that it was a bar, and just saying my CD's disappeared one night when I had been deejaying, I asked the students what they would do in a similar situation. I got some interesting answers and no one told me the assignment was boring, and we had some fun discussions about it. Back to one of the original points of this chapter, much as I tried to hide it, and others might do the same: it is important to open yourself up to students, and let them know a bit about you, since they want to know so much anyway, if it's what they want to know and it serves as motivation and connection, so be it! It all goes under the heading of using what's available. And back to the point of this paragraph, they got an extra kick out of these types of assignments for several reasons. They loved knowing about the deejay life, and this was before being a deejay broke into the mainstream as technology allows anyone to be a deejay; they liked knowing about my life; and they liked thinking about how they would react in a real life situation with real life choices. The ending of the story is that a week or two later, when I went into my trunk for something, guess what I found. It was not easy admitting to the students that mistake I had made, but I figured if I was going to lead them down the road of figuring out how to deal with someone who had wronged them, I should continue down the road with cleaning up the mess I made and admitting the personal mistake in blame when I found my CD's in my own trunk, and solved the mystery. I think they liked knowing it was OK to be wrong, though I'm still working on that myself.

In many of my classes, when I teach English at least, I like to start the day with a quote. Here is one of my favorites, "The fly sat upon the axle wheel of the chariot horse and said, 'Oh what a mighty dust I raise'", which is quoted by Aesop. When I do this activity, the quote is on the board beforehand, or the teacher/parent can write it up there for the student while the student is there; it might even be more exciting that way, the anticipation building. It is important to get a quote that is up to the level of the students so that the meaning is not terribly obvious: one which makes them think a bit, but hopefully one that at least someone will get, although one that is very obvious may just be so profound that it is alright to put up there once in a while. It should take them a little while to think of it and understand it and if a good quote is picked, only one or two students will get it, and it is the ultimate "Aha!" moment.

An alternative teacher has to vary everything, and be flexible with everything, and use a whole array of teaching tools, methods, and practices: traditional, non-traditional, technological, and primitive. Learning the Smart Board, which was something I wanted to learn for a while, proved to be very useful and I think that will be a fantastic tool for alternative education students and all students forever. It is dynamic, exciting, fun, and cool, and it keeps their attention. It is easy to get students involved with learning and actually have them show work and understanding in a fun, fast, interactive manner that keeps the class moving; it is limitless in its application. While it's important to use whatever you can, it is also important to recognize the limits and functions of the tools you have and use, and not to overuse them, as in the usefulness and limits of the smart-pen.

My smart-pen wasn't a true smart-pen, and when I was interviewed for the position where I got a smart-pen, I was told the class would have a smart-board, which doesn't really require the use of a special pen. A smart-board, for those who don't know, works like a giant touch screen, and the computer screen is projected onto the board, so that one can interact with it at the board like a regular computer; it's kind of like a giant touch screen pad. A regular smart-board has a few trays at the bottom: one for an eraser, and then a few for the different color pens. The pens and erasers, though, are really useless pieces of plastic: when you write with them, you're not really writing with the pen or eraser per se. The way the board works is that, when, for example, the red pen is lifted out of the tray, the sensor notes that it is gone, and the sensor indicates that the pressure on the board will write in red. So if you lose those pens, or just want to impress your students, you can write with your finger. And if you lose the pen, you can cover the sensor with a piece of paper. So the pens don't really matter at all.

My board, on the other hand, was a Promethean board, which operates with a $90 electronic pen which has electronics inside that activate the board, so the pen has some intelligence, in a manner of speaking. So when I lost the pen, I was out of luck; the board is then useless other than as a nice white movie screen. But I learned something when I lost the pen, because I had to write in chalk again, and it was in a class that liked to joke a lot. While I was writing on the board, one of the students was tuned out while I was teaching a concept. Later on he was looking at the chalk board and had an "aha" moment about something I had written ten minutes earlier, and pointed it out to the class, looking at the board, saying, "oh that's what that means on the board?" And I had an "aha" moment as well, because I realized that if I was using the Promethean board to teach that concept, that slide would have been long gone and that student would not have had the chance to see the concept the he had missed. I then realized I had to alter my teaching style a bit and become a little less reliant on the Promethean board. It was actually a bit of a relief because writing on the Promethean board I naturally write faster, and I rush more, and it's probably to students' benefit that I slow down a little bit. Therefore now I use both boards and try to determine which suits the learning best, and I think it has strengthened my teaching: using what I have, but knowing its limits.

My position in the Catholic High School was where I received my formal training in Smart Board. When the Commission I worked for during that time first offered training on Smart Board, and I knew I was getting a Smart Board in my classroom, I wondered how much they could teach about colored pens in two days of training. I figured at that point that a Smart

Board was nothing more than a glorified dry-erase board. Once I went to the training I realized just how much potential a Smart Board really had, and understood why there was so much training. It was actually difficult to understand how to use it at first, in that a lot of the program operated and looked different than the typical Microsoft and PC programs. Once I got the hang of it, though, like any new program or system, it was pretty smooth. The Smart Board really is a great tool for the 21st century student. Much as I want to, I won't say it is essential, because there are students and times, as I mentioned, for whom and when the Smart Board isn't the best tool; also, I believe anything can still be taught with minimal tools, by the right teacher.

Another interesting lesson resulted from the breaking of the Promethean pen, which actually happened a couple of times. At one point, the pen broke, and it took a couple weeks to get replaced, and somehow I ended up getting two pens. I locked one in my closet on which I have my own padlock, because I didn't want to be at the mercy of a pen if it broke or got lost by someone else using my class, especially if I was going to have an observation from an administrator in which the lesson was hanging on the pen, so to speak. Alas, my strategy was only successful to a degree; the strategy worked when the pen got misplaced, until one day. The after-school program used my class daily, and when I walked into class, and my Promethean Board had worked the day before, (without making obvious inferences or accusations), I went to use the Promethean Board in the morning and it suddenly didn't work.

I went through a whole song and dance, several times, with the tech people back and forth for weeks, months it turned into; the tech department thought it was the pen that didn't work, and they tried the pens on other boards so they knew the pen worked. I knew it was the board that was broken. The tech people finally took the board off the wall and cleaned it. I was pretty sure that wouldn't work, because I suspected that it happened from somebody throwing something at it, or bumping into it, or some physical action like that. Sure enough it still didn't work after they cleaned it. The good thing about it being broken was it forced me to be less reliant on it, and to use it as one of many tools instead of the only one. Some things are better written on the chalkboard, like I mentioned earlier, especially in alternative education. After my board broke, and I got a new one, I started using my favorite function of the board, the Smart Recorder, which allows the teacher to record the writing on the board for any amount of time. If, for example, I am demonstrating log equations, and I know that some students aren't going to get it the first time, or some students aren't there, etc., I can record the instructional component, even though it doesn't record voice, which is probably a good thing.

Another fundamental strategy of using whatever you can is the ability to think and act on the spot. A person must always be creative and use whatever is in the moment to enhance it, and make an opportunity out of whatever is available, and this is like the teachable moment, as the expression goes. A good example of this strategy was toward the end of this year. I had one student in geometry two years in a row; I think he was the only one that had to retake that class, and he was one of the toughest kids I had ever taught. The year before this, he was still literally growing into himself and I think that was a big part of the problem, I have experience with students like that, who feel bigger than they are, and, in reality, are going to grow into big boys, and maybe they sense they will be big. Don't trust this dime-store psychology though; I have no backing for it. I had a lot of struggles with this student every year, and I didn't know if he was going to make it. I found out midway through the year, when he was at his worst; that he had been allowed back into the program after being suspended from school and placed in the after-school program, as some kind of gift or test. It didn't stop him from failing though.

When he started that year, he was a different student altogether. He was calm and generally happy, and doing work. He was in a class of sophomores as a junior and I think he knew he would look like a chump if he tried me again, and so he sat in the back corner, and didn't cause too many problems. In fact, he was doing very well, and he got a B in the second term, with which I was very impressed. He was actually very smart, and one of the top in the class when he applied himself. A little over halfway through the year things started to change for him. My theory is that he realized he had enough credit to pass for the year, so he didn't have to try anymore. Whatever warning he had been given by administration in the beginning of the year started to wear off, and all of the sudden he was coming into class in the morning with headphones on, and singing loudly whatever song he was listening to, not editing himself if the lyrics were inappropriate. I started correcting him, and we had a few battles, with him being removed from the class. Eventually, I had to move his seat from the much coveted and highly cherished corner seat to the exact opposite corner, in the front of the class, close to my desk.

I didn't realize this would be slightly annoying to me too, but, at this point, I had to do what I had to do. I told him he was going to have to start tomorrow in the front seat and there was no discussion on the topic, and that was it. A few periods later, when I was teaching another class, this student came in, which was out of the ordinary for him. While we said "hello" in the hallways when we passed each other, and were on good social terms outside of the class, he had never been in to visit during another class. I said, "Hello," and asked him how it was going. After he had been there for a minute or two he asked me, (in front of the whole class), if he was really going to have to sit in the other seat. I told him he was going to have to because first of all, he just had to, and second of all, there was no way he could sit in the back without talking to the girl who was sitting in front of him, who was the only other junior in the class. He thought about it for a second or two, and said, "Alright, I'll sit in that seat, if I can touch your beard." Just as in my second year at the Catholic High School was the first time I wore a yarmulke in school, so the second year of my time at West Orange High School was the first time I let my beard fully grow, so that it was a couple of inches long. Now it was my turn to pause for a second or two, before replying, "OK". I guess he just wanted to see, and I was OK with that; in Chassidic thought, a beard is supposed to be a segulah (treasure); I never thought it would be a segulah for the peace and happiness for my students!

In seizing the moment, to make the most of what's available to you, and making learning moments out of opportunities, there are many opportunities to utilize all of the other strategies in this book to their best potential. In that respect using whatever you can, means using all of these strategies and whatever strategies you have on your own, and whatever new strategies, ideas, lessons, or activities you may think of at the moment. The art is to think of them on the spot and apply them right there, and that takes an experienced mind, full of information and ideas, and at the same time it takes a light and refreshed mind, ready to draw from those banks the best choice and response. And while I mention the advantage of waiting a few seconds before speaking, there are times when speaking instantly turns out to be the best method for dealing with a situation. It's hard to describe or teach how to think in the moment and make the best, cleverest, most instructional statements, remarks, or responses that affect people in a positive way and don't have a negative effect. There is however, one word, in the previous sentence, which, more than any other, should frame the state of mind of a teacher or parent at all times, and which, if so employed, will lead the teacher to speak, respond, or answer in the best of all fashions at all times, and I will pause mid sentence to allow you to search the last sentence to find that word……the word is………don't give up yet……..the word is……."positive", but that's another chapter!

Like I said, there is no recipe other than experience for coming up with quick witted replies and clever remarks and the best answers and questions to drive attention where you want it to go. Make sure to learn from past experiences. Some people are brilliant and some are born with the gift of gab and some people always know what to say at the right time and with the right inflection and tone, and some don't! I assure you, however, speaking from my own experience, as a person who, as I recall, didn't know the right thing to say in many situations, that experience and positive attitude greatly influence success here. Two other important qualities in this area that can help develop this skill are confidence and bravery. Confidence comes with practice and time. If you are confident students and children read that like a book, and thrive from it or attack it depending whether it's there or not. It allows you to be your best and allows your best qualities to shine through. It's not that you should be singing your praises or thinking how great you are or mulling over your best accomplishments in life. There should be a quiet surety that you can do the job, that you can succeed, that nothing will deter you, that you will make it through the day, that you can't be derailed by anyone, and that you are OK and chill, and that everything is alright, even in the most difficult situations. Bravery will be discussed in Chapter 12.

3
USE REWARDS AND CONSEQUENCES

As difficult as the following sounds, in reality, as a parent, and as a teacher, you have to have things you can take away, as well as things you can give and offer. Sometimes this can backfire, or not go the way you hoped, as in the case of the fight between a girl and a boy when I took away the free time I had given them, which I will discuss later, but it's best to start on a more positive note. The most illustrative case I offer in this arena, though, comes from one of my favorite TV shows, *Malcolm in the Middle*. For those who don't know, it's a show about a family of five boys, of whom Malcolm, a genius, is the middle-aged boy. The boys are always getting into trouble and mischief, and the worst of them, (discounting Frances, who is the oldest, and rarely on the show, as he has been shipped away to military school due to his horrible behavior), is Reese, who is older than Malcolm. After Reese does something terrible, and the parents are at a loss what to do, they enroll Reese in a cooking class to try something new and a new experience, and it turns out he excels tremendously in it. Though he is obviously by far the best student, (he loves the knives, blood, fire, etc.), he still wants to assure his victory in the cook-off, so he sabotages everyone else's dishes. When the parents find out, they are furious, and, in trying to punish him, they tell him there is to be no more cooking allowed for him. He seems unfazed, till they point out this includes baking, brazing, etc., at which he really gets upset and stomps upstairs. The parents finally find relief and poignantly note that since they can punish him, they are parents again. It sounds cruel when you put it that way, but every education and parenting book mentions reinforcements and punishments.

As I learned in my Master's of Education Program at Rutgers, according to B.F. Skinner's theories, there are basically four types of reinforcements and punishments. They fall under the categories of positive and negative reinforcements and punishments, and it's an important concept to understand and utilize. In a nutshell, reinforcement aims to make a behavior happen more; punishment aims to make a behavior happen less. Most people think in the most basic terms: you give a reward for good behavior, and punishment for a bad behavior. Put differently, for a behavior that you want repeated by the student/child, you want to reinforce that behavior. You want them to repeat that (good) behavior.

In order to reinforce that behavior, which is positive reinforcement, you have two main options. You can either add a positive, or remove a negative. For example, in one option, if I want my students to participate in Math Jeopardy, I can give a prize to the winner, random prizes during the game, or credit for participating, (or a newly discovered and highly prized motivator: extra-credit to the winner, which is a lot cheaper than buying prizes!). This is an example of a positive reinforcement because I'm adding something to encourage behavior, namely, a prize of some sort. To demonstrate the other option, it's not so easy to think of times I remove a negative in a classroom, because I don't like to have purposeful negatives in there. For ease's sake, in general, there is a rule that students cannot have out or use cell phones during class. If, during midterms and finals, students behave and, when they finish their tests, are respectful to others, I remove the "negative" rule of no cellphones, and allow them to text away.

If, on the other hand, I want my students to stop a certain behavior, my strategies for making the behavior stop fall under the broad category of punishment, which is really the opposite of reinforcement, since my goal is the end of the behavior. If I want my students to stop goofing around, (especially when they are acting poorly as an entire class), and they have passed the point of my warning them, and still won't listen or stop, the most surefire way to make that happen is to give a surprise quiz. If they're acting so wildly and freely, sans care, they're telling me they that they know the material, and don't need a teacher to learn it; therefore, let the quiz judge between their knowledge and lack thereof. This is called a positive punishment, since I am adding a punishment to their situation, though a positive punishment sounds like an oxymoron. Should a quiz be a consequence?

The fourth and final behavior shaping technique as outlined by Skinner is the negative punishment; this is an interesting concept, and the goal is still to make the behavior stop. This is what happened in Reese's (from the TV show) case discussed a few paragraphs earlier. The behavior they wanted to stop was for him not to sabotage other people's success. In order to accomplish this task, they took away something positive, namely, his cooking. The point illustrated by the show is an inherent fault of this system, in that eventually, you might find people who no longer seek any rewards, and feel no threat from any punishments, no benefit from rewards, and don't care whether a parent or teacher applies these stimuli to the situation. In that scenario, I would recommend meeting with a professional!

That said, here's a controversial start to a paragraph from an educator: people and animals learn in much the same way. Parents of some of my students would be offended by such a statement, because it is wrong to compare animals and humans, what with humans being so intelligent and all. Point of it is that positive praise works wonders. It requires a quick eye and quicker action and response. Praise the person when they are not doing anything wrong, especially at a time when they normally would. Dogs beg for food if they learn it works. Once they learn the behavior it is difficult to undo, but possible. My dog learned to beg from a guy who used to watch him when I went away, and he would feed him cooked steaks from the table! It took years to undo that habit. When you eat and the dog is not begging, praise him for being good, *right then while he's not doing anything bad.* Remember how hard it is to catch someone being good, and that might make it easier and more common a habit. It is one of the most important strategies of a good teacher or parent. Catch your students, children, pets, friends, and family doing good deeds or actions and let them know that you appreciate their actions and that they themselves are good; compliment them when you can!

While consequences are very useful, there is one little caveat to point out, and that is to not use someone's name in punishment and/or yelling. In other words, it's better to say sharply "Stop!" than to say sharply "Mike!" If you say a person's name sharply, or if you yell it, this teaches the person that his name (and hence he) is trouble or a bad thing. It will stifle self-confidence and can lead to a series of problems that will make your life and their lives much harder. It is a negative association situation, which you can research in detail if you like, or trust that it is not good to yell a name, unless imminent danger is in the way and you need to call a person's attention to get them out harm's way, G-d forbid.

Interestingly, I went to a continuing education seminar once in Oregon where the presenter was against using any kinds of rewards at all. He was determined to use stimulating, funny, and cute activities, which are great if you have a full toolkit of them. Of course, a weakness in his theory and a point of contention was the use of verbal rewards, and I think he was even against those, though not as strongly. He was a fantastic teacher but as I said, you have to be a superstar to have those kinds of ideas and inspiration and I'm writing this book for the average type of people like myself who may not be a wizard at comedy and wit.

Some of the reward methods I employed both in Oregon and New Jersey might be obviously recognizable. The 100 penny jar system is when you keep a jar somewhere in the class or the house, and you add a penny to the jar whenever students or children are handling their activities and behavior properly, (based on whatever criteria you establish and clarify to them). When the total reaches 100 pennies, they are granted a prize activity of their choice. You can never take a penny out of the jar, even if they put a cat in the microwave. The 100 penny jar pretty much worked in New Jersey well as it did in Oregon and, to my surprise the students never took the money from the jar! They always opted for the same choice here, and that was a party. A couple years ago they earned the right to have two parties. Every few weeks or so, someone would ask how many pennies were in the jar. If I said I didn't know they asked if they could count. I was very happy with the system. I need more jars.

Another method that had funny results was the tracking system. This is a system I devised on my own, which works from a spreadsheet. I have all the students' names listed in a column on the left, and the days of the week horizontally across the top. There are generally three categories, which I track them on: getting to class on time, being on task, and participating in discussions. Each day a student meets all the criteria, he gets his name entered into a drawing, which happens at the end of the week. If a student gets entries every day of the week, he gets a bonus entry. At the end of the week I draw from all the entries, and I might draw two to five names depending on the size of the class and the number of entrants. This method has differing results with different types of classes; it depends whether students prefer to work as a team or alone. This method works best for individual success and for parents with small families; the hundred penny jar works better for making a class function as a unit, or in a household with a larger family. A question with the tracking system is whether to post the chart publicly or not, and again, that will vary with the situation. I prefer having the chart public for those who are willing to have their names on it. Then they can see and recognize their progress. Most of the students like it, and get the hang of it. They enjoy the drawing part as well. The question still remains to me, of when to give the prizes. On one hand I want it to be connected closely in time to the success, which would make Friday the logical choice for the drawing. On the other hand, Monday would make more sense because it would get students to remember the whole process and would affect their week in a positive way. The other question is the selection of criteria for entry, just be sure to clarify for students and children.

The reward system that was the funniest bumble of the whole year came from out of nowhere. I reconnected with an old friend, Dwayne, my dad's former client, who owns a couple of hot urban clothing labels, "Dada" and

"Cezer". The gear is all ace and I recommend you pick some up; it's hot. He grew up in an urban setting in Baltimore and wanted to give back to the kids in school; he knew I was a teacher. He told me in the winter that he would be sending a box of shirts, and I would be getting a shipping confirmation soon. I made a mistake in that I was so excited, I told the kids about the imminent arrival of the shirts. Something got in the way on Dwayne's end, and it was months before the shirts came, which I think led to some problems and outbreaks in the classroom. It was a real life example of "don't count your chickens before they hatch".

The funny part is that when the shirts finally came, I had absolutely no desire to share them with any of the classes, because they had all become such jerks, which made my position awkward. On one hand I had an obligation to Dwayne to give the shirts out to students to fulfill his desire of giving back to the kids. On the other hand I had no students I wanted to give them to! I had a couple students that had always been great through and through, but there was no way to give it to them without the whole class knowing and getting them more up in arms with complaints, and I was not about to start obligating my students to secrecy. Then I even started getting nervous if this could cause me problems, because what is a teacher doing giving clothing to his students? I actually seriously considered giving them to my Hebrew school students, (who I taught twice a week for about 2 ½ hours), especially since the shirts, which were labeled XL and XXL, were kind of small. The XL just fit me right and I'm only 5'7 on a good day; which also meant I really couldn't give the shirts to some of my bigger students. In the end I waited it out till one of the classes who had come around to being good, asked what had happened with the shirts, and I told them they were in.

I think the most fun giveaway for the shirts was with that class: I came up with a pretty creative, exciting idea. We were studying probability and I had the students trying to design their own probability games of chance. The hard part about that was that the games the students designed were more based on skill than chance. A true game of chance involves no skill. For example, some of the students, in using the limited materials I allowed them to use, (11 plastic cubes, a piece of paper, and a pen), created games involving flicking a folded up paper football through a field goal: great game, but not a game of chance; just a game of skill. The student who sought after the shirt the most, and who was one of my toughest students, (who I hoped would win a shirt), designed the winning game. See, the contest was really a contest within a contest. I divided the students into teams of three or four, (randomly), and then set them to creating the most exciting game of chance. The students would then all vote on the game they thought was the best. I had a specific voting method to bypass their tendency to only vote for themselves. I gave them scoring sheets and they had to assign a 5, 4, 3, 2, and 1 to all five teams, and the team with the highest score would win. Then, the team that won would play their own game, and the winner of that game won a shirt: pretty cool, right? The only effect on the process I had, was that they wanted me to vote, and I did, and I think I voted for the team that won and might have affected the scoring that way, but they asked for it! I was very happy with that situation and have done it again every year for my seniors with nice results; this past year they came up with some really fun games that could sell! Hopefully I didn't break any school rules on gambling in the process. It is a real question about doing drawings like the one mentioned, and like these games. That's because on one hand, we should give rewards to hard working students for their hard work, like the normal way of rewarding students we have always done; on the other hand, we should do it randomly as well, to keep them working not just for the reward, and to give everyone a fair chance to get rewarded for their efforts and work, even if they're not the best. This system seems to accomplish all of the above in a functional, educational manner.

The best part of this whole thing was that toward the end of the year, I was having trouble getting a single thank you note from any of the students for these shirts that Dwayne so kindly donated. I could have written a note myself but I would have been embarrassed on behalf of my students, their generation, and my school: not a single student who had received a shirt was willing to write a note. In the beginning of the year the standards for getting a shirt were pretty high; by the end of the year, when I was trying to get a thank you note, all a student had to do to get a shirt was write a thank you note, and not one of them would do it! In the end I finally got a note from one of my best students who I don't even think took a shirt! It happened to be a very cool note that I finally sent to Dwayne a few days later; it was so cool because it was micrography inside of the word "Thank you" written in bubble like letters; within those words she wrote the letter explaining what we had done that year. Micrography is a very cool art, which I have done with my Hebrew School students, which maybe I can figure out a way to do within math. Math Micrography might be the first original idea born, so to speak, of this book; maybe I could do it with numbers. For the record, there might be a couple shirts in the bottom of the closet in class.

Rewards and consequences are not only effective with those you teach and raise. In order to become better at using these skills with children and students, it is helpful to apply them to yourself. Some of those reading this work may be perfect, and require no improvement. If so I commend you. If you want to get yourself to do something, then reward yourself after you do it. The way to do it is to get yourself to act, and then give yourself whatever appropriate positive reward you desire at the end of or even during the activity to keep you repeating that desired behavior. For me, right now, in getting myself to write and edit this book, that reward is more tea, and I think that's all I need; at another time the reward for me might be going out for pizza. Maybe I'll even decide to read something I really like; on other days I'd play guitar or maybe Nintendo Wii to reward myself. Whatever it is, reward yourself and then the next time, I'm sure you won't even need the reward or it will be less necessary.

In my case, in my original writing of this novel, as I am writing it, I only need another page from the beginning of this paragraph to meet my goal of six pages, which usually takes about two hours, (which I have not done at one "sitting" this summer), and by the time I get to the six pages, the tea may not even be ready yet! But that is fine: the point is I made the tea to encourage myself and knowing the reward is there was enough to keep me easily going, so that it wasn't a struggle, and it is enjoyable. For clarification, we're talking about a whole pot of tea here. On a normal day after I do my morning routine, when I first check my emails, I make a pot of tea, and that's all the caffeine I have all day, which is a good amount. When I started writing this today, I made a second pot of tea, and now I'm considering making a third. I am determined to get to six pages. Once I do it once, to use some funny grammar, I know I can do it again, and it will most definitely be easier, faster, and more fun. Believe it.

I remembered an idea that is useful for parents especially and obviously used by teachers in varying form. This was based on a request by my cousin, who I was impressed decided to ask me for help, to help him in "fixing" some problems his son was having. At that time his son was about five, and was being nasty and picking on his sister and generally not being a good boy. My cousin said he had tried everything he could think of, and nothing was working. Knowing that I was in education he turned to me for advice on any methods he might use to help guide his son in a more positive direction. I was quite honored by the request. I thought about it and told him he should set up a reward system, which included a chart that his son could look at, and see his progress. It was loosely based on the 100-penny jar system mentioned earlier; elementary teachers use these systems all the time, but parents may not be aware of them; I therefore figured to bring this across for those who may not know. I said that every time the boy does something good, he gets a sticker on the chart, and that when he reaches a certain number of stickers, he can get a prize of his choice, and when he gets to bigger markers, like a hundred stickers, perhaps they take him on a trip or do something extra special. There are many ways of varying this reward method but it works. Too often we are focused on the negative and as I wrote earlier, we have to get busy catching children doing the right thing and reinforcing positively that behavior. The important thing about this method which I told my cousin is that once a sticker goes up, it cannot be removed. In other words, a good deed is done and cannot be undone. He used the method and never told me about its success; but I checked in on him from time to time and his son was doing very well, and is now a very positive, friendly boy who tolerates his sister well; he's actually super cool!

4
BE POSITIVE

In a nutshell, this means to redirect negative energy; see the best in people; give the benefit of the doubt. There are times when I think you can be too positive, but there are not too many of those times, and it's almost impossible to be too positive when dealing with education. This concept includes being optimistic and seeing the bright side; the cup is never half empty; it's always half full; or else figure out where to get more liquid to fill it to the top. Highlight the situation for its positives, and I think the best way I can illustrate how positive you can be, is to tell the one case, in my education career, and in my entire life, I might say, where I feel like I may have been too positive, and possibly too tolerant.

Once upon a time I had a group of students in my alternative education; they were cool and alternative; it was my first full time teaching job. After doing well in that position for two years, I was invited to teach a mainstream classroom in the middle school, in a grade five/six split class. One part of that plan included taking some of my alternative students with me into that classroom. One of the students was one of the nicest kids I came across, though he had a bit of a streak in him for getting in trouble; but it was really always to make people laugh. He was very determined and persistent, and there wasn't much logic or talk that could sway him from his path of doing what he wanted to do. He was also charming; he was magnetic for people, they just wanted to be around him. I recall once when someone brought a puppy into that classroom, the puppy went directly to that boy, out of all the kids in the class, and I didn't think that surprising at all; I guess I would have been surprised if he went anywhere else.

One day, we were in the library, and we were doing presentations on various countries, and I think someone had done a presentation on Germany, and this boy came up to me at the end of the period, and seemed kind of nervous, which was very out of character for him. He said, "Mr. Miller, I have to tell you something: I'm related to someone who's bad." I told him to tell me whatever he had to tell me and not worry and he said, "I'm related to that Adolph person." I was kind of floored and I honestly don't remember if he said he was a descendant of his, or he was his great grandfather, but I wanted to respond quickly. I could tell the nervousness in him; I think he felt that he had those same bad genes in him, and that he was going to be a bad person like his ancestor. So this is where I might have overdone the brighter side, when I told him that his ancestor "Was just…. Very…. confused."

I'm sure there are better answers but, in that moment, a child's health and sanity seemed the most important thing. I can't say what I should have done in the situation to make it better, though I now have a few more ideas; I would like to think that was the best way to respond way I could respond at the time; but I can't really fault myself for being too positive. I believe that to be the lesson: on one hand, there is a limit to being tolerant, and how tolerant a teacher or parent can and should be; being too tolerant can backfire and make students or children think you have easy boundaries to cross. There are not too many instances, though, where I can say a person was too positive, or too optimistic; it seems a quality that has no limits, which I guess is really what true optimism is all about. So use it, be it, see it in the best light, let it flow, and let the positivity and optimism spill over from you!

Being positive is not easy to persuade or define. It's a learned habit, and it's always a struggle. I write quotes on a paper and hang it on my wall with easy reminders for times I might forget how to be optimistic in the easiest way. When I graduated high school I was ranked second out of a class of 400 and as a result I spoke to an audience of thousands. I wrote a speech entirely in poetic verse, and came up with some interesting quotes from various sources. One of my favorite quotes puts positive thinking in a simple frame, and I am not sure where I got it, so if someone knows, they are welcome to connect to me and I will be happy to credit the appropriate source. "If life gives you peanuts, make peanut butter; if life gives you grapes, make jelly; if life gives you peanut butter and jelly, make a sandwich."

Every person who is bold enough to become a teacher is going to have to use everything in his or her history and experience to succeed in the class, and more than anything, he or she will need to stay positive about whoever he or she is. It will need to become part of the personality if they really want to improve students and children. Students will want to learn about their teacher and bring these things out of him or her, so it is useful for a teacher to be aware of his or her history and how it has shaped and affected him or her as a person and a teacher, and how it affected him or her as a student. The way they were as students probably has a lot to do with the way they view their own students and what they will and will not expect of them in their actions, thoughts, and words. Yes, we have the ability to expect certain thoughts of our students. If we can control our thoughts, and work hard to do so, they can too. Better thoughts lead to better words and better words lead to better actions and those are the facts of life; start with the thoughts and the words and actions will follow. Not to worry that we are going probing people's thoughts, just to know that we can have an expectation of clear, peaceful, honest, and pure thoughts. It can be done, even if it is not easy, and it will lead to a great attitude; give it a shot.

I used my teaching tricks extensively in becoming Orthodox in the Jewish religion; I especially used rewards and consequence. In exploring Orthodoxy, I wanted to know if these people who were so strict and observant were truly happy. The person who connected me in this vein was Rabbi Goodman from Chabad of Rutgers. I have always been a very happy and optimistic person, and when I went to his Friday night services during my early college years around 1995, I noticed him beaming, glowing, and exuding joy, and I was curious, because he seemed at least as happy as I was, and maybe more. This was combined with the fact that I knew some orthodox people growing up and I wondered how they could be happy with what looked from the outside like so many constraints, restrictions, and rules. I wondered if indeed they were indeed happy. I have always had a certain excitement about being a positive person, and these people seemed to have a genuine truth about their positivity that I was very curious to explore and research.

In trying to determine if Orthodox Jews were really happy, I realized that the only way to answer that question was to become one. Anyone can tell you they are happy but only the person himself knows the truth to the answer of that question. Now in becoming observant, (orthodox), there were other reasons and motivations as well, and those are the storyline of another book I'm not sure I will ever publish, the title of which would most likely be *Porch Stories*. The point is, I really wanted this observance to stick, and so I used my teaching tricks and methods on myself in taking on this observance, because contrary to what people might think, it's not an overnight process. Even if a person decided he wanted to be fully observant, there are a whole bunch of things he needs to both learn and integrate into his life, and it's not all that easy. At times it can be frustrating. I won't go into all the details of it to stray too far from the point of this book, except to write that besides rewards, I used such methods as scaffolding. I would integrate small practices at a time, in a pleasant and enjoyable fashion, so as not to overwhelm myself, and when I became comfortable with a practice, I would add a new habit, activity, custom, etcetera at an appropriate, slow pace. I would regularly reexamine the practices and new teachings I had taken on. This made the process fun, and made me enjoy the process and the practice, so the whole experience was a positive one, and I wanted to make sure that, no matter what, I didn't rattle my optimistic attitude, which I didn't. Fortunately it worked!

The same method is the one to use with alternative education students who are rebelling against authority, or hate learning, or don't want to be in school. When those students' walls are up, learning is not going to take place, so the first thing to do is get them to enjoy being in school, to enjoy being in the class, or at least, not to hate being there. The goal is to make them happy and positive about the experience of learning, which might be difficult for some people to relate to. My own parents made me work hard and I never hated school, so it was a little tricky for me at times to relate to some of these students. I could relate to training change, though. That's what alternative education and good parenting is about: if you can keep your children with a good attitude about learning and education, a lot of other things will naturally fall into place. You can start to build success by little steps. Impress on them the desire to learn and pass on information so they get into the learning mode. It may have to be done slowly, and more than anything, it requires great patience on the part of the parent or teacher.

Building this positivity and attitude is greatly affected by the relationship and bond between student and teacher, and it is pivotal for the success of the student. It takes a special understanding of these types of kids to connect with them, and especially the realization that before academic success, or more aptly, above academic success, rests the importance of this relationship. As I mentioned regularly in interviews for alternative teacher positions, the difference between success in alternative education and regular education is this: more often, in alternative education, when you succeed with a student, it's not only in their getting smarter or better grades; it's more like they are learning how to live, be happy, and be productive people. To help make a change like that in someone's life is quite amazing and fulfilling, and drives a person to keep coming back for more. Having that focus of goal above all else allows the alternative education teacher, or requires the alternative education teacher, to have a different set of perceptions, ideals, and attitudes towards his students, because he is really looking at academic education within a much broader picture than a standard teacher. Not to say that regular teachers don't consider other life factors of their students when teaching or on a day to day basis; it's just that alternative education teachers are really required to do this sort of evaluation and application more frequently and intensely, with more profound results based on more pressing and immediate needs. It's more often a matter of immediate attention, and the results are generally more significant.

The following incident shows a good comparison of what a difference an attitude can make. In the middle of the year, one of my seniors from my first class at West Orange High School, (which was a very difficult class), came up to me at the end of class. In his general conversations with me throughout the year, I did not get the sense that he was being real to me much of the time; he seemed to operate out of fear and worry. While he was a quiet hard-working student for the first half of the year, he became a little difficult during the middle of the year, and I got the feeling that he was trying to butter me up when he was being good. In general during the middle of the year, he seemingly became friends with some of the tougher kids in the class, and tried to act a little tougher than he really was, but he was still the same kid. One day he came up to me at the end of class and asked me if my dad would be able to introduce him to the accounting world, which is my father's career. He used the words, "take me under his wing", which was very open of him. It was hard to figure out the right response.

I told the students about what my dad did at some point earlier in the year, and as it turns out this student wanted to become an accountant. He told me this fact, and he was asking me to connect him to my dad, which would not have been so unbelievable, if it wasn't for one fact. That class had been together for a long time, and had another teacher together in the program for two years before I got there. The class was super tight and had that going for them in that they operated as a team, and they all really had each other's' backs, especially when it came to being against the teacher; there had been a couple of revolutions in the class, or mutinies might be a better word, which were the most powerful united fronts I came across in my career. While this boy wasn't leading these mutinies, he certainly wasn't staying out of those revolutions. The class had a couple of really bad days, and there were times where he joined the argument against me, which is fine, but it takes a lot of perfection as far as I'm concerned to ask me for a personal family favor like that. So I told him the truth, that he had slipped some, and that his grades had slipped somewhat, and that if he wanted that kind of connection, in which I would be recommending him to my father, he had to be perfect. In that respect, there is no room for errors and I certainly won't have a former student causing any kind of problems for my father.

So if he wanted this kind of recommendation and connection he was going to have to shape up to perfection and demonstrate that he was amazing, and then check back with me. I kept a special watch on him to that end, and if he had become amazing I would have made that recommendation, but I didn't have too much faith in it, based on the way he asked me the question, and based on his experience; it seemed he wanted the connection for the wrong reasons, and didn't really want it enough. I didn't know if he had the will and stamina to follow through on commitments and that was the reason I was wary to recommend him. As it turned out I was right, not that I let my assumptions get in the way. He still showed up late to class, still had troublesome days, and non-productive days, which doesn't fly serving the garment district: to get a recommendation from me to New York City, he had to be amazing.

Then again, I had a student who all year was just fantastic: one of the most, if not the most, positive students, (and positive people), I have ever come across in my entire life. I don't think she was ever negative all year, except when this boy said something to her, and she said something back to him, and both remarks were smart remarks, and neither was negative, and they were both funny. This girl was so positive and enthusiastic, that she was beaming and glowing every day. She was an absolute joy to have as a student and I hope to have more students like her in the future. She would come into class every day, with an excited greeting of "Hi Mr. Miller!!" She was so happy, and you could tell she was making an extra effort to be happy and positive. That's how she was all year, and she always did her work and homework, and if she was absent she made sure to make it up, and if she didn't do well on a test she did whatever she could and had to do in order to get the grade up. She was dedicated and hard worker.

Towards the end of the year she asked me about the possibility of connecting with my dad, as she wanted to go into accounting, (which she had told me about during the year). I checked with my dad, told him about her outstanding qualities, persistence, hard work, and positive attitude, and asked him if it would be alright to give her his work email, which he was happy to oblige. I told him I wanted to make sure that she succeeded, as she was such a positive person, and she had the right ideals and habits, and that I knew she would be a great model in the business world. I didn't want her having any unnecessary obstacles getting in her way, and if there was any way we could help that process along, I thought we should. A positive attitude makes a big difference. Someone who wants to question me about my decision with the first student should know the following: If I'm going to be able to use this avenue again in the future, in terms of my dad as a connection and recommendation, the connection has to succeed from the first student. So while it is tempting to be so merciful and let the boy connect with my father, in reality, if he messed up, (which in my estimation he was likely to do), he was messing it up for all future students who might benefit from that connection; that was not a chance I was willing to take. These are tough decisions a teacher makes regularly; but we must try to have the biggest ethics in mind.

Being positive is often about making the best of the various situations we find ourselves in. This is a skill that really can only be taught to students and children by modeling. It therefore also links closely with the "Be in control" chapter. If you really believe everything happens for a reason, and for the right reason, then you should be positive about all that happens to you. Nevertheless, it's important not to let surprises or seemingly negative events get you down, and to make the best of the situation, as difficult as that may be. I think the beginning of my career as a teacher and my embarking on a career as a professional teacher illustrates these points pretty well. I worked in teaching children since I was at oldest sixteen, at which point technically I was a child myself. Regardless, I taught swimming lessons as a lifeguard in Rolling Hills Day Camp in Freehold, NJ, and did that for five years. I really enjoyed it, and never knew whether my enjoyment was the more from the weather and swimming, or from the teaching, (or the girl-chasing). However, I learned a tough lesson about reality after graduating college and then working in Starbucks for a year and a half. This was not the glorious career I expected as a youngster. While I was also a deejay for Star DJ's, (with my double major Bachelor of Arts degree in philosophy and sociology), I saved up some money. I then went to Israel for five months to learn Hebrew and see the Holy Land. I had to return suddenly at the end of my program, when I was about to go on an extended trip through Africa. That was when I found out that my mother, may She rest in peace, had passed away from a seizure. Returning to my empty-feeling home, and feeling like I was the most secure, confident, and relaxed of my two other brothers and my father, I realized I would need to stay in New Jersey, and specifically in that house, for a year or two, which did not hold quite the allure of a wild trip in Africa for me. I knew I would have to make the best of the situation, whatever the case.

I was to be in that house for a while, so I had to decide what to do with my time and I figured I should try something in life like a career. In thinking what I should do for a career, I kept hearing my mother's words in my mind: when I would press her asking her what I should do with my life, she would say, "Why don't you try teaching? You always loved working with kids." This was true, and I finally accepted that I would have to try something long-term to see if I really liked it, and I enrolled for a two year Master's degree program in Education at Rutgers University, my alma mater, for the Elementary/Early Childhood Education K-8 degree. I must have dropped out of the program mentally eight times before and during that program, and I kept getting nervous, especially when I would be in the classes: me and two other guys, and 40 girls. I was wondering how I would do the insane amount of lesson plans that seemed to be required of regular teachers; but I persisted in any case, with the idea that if it was meant to be, it would somehow work out; otherwise, it would work out another way. I hoped and pressed on.

To make matters more challenging, by the time I finished my Master's degree, my younger brother had moved out to Oregon a year earlier. The Miller brothers shared a common dream of living out west. I went out to visit him. I found that Oregon had everything I dreamed of, (fresh air, big mountains, less traffic), when my twin brother, (rest in peace), and I went out to California in search of a place to live in 1995, after graduating college. So I moved out to Oregon in August of 1999, and sought a teaching job, having effectively severed all the great contacts I had developed from successfully navigating the New Jersey public schools system throughout my education, including substitute teaching in several districts. This was aside from all of the contacts I developed in my Master's of Education program. How was I supposed to find a teaching job in a new state where I basically knew nobody? Too make things even more difficult, upon moving out there, after jumping through all of the reciprocity hoops that would allegedly get me an Oregon Teaching License, I found out some surprising information. Oregon Teacher Licensing told me that New Jersey fingerprints would be fine for my Oregon license; when I got there I found out they were no good. As a result, by the time I got my Oregon fingerprinting done, it was already October or November, which was too late to get a teaching job for that school year. This made things a little scary and slightly annoying since I had moved out specifically in August to find a teaching job for that school year. As it turns out, it turned out well, and it was for the best, and so it goes.

In completing my teaching license in New Jersey, I found out towards the end of the program, that after the two years of work, my practicums, student teaching, and all that fun stuff, after all that, my license wasn't truly going to be legitimate until I completed another year under the tutelage and supervision of a mentor. It annoyed me to considerable degree: that New Jersey would stick it to me like that, though I should not have been surprised, considering the state of the state I grew up in and know so well. The nice exception to this process was that in moving to Oregon and getting a new license, I wouldn't have to be under a mentor, which was great, except for the fact in the back of my mind that, I really wanted that New Jersey Teaching License to be official, as if I had completed the mentoring program. Then there was nine years teaching in Oregon, which is the writings of a whole other book; then I came back to New Jersey, with seven years and vestment in the Oregon Pension System. End of the story in a good way is that, in applying for my New Jersey Teaching License, I finally got it. When I thought about it a bit, I realized that goal took me from 1997 till 2008 to complete, a whopping eleven years, a mega-long term goal, if you will. I stayed positive. But this book is competing for a close second in length of years!

I tutor a boy right now in math, a high school junior, who is studying for the SAT. This past year I was tutoring him in geometry and his dad told me he wants the tutoring to occur regularly and for the boy to transition into SAT prep. During the year the boy and I were still getting to know each other, and it didn't feel like he opened up so much, but in the summer he seemed to get more comfortable, so when he said, as he often does, when he makes a mistake, "I'm so stupid", I finally told him he wasn't allowed to say that anymore. If someone keeps telling you something negative about yourself and you don't do anything to deflect or reject it, or if you keep saying these negative things about yourself, you're going to believe it, and it's going to get in the way. The ego can be a powerful force, and it pulls all kinds of tricks toward an end I don't fully understand, but I know it gets in the way of learning in more ways than one. When a person is sitting wondering whether he is smart or not, or thinking he's stupid, or anything else of the like, then that's going to get in the way of his thinking about the material he's supposed to be learning, and he'll be absorbed with those meaningless, useless ideas, instead of the cool stuff he needs to learn. I can't really say it enough and I hope it sticks in your head solidly: please, be positive, people.

The positivity aspect is so worth emphasizing and understanding, in order to bring across the point that you have to be super-positive, with the best attitude, and nothing should phase this positivity in the long run and in general. It should be the underlying current or motif of an outlook, if you want to be the best parent and teacher possible. There's a lot more to it, for sure. One more thing to point out is to give the best outlook and benefit of doubt, so to speak, that is possible, and to give every day a new chance and a fresh start. Every day should be a brand new beginning and your students and children should have a fresh slate every morning without worrying that you held on to their words or actions from the day or week before. This is the best way to approach them daily, if you want to see them make the best and fastest change and improvement. This involves the utmost humility and fresh perspective on your part, but I can tell you it will make you a better person, and it will make you a happier person, and your students and children will reflect that growth and happiness. Their change and improvement will happen quicker and smoother; if it's not immediate, it will occur eventually; if not then, most assuredly down the line. If there are people who won't change for the better, there may be little you can do about it, other than going to a professional, but you must try and continue to believe you can do something about it; don't worry or think about the possibility of not succeeding; it gets in the way of success.

5
IT IS ACCEPTABLE TO MAKE MISTAKES

You are not perfect, though you should try to be. If you make a mistake, you can make something wonderful out of it, and then it's not really a mistake, because something better came than if you hadn't made the mistake. In education, especially with alternative and difficult kids, and with all kids, it's much easier not to make mistakes. The mistake usually creates more opportunities for students to make further mistakes, even, for example in pointing out the fact that you made a mistake. It makes opportunities for distraction and more problems on their part. It seems unfair to get them in trouble for making mistakes, which stemmed from a teacher or parent's mistake; so it's easier not to err!

Working to this level of success is an aspiration, and it's not easy to achieve; it requires being on point a lot and if possible, all the time. Then again, that's why I used to drink 24 ounces of cold coffee pretty much in one long gulp as I started my school day and that took me through the main part of the day: because I want to be amazing and perfect if possible. Mind you, I'm not saying that I don't occasionally make mistakes and do any of these things wrong, and that mistake-ability can apply as a general disclaimer to this entire book. I try my best, and I try hard, but there are times where I make mistakes. That's all right: I own up to them, (most often not begrudgingly); it serves as a model of learning to make mistakes for kids. The following story illustrates a case where I think I made a mistake.

There is one girl who has a fiery spirit and attitude never "att'd" off to me, which is a word I'm making up to mean, "shot an attitude in a nasty way", (the verb form of "a negative attitude"). The first time I corrected her on her attitude was tough for her and me; she responded well to me those first couple days, which were my first at West Orange High School. Even the arguments she gave me were obviously to test my waters; and really it seemed she meant to tell the rest of the class that she was unafraid. After that she had major breakthroughs, and she became one of the sweetest most hard-working students I had. While she had her days when she didn't want to work, or when other things were going on, she always maintained composure in class, despite what seemed to be a heavy weight in her life.

I always wondered if she was going to get back to that original very fiery side of herself again; or if she would open up and let off steam again, and I could sense it coming on with a student who, in graduating, did not succeed in my class as far as I was concerned. This boy, who even had issues with the auto shop teacher, (more on that later), was pretty annoyed when his senior year did not work out how as he meant for it to go. It was getting close to the end of the year, when students were making their plans to go to college. He was getting a little frustrated around the edges, and it was showing, and his previously successful strategy of dragging others down to the pit of misery and anger with him, was no longer effective on anyone. It was the end of the year, and everyone was in good spirits, sans him; so he was kind of on his own, and I was having trouble feeling any pity for him after what he said and put us through that year especially, besides other years, which I will discuss later.

Now one day around May he said something obnoxious to this girl, so she took a possession of his that he cared about; I only realized this after the fact. Though I had seen confrontations between boys and girls, I hadn't really seen this kind of confrontation between a boy and a girl. It was new to me, so I wasn't sure what to do, but I thought she could handle herself so I figured to let it play out. In reaction to her taking his item, he stood over her menacingly, less than a foot from her face, it seemed, like he was going to beat her up, and said something to her that I couldn't fully hear. The girl that sat next to her, who was one of her best friends, said something to her like, "He will! I did something to him last week and he punched me". So it was clear, (but without evidence, which this boy was very good at skirting the line on), that there was a threat of violence there. She gave back the item, whatever it was, and he said whatever he said, which I didn't hear, but I had a feeling the issue wasn't yet complete.

About a week or so later, that class, which, for the record, (while I wouldn't tell them so), was one of my least favorite classes of the year, had slipped very low. They were in a very bad way and not doing well, but we had made some progress. More importantly, I had just finished, right before class, monitoring the Biology State Standardized Test, which was one of the more stressful work experiences of my life: I had no break, and was working a ridiculously long day. To deal with my increased stress level, I gave the students a situation in which they would not have to get any new work, if they could maintain a quiet volume. All they had to do was sit relatively quietly. Now this same boy was pleased as could be, because he had his gaming cards with him, which I made the mistake of letting him play. There: I said it, in print, no less; I made a mistake, though the first mistake was really even letting them have that free time. I should have toughed it out and put them to work, if I'm looking at it in clear hindsight; but sometimes you get worn thin in school, and that was one of those times for me; I went easy on them.

I should have only allowed learning games but I was burnt from proctoring: I had never been lead proctor like that before; you would think you were handling radioactive waste the way you had to deal with these testing materials. Literally, only I was allowed to touch the tests before they got to the students; the procedures and organization are insane. Back to the real story: he girl didn't have the full range of personal gaming activities with her to entertain herself; and her voice, which was naturally strong, elevated a couple times to the point of my having to correct her and warn the class that if they didn't keep it down we'd be going back to standard operating procedures, so to speak, (where they didn't get to do no work). The class naturally kind of amplified itself: if one person got talking and noisy, then they built on each other's volume, getting louder and louder. It happened again and then I had enough, and said that was it, and told the students to get back to their regular seats. This boy flipped his lid and something to the girl sarcastically along the lines of "Nice job, thanks a lot". He said it, though, in a really mean and nasty way. I don't remember what the girl said next, but she was trying to defend herself; he then egged her on and he said something loudly like, "And you're still talking!"

That was when she had enough and boy, did she yell. I don't remember what she said but I think I saw flames coming out of her mouth and off the top of her head. And it was loud! After her words, she stormed out of the classroom. I said something disciplining to the boy because he kept talking smack and I got him to stop; he left class in a huff after that. I apparently pushed him with my words, but I don't like when other students are bullied and this was obviously part of a clear pattern. Then I went out to talk to the girl and make sure she was OK, which she was, and we wrote down the events as they had happened. When I told my boss, she told me to have a talk with the girl and remind her to keep her temper in line; there are mean people in the world. It's no easy question to resolve fault in cases like this; people do annoying things; nobody has the right to bully another; in school, we strive for the ideal.

Mrs. Wall, my third grade teacher, in explaining another concept, expressed this concept of making mistakes, learning from them, and being all right with them, to me most profoundly. She would never let us use the word "can't". If you think about it, it really does make no sense as a word. There is nothing that can't be done, except maybe to come up with something that can't be done. Regret does not come from generally from mistakes. It more often comes from missed opportunities, which is really avoiding taking a chance, in order to avoid making a mistake. Mistakes are useful as a tool to learn. The point of Mrs. Wall's lesson, in my mind, and according to Jewish teaching, is that if you learn from a mistake, it is no longer a mistake, and can actually bring you to a higher place than if you never made the mistake in the first place. They can help you grow and mistakes become instructors and merits. Mistakes are good because you can look back and say, "If I do this thing again, a bad consequence will happen." You can learn a lesson and apply it to your life, move on, and be a better person, thanks to your mistake.

The following is a simple example of the benefits mistakes can bring to life if they are used in the right way, especially in learning lessons. In selling the first house I ever owned, the closing was backed up to the date that was the last date I could make my regular mortgage payment without getting fined. While I did not want to hurt my credit, (which, by the way, was already pretty bad), I wondered whether I had to make that payment. By this I mean that it was the time when the house was changing ownership and I was not sure who would be responsible for the payment. I asked my realtor if I had to pay, and she said I should because the mortgage company would give me back the money anyway. I asked my title lawyer; she said I could probably skip it but that "I didn't hear that from her". But I was really curious.

I thought to myself, "If I make the payment, I will be safe. But next time I go to sell a house or someone asks me this same question I am currently pondering, I will not know what to tell them/me about that blurry time when two people own the house, when it changes hands. If, on the other hand, I do not make the payment, I will know for sure what happens and I will have a good answer." So I skipped the payment, (Bad Larry). Turns out I did not have to pay it. I still got checks for the sale from the mortgage company and the title company on top of my regular sale price. Go figure. And now you know without ever having to try it the hard way, that you can skip that payment. But it might not be as fun for you.

Loss comes from lack of trying, and so does regret, as far as I can tell. Regret comes, as I mentioned earlier, from an opportunity to learn when a person missed it because it was too difficult to make a choice, or some fear made the person back away from the situation and not act. Nevertheless even that missed opportunity can be an opportunity for learning if it is dealt with in the right way. If we recognize that we missed a chance, look at the places we could have exerted effort or done something better, and try to teach ourselves something for next time, then learning took place and there really was no loss. As a side note it seems to me that the brevity of this chapter highlights my dislike of making mistakes, and how much better I feel about not making them at all in the first place, even though, as my official position, it is all right to make mistakes, just make sure to use them the right way, and learn from them!

6
PERSIST

Believe in the ability of people to change, despite what anyone tells you about how people don't change. Believe in the seemingly impossible. Believe in the best possibilities for your students and children, and aim for that. There are so many sayings about persistence and ways to teach it. This is another of the qualities I pretty much always give as an answer when asked my best attributes by an interviewer, and for a teacher and a parent, persistence means persistence to the tenth power. There should be no limit to your effort and will, and you should continually push yourself to do more, and handle more. I have managed to stay pretty non-religious in this book and there is a maxim that G-d doesn't give us more than we can handle, and without comparing life stories, I have had my share of troubles, and I truly believe that maxim. We should stretch our limits, especially in perseverance.

The following two prosaic paragraphs, starting from the period after this sentence till the end of the next paragraph, were the first I wrote in this book; I feel I should include them in order to illustrate this point of persistence; these are the first things I wrote after I lost all that work and kept persisting, so here goes. I used to hate flowers. They always die. All will be lost with time. The cliché sounds quite depressing. Examples prove the best truth. The first chapter of this novel has been lost to the winds. It was quite profound and creative but not properly saved on the computer so it is gone. So, I write again despite this loss, hoping to achieve something great, something, which will not be lost. Why bother? The story must be told, as long and difficult as this process may be. I write to give light to those who might be seeking it and have no other way to reach it. We all have great stuff within and gifts worthy of others. To find these gifts and utilize them in the right time and fashion is a challenge. Good luck.

I still plant flowers even though they are such a pain and I know they are going to die eventually. The time they are there makes a difference to me and maybe to others. It is worth the risk to put in the effort and see what happens. It is much better than not trying at all and wondering if there is something you could have done. I do not wish to experience that feeling. I do not think I have had it yet. I think people call that regret. Regret can only come from not trying something, or giving up.

I hope the prose wasn't judged too harshly, but to be more focused on the topic at hand, I would say that consistency and persistence are essential. Once you pick an activity, method, etc., to do or try in teaching students and children, stick with it, even if it seems like it is not working. Give it a fair shot. Students and children will learn eventually, and they respect persistence, and connect to it. Most things take a while and practice to learn and apply. Persistence means keep trying. Do not give up. Do not get frustrated, as you only end up not thinking clearly. If you do get frustrated, take a breath or take a second before something comes out of your mouth, and that's a whole chapter or two in itself, later in the book. That is usually all it takes to get the right words and actions to take place. In being persistent, you must repeat the same routines for people to learn them, and you must follow through with the consequences and/or rewards you assured would come with the behaviors if you expect it all to stick. It may not seem to work at first but it will eventually. There will come a certain point, at which you may decide a strategy is not a good one, but you must give it a really good try, and if you do give it a fair try, you will know that you have tested and tried the strategy long enough when you finally abandon it.

As to where my thoughts, words, and actions are coming from, with respect to persistence and determination, I need to tell a bit of background on my journeys through the great public education system of this country. When I started elementary school, in first grade and/or maybe kindergarten, I was pulled out for speech, along with my twin brother, Jon. I think he got out of "pull-out" faster than me, and I was there for a while. My mom was a trooper and determined to make it work for my speech and she got the job done. I can remember being in my house and trying so hard to say my friend's name "Robert Theil" and being stuck saying "Wobert". Now I think part of the difficulty of saying "R" is that you kind of have to get a little mad, like when you growl, you make an "R" sound, and maybe I was just too happy in life, but that is a wild theory with no grounding in research whatsoever. I could not say my "L's" either, so try to say my name where all the L's and R's sound like W's; it's like a joke, and I think this is why I went through my life the way I did, but I leave those stories for my book, *Porch Stories*.

So I finally got out of speech class and yet I was still in the lower reading class! My brother Jon was in the high reading class and to this day I have to give credit for my success, even starting in first and second grade, to him. He was always a beacon for me, ahead and pushing, and never giving up. I have no idea how many times I wanted to quit or give up, be it in studying for a history test, or learning to snowboard, or sticking with a job, that I fully would have stopped, except Jon was going to go on, and if he was going to go on, there was no way I was going to stop. I give thanks, respect and honor to Jon.

I worked my little tuchus off to quote a Yiddish expression. I just wanted to do well. I remember being in third grade, when Mrs. Williams, my rosy cheeked, sweet Reading Teacher, asked me to speak with her at the end of class, and it was weird; as clear as if it was yesterday, I remember knowing exactly what she was going to ask me, before she did, and I was right. She asked me if I wanted to move up to the highest reading group, (which was where Jon was!). I was never so overjoyed in my life, what a feeling! Of course I accepted and then I was in the high reading group. The next thing I remember thinking along these lines of early academic aspirations, was on the playground within around fourth grade, and it must have been after a kickball game, because I was feeling pretty average. I remember thinking I wished I could have all my teachers' knowledge somehow implanted in my brain and wishing that I would be anything but average. I was so sick of being average. I say it must have been after a kickball game because I recall feeling a little down since I was never really picked first or second. I was always a solid fourth round pick, which was not so bad, considering there were like fifteen kids on a team, but I was tired of being average. I had a friend in ETC, which was "Education Through Challenge", the precursor to TAG, (Talented And Gifted), and I just felt in the middle, and did not like that feeling.

I worked and worked and got good grades, mostly A's, in fact almost all A's, and I recollect in middle school my parents were giving my younger brother money when he would get good grades. I was wondering why I did not get any money when I had been getting A's all along, and I think I figured it out: I did not need the reward or motivation to get the grades. I was happy I was willing and able to do it, and had the drive and ability to be very good in school. Or maybe they just wanted to save some cash! Well I just kept chugging along, and so did Jon: we were both getting mostly A's, and I did not realize all the grades all added up and that the schools kept track over the long run of what we had been doing over time. In high school I was in all the honors and advanced and Advanced Placement (AP) classes, but I never took notice of what that meant. I recall feeling proud to be student of the month once, which was very cool, but it took me a long time to get to be student of the month. It seemed to go more often to a lot of popular and football type kids first, but whatever, I didn't take it personally.

The next thing that happened in this path was that one day I heard a couple people coming to me at different times, asking me if I could believe it: Jon and I were ranked really high in the class, like top ten or so. Like I said, I did not even know there was a ranking, but to be in the top ten out of almost 400 students sounded well enough to me. They told me I had to go to the guidance office to find out my rank and I did and found that, sure enough, yours truly was ranked number two! I could not believe it! I was overjoyed once again, to tell the truth; it was probably the closest thing to that feeling from when Mrs. Williams asked me if I wanted to move to the high group. Jon was ranked four, and the other two twins that we had gone to kindergarten with, who are now both doctors, were ranked number one and three, which made for a neat newspaper picture and article that still hangs in my grandparents' house. The greatest part of those events was probably going home and telling my parents; they were proud.

The funny side note to this story is in learning how much difference in points there was between the number one student and me, I learned that it was possible for me to take the lead. It actually came down to one math test and at that point, near the end of the year, I was already accepted to Rutgers College and I was going there. So there was no reason, other than pride and glory, for me to work for the number one spot, and it seemed important to that girl to have it. For myself, I just wanted to have fun: it was my senior year, and I had worked my tuchus off for the last thirteen years. So, knowing that I did not know when I would get a break in the future, I wanted a little break now, and a chance to smell the roses. I am proud to say I let slide my pride and enjoyed senior year. I settled for number two: yay!

I did not realize there would be so many side notes to this story; so here's another one for your hopeful reading pleasure. The position of number two would still put me on stage at our graduation and allow me to speak to the thousands of people in the audience: the salutatorian spoke first and the valedictorian spoke second. I was not the lone member of my family on the stage, though: Jon was on the same stage for graduation delivering in front of the audience not a speech, but a gift to our Principal and to our school, in the form of a trophy case, on behalf of our class. While this is linked in a major respect to the main point of the story, in being persistent, I should point out that this is probably my favorite story in the history of life. And the following, linked delicately through a chain of confusing clauses, and weaving storylines, is an example of the concrete benefits of persistence.

We had some issues with authority, my brothers and me. We did not like authority randomly or illogically imposed upon us; in general we did not like authority at all, but especially when it did not make sense, and was not fair. That was just not cool and we knew it. One of the rules that had been imposed in school was that we could not wear bandanas on our heads, or as my grandmother referred to them, to dip back into the Yiddish, "shmata's" which she insisted were for cleaning tables and what-not. We were allowed to wear hats to school and other things like hoods on our heads, but not bandanas. Gangland had not yet entered our suburban school and looking back, I can only imagine that was what prompted the fierce opposition to this particular type of cloth on our head. I do not recall where we noticed this style; it could have been from rap we listened to at the time; I know the rap group NWA was wearing them at the time. I specifically reminisce on one time while I was wearing one, and like the hundred other times the same thing happened, that my friend Jay made fun of me for wearing it, only later to don one himself, which I called him on later and call him on now. It was only a year or two ago, by the way, when Jay, dressed in baggy pants like I would have seen myself wearing ten years earlier, finally owned up to his "behind-ness" or my "forwardness": I called him on his dress style, saying that he would have made fun of me for wearing those same clothes ten years earlier and he said, "What can I say, you were ahead of your time." So he finally came around: way to go, Jay.

There were other clothing issues in school that I was fighting about also: enough people had taken up the bandana cause. I was busy fighting for my shredded pants. I had pants that I shredded in seventh grade, when my mom would not buy me pre-shredded pants, insisting it was a waste of money, rightly so: half the pants should cost half the price and not double. These shredded pants from seventh grade still fit me and I still liked them. At one point, the principal, "Crazy Joe" Sweeney, who I was on good terms with because of my standing within the school and in the top classes, said something to me about wearing the shredded pants; a teacher had said something to him about them. I had a good discussion with him about the pants, and I was kind of shocked at his opinion and rule, but he did not seem too strict or concerned about it, so I wore them again, less often, and tried to stay discreet when I wore them, or chose my corridors particularly, and he said something to me again about the pants. Go figure. I engaged him in a discussion, to try to understand the logic of it, and when we finally got down to it, it turned out to be the issue of skin exposure. I did not like that since girls were wearing skirts that were higher than the rips in my jeans went, but he said something about gender styles or whatever.

I think I was going along with it well, and I am not a hundred percent sure of the order of events here, but things took a serious turn on the subject when Crazy Joe saw me at a Friday night football game wearing the ripped jeans. He said something to me the following Monday about the jeans, along the lines that if he saw me wearing them again at a football game he would have me kicked out of the game. To me that was taking the battle out of school, and taking the battle out of fun, and it became a different ballgame to me. Therefore, the next time, I chose a different strategy, since I also had a pair of ripped black sweats by this point, which were shredded up the front and back, so much so that they were tricky to get on. I wore the sweats with yellow sweatpants underneath, and then I did the same thing with my jeans, so that I wasn't even exposing skin, which was the only reason I had been given not to wear them. So you can understand my shock, surprise, and anger when I was told I could not even wear them that way! Whatever reason he gave me was at that point irrelevant. The battle was on.

Sometimes persistence shows itself in the funniest places and ways. Jon took on these battles too and ran with them like a champ. There were elections for student council coming up, which were usually won by the most popular people. The same people were running for offices senior year that had run for the offices the year before, and had always run, and always won. I do not know what prompted us to run but Jon and I did. I gave some regular class office speech and ended up as secretary, which was pretty cool. Jon gave this speech about bandanas, only it was not only about bandanas. It was a battle cry about rights! It was an epic rally!! He had kids standing and applauding and screaming and he was talking to them from the depths of his hearts about our freedoms, our rights, and our rights not to have our freedoms trampled on, and it was the best speech I ever heard in my life. What I would not give to have a recording of that speech. The kids went wild and they applauded for days, it was straight out of a movie; they were talking about it for weeks. He won President by a landslide and it was the coolest thing I ever saw. I do not know how much prouder I have ever been of anyone. It took guts and courage and strength, and wisdom and writing skill and charm. He rocked the school to its core foundation.

Back to the original story, that is how Jon got on the stage at our high school graduation. That is not the point of the story though; the point of that story is the possibility of our being on stage. I say this because, the day before the end of school, there was an awards ceremony at the other high school in our town for all different kinds of things, honors and scholarships and a nice dinner. Crazy Joe Sweeney was there, along with the top forty students in our class and some others who were receiving various awards. A few of us were talking to Crazy Joe in a circle, including myself and Jon, and Joe says to us, and looking specifically at me, and I quote, "So, are you gonna raise some hell tomorrow?" I had no idea what he was talking about, and I said as such. He continued, "You know, it's the last day of school, so are you gonna wear some bandanas or something?" I've never been so egged on; and it was on.

I honestly never considered the idea, but it did not take much to goad a seventeen-year-old Larry Miller into action. I got an idea and Jon and I spread the word to the students there at the meeting, and the students at the meeting were to spread the word to the seniors. The next day, at 10:00 AM, Jon and I went down to the guidance office. Jon distracted the guidance counselors and I walked over to the microphone broadcasted throughout the entire school. I hit the red button, and said, and I quote, "Attention Mr. Sweeney, it's 10:00; do you know where your seniors are?" Jon and I then strolled out of the office like kings of the world and got about twenty feet down the hallway before Saul Brodman, a guidance counselor who I never saw outside of his office seat, came running out of guidance yelling something about "You Miller boys get your a-s back here" and if it was not that cuss it sure carried the weight of it. He yelled at us and sent us into Crazy Joe's office and I was totally bummed because I was totally looking forward to going outside and meeting everyone there for the walkout. When we got to Sweeney's office we had to wait there because he was out trying to clean up the mess we made.

Apparently the word spread throughout the whole school to everyone, not just seniors. There were teachers blocking doors, and students trying to get through the doors and the teachers, and somewhere between five and seven hundred students left the building sans permission that day at 10:00 AM. It was possibly my and our proudest moment. When Joe came back into his office it was like seeing a person I had never seen before. He was furious. Until that point that I knew him, he was always the pinnacle of control and discipline, and here he was in his office yelling like a crazy man and kicking his garbage can and totally freaking out! It was bonkers! When he finally settled down to talk he was still mad and I tried to explain my side, that he told me to raise some hell, but he did not get it. Go figure: authority.

He called my mom in and that was the worst. She was crying when she came in the office. I do not think she had ever been called in to the office for Jon or me. I have no idea what they said to her when they called her, but it did the job. She calmed and pleaded and placated Crazy Joe, because, to get to the main point, Joe said that if it was not for us being who we were, meaning myself as Salutatorian and Jon as President of the Senior Class, we would not be graduating or going to prom. It was only our positions and hard work that had saved us from missing graduation. See, and that's the final point: persistence pays off. Missing graduation would have devastated my parents, which would have resulted in devastating my social life, I can imagine, among other difficulties. I was consequently glad to know that my hard work for thirteen years in the public schools finally paid off for something besides academics. I say that because all my friends, half of whom totally slacked their way through school, were also going to Rutgers. Until that moment, I hadn't really seen the value or benefit of my having worked so hard all those years of school, since we all ended up going to the same college! What did all my extra hard work and dedication and effort get for me if we were going to the same school? I could have worked a lot less hard with the same result. Here, though was concrete reward for my persistence. Also, along those lines, I always had in the back of my mind this weird desire to get suspended, because it seemed cool and fun, and in my thirteen years of public school, I never once had this honor. So I got the honor on this day with my brother Jon. We went home with my Mom from the meeting with Crazy Joe, suspended, and that was how we finished public school. When we got home and talked to my Mom, it was one of the rare times I was able to convince her of my side: she saw my point of view, that he had egged us on, and she said something like, "What is a principal doing egging on a 17 year old?" If that's not the exact quote, she was at least on our side, which was the most important thing to me.

That is how Jon and I did not destroy the possibility of our being on stage at graduation. The next time I was on stage at graduation was making a speech to my graduating senior of IPASS, in the Harding Learning Center in Coos Bay. He was the first person in his family ever to graduate from high school, so I had a keen perception of the value of that graduation. I had a keen idea of the value in persisting to get students to make it to that point, and to graduate from class to class, and to keep learning through life. The following year in Coos Bay, I would be given the honor of giving the commencement speech as the choice speaker to the audience. This speech never held the same punch as my high school salutatorian graduation speech which was entirely written in rhyme, quoting lunch foods like peanut butter and jelly, and quoting the Beastie Boys and Led Zeppelin among others, but it still has a special place in my heart.

Persistence shows up in interesting places. It's funny how I got the job working for the Union County Educational Services Commission, so here's a bit of that story. It was my first real teaching position in New Jersey, which was also the first job I got here after moving back from Oregon in 2008. It was the most laid back teaching job you could imagine in Union County; and the truth is, when I say that, I mean it was the ONLY teaching job I ever had that was relaxed; it was the most like a regular person's nine to five job of any teaching job I've had. I had been there almost two years; three days before I was about to close on a house in West Orange, New Jersey, I got an email from my supervisor, telling all of the non-tenured teachers that we would have a meeting that Thursday. It was Monday, March 22, 2010, and another teacher and I were in the Commission for some kind of training. She was very nervous and sensed from the recipient list on the email that something was up with regard to our jobs. We asked our supervisor if they could tell us whatever it was they had to tell us right then, instead of Thursday, since it was pressing. We had a meeting right then and they told us that they were not renewing our contracts. It was a little rough. I found out it was too late to get out of a house closing without risking bigger losses, so I proceeded with hopeful optimism in my job search. It was pressure for sure: having settled into Jersey after moving back from Oregon, I really wanted to succeed. The short end of a long job search, (though not the longest job search, which I don't think will fit in this book), was that I got offered three jobs within one week. One was for a Middle and Elementary School Science Teacher position in Hillside; one was up north, in Rockaway, with kids in a restricted environment; and the other was in West Orange, teaching math at an Alternative High School Program, (set within the actual high school building), of the town where I just purchased a house and chose to settle. All lights were green.

Contrasting to the relaxed atmosphere of my position with Union County, was my next position teaching math in the Horizons Alternative Program in West Orange High School: it was one of the toughest teaching jobs I ever had, and my first year there was one of my toughest years teaching ever. I had to thicken my skin and toughen up. These kids were not easy. On one hand I have had some great success stories in West Orange. One of the best was a student who made the fastest, sharpest turnaround and change I have ever seen in my life; it was the same girl who, earlier, I wrote about having an argument with a boy where he confronted her in a menacing way and she flipped. She started originally in my first period geometry class, which had nineteen students and sixteen desks. I should have used that to teach the concept of negative numbers for students who didn't get it so well. This girl was very loud and angry when I first got her, and I had battles with her a couple days, and then she settled. Shortly after that my boss moved her into the other geometry class which only had nine students. It was a much better fit and she was much more settled. Regardless, she still refused to write or do any work, despite the fact that from her answers, I could tell she was very intelligent, especially with respect to mathematics. But whatever I did, she was refusing to write; I didn't press too much since she was still doing alright and giving answers, and it was definitely a huge improvement from her first few days in my classroom.

One day she asked if she could use the colored chalk to write on the board. I said she could, and she drew some pictures including the "Pink Floyd Prism" that stayed up there for the majority of the year. A day or two later she asked if she could write the answers on the board, (this board was in the back of the class, so don't get too excited), and of course I obliged. Then a few days later she asked if she could write in marker on paper, which I allowed. Then suddenly, out of the blue, she was doing all the work in her notebook and she was one of the two brightest students in the class: more eager, enthusiastic, and excited for math than anyone I had seen in a long time. She was fantastic for me for the rest of the year, though she did have difficult spells and she would fall off a little. Nevertheless she still asked engaging, exciting, original questions that blended various aspects of math she had learned, and shed light on connections I never saw. It was fun to watch her learn and she really was one of the best students I had. As a side note, later in the year she made it to the school-wide poetry competition, which was big news for a school of 2200 students. She competed on stage in front of a large audience in our auditorium, and while she didn't win, she gained confidence in a way she would not have believed possible in the beginning of the year. Her quote to me at one point when I had been trying to get her to work early when I knew her was, "Why bother, I'm just dropping out of school when I'm 16 anyway?" I almost believed her, but I didn't let it phase me, and I believed in her, and persisted, as did she, and it paid off.

The story that stands out at the other end of the spectrum is with my senior class in my first year. While the story is funny, it shows on persistence in that in the end, they finally came around, even after they had been with another math teacher in the program for two years. I was able to turn them around with a lot of hard work and persistence, and I really mean a lot of hard work. I had to change their habits, and stay constant with my rules and methods which were different from those of the teacher who had the class before me, but it worked in time. This senior class was tight and tough; it was the class I was discussing earlier with the student who asked me about having my father mentor him. They all had each others' backs, and especially when the common enemy was the new guy who was doing things differently and not taking any guff, but doing it while looking smaller and less threatening than their 6'4 former teacher, (I'm 5'7 on a good day). One of the other three teachers in the program said that they were the toughest class she ever had in forty-something years of teaching, and she's a good teacher.

One day things were going badly. I don't recall why or what caused this bad day; in the first half of the year, I had a lot of tough days with that class. Pretty much every day it was either that class or my first period geometry class that gave me a big problem. Some days both were tough, to put it nicely, and those weren't fun days. And on the days when no one gave me a problem I was so thankful. Well, on this particular day things were not going well at all; and at this time, I was in the habit of giving my classes regular "progress reports" before the real progress reports came out during the middle of the term that got mailed to their parents. I gave them these pre-progress reports so that they were able to get caught up on missing assignments. I had done this in Oregon and it worked well there for empowering students to take ownership of their education. That ended in New Jersey for me this day.

I guess I made a small miscalculation, which some might call a mistake, in that I figured things were going badly, so how much worse could they get? I figured since we were in a fallen, failed state already, it was a good time to give them their progress reports, which were not good. I was totally wrong about things not being able to get much worse. They flipped out. They all had a lot of work missing, and they all had low grades, so they assumed the problem was me. They complained, argued, got angry; they were gathering around my desk. Finally I got them to settle down and quit freaking out and one of the students, who was a star football player asked me, "Mr. Miller, who do you think would win in fight between all of us and you?" I don't think it took me two seconds to ask in return, "That depends: would the girls be fighting?" They all cracked up and that nicely diffused an almost difficult situation. Somewhere around January or March they got in line and finally accepted me as their teacher and leader. I really did not know before that if I was going to pull it off. I had really tough students before, but I never had such a tough class which was so tight and unified. It was not easy to break through it and gain control. It was a great exercise in education, and it was a proof of the power of persistence.

One quick neat story along the lines of positivity in persistence: it was towards the end of the first year in West Orange High School. One of my fun students who had a barreling voice had transferred from the crowded first geometry class to the emptier second one; his father was a teacher, and the boy asked me if I was going to bring my guitar to class, as I had mentioned to them earlier in the year that I played. I was hesitant about it, and said something like I didn't feel that open with them to do that. He reminded me that I had said earlier I would bring it at the end of the year. I honestly didn't recollect saying that, but I could imagine myself saying it in the middle of the year, when things were very hectic and thick. I would have been thinking that if I made it to the end of the year, I would be so thrilled to be there that I wouldn't mind playing guitar for the class. So I brought it in and planned to play it on one of the last days; but I was still waiting for him to ask me; I was really hoping for any kind of way out I might be fortunate enough to get. On the day of the final, at the end of the class, (his class had been working the whole period, and then talking for a while after that), as he was leaving, he asked me about the guitar and I told him it was here in the class. He planned to stop by after his next final and I wrote his teacher for that final an email giving permission for him to come to my class when he was done. Apparently by the time she let him come it was too late, but I even left the guitar in the class over the weekend, just in case secure in the cubby behind the speakers where no one imagined a guitar hid.

The beginning of the next week he came in when I was done with my finals and I played a few songs with him there. He wasn't that into the Green Day song that I was playing, but it was still cool playing. He played a little after that too but he'd forgotten most of what he learned. That was the first time I played with students here in New Jersey. The last time that happened with students was out in Oregon in like 2008. Good to know there's still the positivity. His persistence and determination were what got me to play with him and I am glad to know students have that kind of motivation, because even though the motivation is regarding music, that kind of motivation will transfer over to other subjects and areas in life. On that note, with two pages written for the first time this summer and for the first time since teaching in a New Jersey Public School, I think I'll go rock a little, (as in play guitar): my new reward.

The tea is made, the six pages are not yet complete, and onward I press because I am persistent! In joining a fraternity one might think I wasted many years or time, and indeed, this might very well be the case. My brother and I spent a lot of time and energy arguing with the brothers of the fraternity of Phi Gamma Delta, or Fiji, about right and wrong, and being better people and the like. For all the garbage that went on in the fraternity, and for all of that which we were parts of, there were two positive things that stuck with me from the whole experience, and to this day, stay with me in my mind and consciousness, and they are both along the same topic. The first is a signature that was signed at the bottom of all Fiji documents, and it was the imperative form of the Latin word pergo: the word is "*Perge*". It means "go on", "press on", or "proceed"; and it is a very positive statement of encouragement, with which I strongly connect. The second involved a poem of sorts, of all things, we learned, written by one of our most prominent members, Calvin Coolidge, entitled "Persistence" which praised the qualities and loftiness of said trait. I relearned this poem just now. Here it is in its entirety:

<u>Nothing in the world can take the place of Persistence. Talent will not; nothing is more common than unsuccessful men with talent. Genius will not; unrewarded genius is almost a proverb. Education will not; the world is full of educated derelicts. Persistence and determination alone are omnipotent. The slogan 'Press On' has solved and always will solve the problems of the human race.</u>

The point is that I'm enjoying writing right now, and when you have that motivation for whatever it is that you are trying to train yourself to do, you have to go with it and keep going. That's because when you're really enjoying the activity and doing it, just for itself, that's when the strongest reinforcement takes place, (to drop back a few chapters). We learned that when you get a student to do what you want them to by using rewards, the goal is to eventually remove the rewards, so they enjoy the positive activity for its own intrinsic value. So right now I'm going with that, and on another note, the aspect of "guessing" is really a great activity for students. Firstly it encourages persistence in that they want to keep trying to get the right answer, and this doesn't even have to be something academic, yet the focus would be building this persistence, motivation, and desire to learn. Secondly it encourages them to be comfortable in being wrong, which is an essential part of learning. A simple example of this is when a student asks me how old I am, rather than just give away the answer, make them work from curiosity to build motivation and determination. I have them guess my age, and this guessing game is something I often do in my outside life as well. We always play "guess the check", or "guess who I saw today", or even "guess who's pregnant". It's fun, it keeps learning fresh and enjoyable, and lightens the process of learning which, in general helps to ensure delight in learning and education.

I can't believe I have written so much. Today the method I used to get myself to write this novel was pitting it against painting the garage. Again, persistence means to keep going, and in a work like this book, I need all the persistence I can get; that means keeping the methods fresh. Now this method of pitting one thing against another, is one which I don't know the name of, because I don't know if it's yet an official education method! Normally we have rewards and punishments, and positive and negative reinforcement, but I don't think this method falls under either of these categories, and anyone with a Ph.D. who would like to research this exciting field of education is free to take the idea and run with it. It's interesting since it's not a punishment: I just don't want to paint the garage. So it's like the lesser of evils, in a manner of speaking, in that I would rather write than paint the garage. Writing in this case is not a reward, though, either: it's really only a better choice over painting the garage; this is a slightly fascinating concept I've stumbled upon. What I think will be more interesting though, is the question of whether I will do any research in this book to go see who else has researched teaching methods in alternative classrooms on both coasts of these United States, and I think the answer is "no". Resultant of the current 90 degree weather, the book writing takes the cake over the garage, and so I persist.

7
PREPARE FOR THE WORST; EXPECT THE BEST

Expecting the best comes with being positive, and involves having high expectations for your students and children; but truthfully, there are times when it seems you have to have low expectations of your students, and I know this doesn't sound right, but hear me out. Students and children go through rough times in their lives, and maybe this applies more to high school students than to those in the younger grades. I had some students who were going through some difficult times in their lives at various points, and to try to force them to work harder than they really could during those times would have been counterproductive. It's better to respect the fact that sometimes they need time and space, and in the long run, for certain students, at certain times and periods, I believe that allowance pays off. On the other hand, it takes a lot of teaching experience to get to a point where you can recognize when it's appropriate to do that, and until you know what you're doing, I would keep the expectations high!

About preparing for the worst, it's not easy to anticipate what might happen, unless you've read a lot of books, or more likely, you've already experienced whatever situation might pop up. An example of this was in my first year teaching, in Jefferson, Oregon, when I had the same class of students for most of the year. It was less than ten students that had been with me, and then I heard I was to get a new boy arriving to my classroom, and he had allegedly been a terror since kindergarten. I heard this boy once bit his third grade teacher's arm, and hung on; I always pictured him hanging from some flab under her upper arm with her holding him up like that, but I don't know what that experience looked like, and I'm glad about that. I should have taken this story more to heart and been more wary of the boy, but my guiding principles of being positive, seeing the best in people, and giving them a fair first shot, won out and I looked at him with a completely open mind without judgment when he came to my class. At that time it seemed like my open mindedness and fairness was the right call, because for the first couple weeks, this boy was nearly angelic. For the record, he forms the basis of one of my interesting educational psychology profiles, (without any basis in study or fact other than my own personal observation), that some tough kids are tough because, while, like this boy, they are small children (for their grade/age), in reality, they are going to grow into larger boys, which they may consciously or sub-consciously know. I never met the boy's father but I heard he was a big tough boxer, and if the boy's athletic ability was any indicator, he had a natural knack for physical activity. I don't know if I ever had another student who was more naturally gifted in physical activity and action than he was.

Like I said, for the first couple weeks with him things were great, and I don't think he caused a single problem; he never spoke up, and he would answer quietly when I asked him a question, and I was surprised at how wrong everyone must have been about him. Here was a genuinely nice, well behaved boy. Then one day, I forget what happened and how it started, but all chaos broke loose, and all of the sudden, everyone was mad at everyone, and everyone was freaking out like I had never seen before; the class completely fell apart like it had never happened before. When I looked at this boy he was sitting there with a certain kind of grin on his face indicating he was very happy with the results of his work; I realized he had been organizing a kind of chaos for a while, and so I realized the child I was dealing with.

To end nicely though on this story about the concept of being prepared for anything, while I had my fair share of troubles with this boy, when I moved into the mainstream classroom, he was already going into seventh grade, and so he wasn't able to join me in my new mainstream class like some of the other boy students did. I do remember, however, seeing him walking down the hallway, and he had grown a good bit, and he was walking proudly down the hallway in the regular building, which was a major accomplishment, both for him and for me. I got one of my greatest senses of satisfaction and accomplishment from seeing that, as I knew how much he wanted to be with other students, and I knew how smart and cool he was, and I knew how much he wanted to succeed and be his best and the best. It was a pleasure to hear from other teachers and see with my own eyes, that the legend, on par with none other than "El Barto" from *The Simpsons,* was doing well in school and happy as a student and a citizen. In the end it shows being positive and expecting the best from your students has great results.

I should really add a subtitle to this chapter, saying "be ready for whatever", but I'm really trying to keep these titles simple so that maybe someone can memorize a few of them to be able to apply them more readily. The bureaucracy that I saw in the high schools in New Jersey was different from that which I saw in Oregon, and it helped for me to have this mentality of being prepared for the worst. It could be a factor as well, of the fact that the high schools in New Jersey are generally bigger and more crowded, on the whole, than those out west; there is less space; regardless, you have to be ready to deal with surprising situations, and react with calm. In the beginning of the year in New Jersey they ran us through new teacher orientations that lasted for a week. It was kind of a funny skit and there were a few pieces of useful information which nearly got stomped to bits by the massive amounts of less useful information they heaped on us, combined with the massive amount of training. Some of it was stuff that's forced on us from above, in the government, like how to interpret test results on a massive spreadsheet program, which regular teachers might not have time to do or use so much. That wasn't such a big deal for me, though, because it really only seemed like a loss of a few days and that was the end of that. I had to accept that my time wasn't being used for what I thought to be the best end, but it wasn't the worst situation in the world, and New Jersey is thick with bureaucracy.

If we stick along the same line of dealing with the hand you're dealt and being prepared to handle it the best you can, we come to an interesting case of bureaucracy which many people reading this book might be most fascinated to learn about, and that is my encounter with some higher-ups in the New Jersey Teachers' Union. Later on you'll hear about my stint as a union representative in Oregon when we almost went on strike, but for now, suffice it to say that the Oregon Teachers' Union seemed a fair organization, the union responded to my needs when I had them, and served the interests of the teachers in an expedient way. It was a nice experience as an Oregon Teachers' Union Representative. We weren't paid as representatives; the most we got was light foods when we were working long unpaid hours on behalf of the district; dues were about $50 a month if I recall correctly. Nevertheless, after almost going on strike, and sleeping the night in school with my fellow negotiators to avoid a strike, and calling out a specific board member in a board meeting over his lack of attention and care about schools and the situation at hand, I felt that one year as a union representative was enough for a decade, and I had completed my duty for the next ten years; but like I said, more on this topic later.

When I had an issue in a New Jersey school for the first time, it wasn't really an issue: it wasn't anything major and it was just some information I wanted to learn about. People always wonder and question but most often give answers and opinions about the New Jersey Teachers' Union.

Regardless, what they fail to realize is that still, as in the old days of unions, it is an "us and them" situation, where the power of "them" far out-measures the power of "us", and that is why this union, regardless of its level of corruption, is still necessary: because we are fighting for our livelihood against the strongest man-made organization in existence, the US government. As far as I'm concerned, "them" consists of the government officials who are trying to impose and implement the goals and will of their own interests onto the teachers and students without regard to what is best for either. Note that this rarely matches the goals, ideas, and ideologies of the teachers and the students and the community in real time and on the ground. They are generally more willing to trample rights of teachers and students for some bigger picture and some larger interests. I hope you don't mind my temporary soapbox, but it needed to be done. I know there are great government officials and governing bodies, and if they would get involved with education for the right reasons and from the right perspectives, everyone would win out big time.

Back to the story from which I digressed: the case of which I speak is when I almost left the teaching profession. Remember, the lines of thinking here are being prepared for the worst and expecting the best. At the end of my first school year in West Orange High School, I hadn't been offered a renewed contract for the following year. I sent out resumes in the middle of the year, with some success; I was very close to having another job offer. An old friend from the Oregon Teachers' Union reminded me I should check into the benefits changes if I was to leave the teaching profession, and to find out how that would affect my retirement savings and such. I called the New Jersey Education Association, because I didn't know our Union Representatives that well. The NJEA connected me to the local county branch after asking which county I worked in, which I thought was out of the ordinary, because why would they need to know which county I worked for? Then, once they transferred me, they asked me further what school I worked at, and my name; all of which put me on guard the way they grilled me, because this was my union, and they should have been helping first, and the way they asked for the information felt like the police: it wasn't asked in the kindest way.

I asked the guy on the other end of the line my pension questions, and as it turned out, if I left the education field and came back to it later, (in a "smooth" way, which I will explain in the next paragraph), I would be coming back at a lower tier in my retirement, which would mean a lower rate and percentage, meaning my benefits and my retirement package wouldn't be as good as they had been at the time I was considering leaving.

The wild part of the conversation which hinted to the state of the union, in a manner of speaking, was that, at the end of the conversation, this guy told me, off the record, that he would say my questions had been asked confidentially. The reason he would say that I had asked him these questions in confidentiality, was so that he wouldn't have to report my questions further along the chain of union command, and that freaked me out a little bit. What was the situation going on here, that something asked of the union, by a dues paying union member, would have to get reported anywhere? What were they there for if not to help us? It's consolation that he didn't report it, and that he made the decision to tell me to make it as if I had asked in confidentiality; and I think that's only because I made him aware of the sensitivity of my situation there in telling him about my not wanting to go through the regular channels. There are certainly some issues with the union, as far as I can tell, but it's good, and it's a necessary self-defense against "them", and you have to be ready for whatever.

I said in a "smooth" way, because the answer they gave me when I called a second time, to clarify on my questions of retirement if I left education, they gave me the answer I wouldn't be able to get back into my old retirement plan at all. This was a different person I was speaking to, and she said that if I left education, after two years of being out of the education profession, I believe it was, I would be asked to clean out my retirement account, as it would no longer grow, since it would not be vested or invested. You get vested by being in the New Jersey pension system for seven years; in Oregon it was only five years. The loophole that I would have been able to use in my New Jersey situation, was that since I had been "RIF'd" (reduction in force, meaning they let all non-tenured teachers go when there was no budget or money), I could apply for a special pass of sorts, to keep my retirement intact. The lady only gave me this information, though, with a little prodding and pressure, and this was my union, for which I paid a good monthly amount. I won't complain too much; it's a situation that requires some mechanical work, but it's still a functional system and succeeding overall in a difficult battle.

Being prepared for the worst and expecting the best means thinking ahead of time and anticipating situations that are going to come up and arise. It means getting ready for these situations and doing something about them proactively, to the best of your ability, and for most of us that means some writing of various plans in advance of classes and situations. You have to use whatever little time you have wisely, and while going through some of our new teacher orientation, I remembered and realized that I was going to have to introduce myself to my classes, and that I would have to have some activities and startup ready for the first day. I therefore began to compose my "introduction": this consisted, at its completion, of roughly 60 points I wanted to deliver to the students to introduce and welcome them to the classroom, and to attempt to connect with them. Within this story about being prepared and about preparing for future situations, there is one interesting point that succinctly clarifies the difference between a west coast and east coast school, for those who are interested. It also shows something about one difference between different types of alternative programs, so follow along.

Earlier in that orientation week, they had given us an instructor who was teaching us specifically about classroom management, and the tricky thing about some of the new teacher orientations, both before school started, and throughout the year, was that they were mainly geared towards elementary teachers, and a little towards middle school teachers, and much of the information was really irrelevant to high school teachers. I don't know if this was because it was easier on their end to set it up this way, or because most of the best practices in education function best in a non-departmentalized setting, or because those were the teachers who volunteered or were hired to do the training, or some other hidden reason that eludes my educational curiosity. It was, however, a fact, and it got kind of annoying at a certain point, like, why am I sitting through all of this? Maybe they could have thought to include high school teachers in the lesson plans more, the same way we they were teaching us we should include all our different learners in our lesson plans; alas, the system is what it is, as the saying goes.

So when they suggested to us that we use the "name cards" activity for students on the first days of school, and have the students crease a paper "hot dog style", I figured I would give it a try. They said it would work in all age groups, and so I was game to give it a go. I could have done this activity in any of my other classes ever before this point in my career and gotten away with it, even with high school students, I'm convinced, but my new kids were too tough for it. I mean, they actually did the activity, surprisingly, even my seniors, and there were just a few complaints along the way. To bring it up to a more closely appropriate age level activity, I had them draw on the back of the card their favorite shape, and the shape they liked least, for geometry; and for algebra, what letter they would most like to use for a variable, and so on. It wasn't the best activity, but it was something different and didn't require a whole lot of hard work on their part for the first week back to school; and it helped me learn their names a little faster. So I expected the best and it came out well, even if I was doubtful about doing the activity in the first place. I was prepared for the worst in that I had other activities waiting and ready; if there was a certain level of negative resistance I could have bailed on the activity; I wasn't tied to it.

Besides folding cards hot dog style and writing our names in marker in those first few weeks of school, we spent a lot of time on problem solving. This is one of those activities I would recommend, coast to coast, fifth through twelfth grade, to parents and teachers, to all students and children. I think there is no argument that learning to solve problems is an essential skill in life. If a person can solve math problems using reason, logic, and thought, he can apply these skills to any area of life and any type of problem that might come his or her way. There are many methods of solving problems, and the best are just that: methods. A person should have a set of organized skills to attack a problem; he doesn't need to use the set all the time, but he should have the tools in case he needs them. One method of problem solving I use in all my math classes, and which I have used for about ten years, is the "four square method"; it works with pretty much any math problem, especially word problems. To use the method, you draw a horizontal and vertical line that cuts the paper into four equal sections, (squares).

In the top left you draw a picture of some type, (chart, diagram, or visual illustration). In the bottom left you do your work, where you actually do calculations, computations and whatever basic math equations or applications you use to solve the problem. In the bottom right is where the communication goes, and that should be in numbered steps that a scorer could read, recognize, and understand; it's basically explaining the different steps you took to solve the problem in sentences, and the easiest way is just to look back at your work and explain how you got to your solution. In the top right you verify your work, which ideally means solving the problem in a different way; you can also verify by solving your problem in reverse, as in working from your answer till you get back to the original equation; in a worst scenario, you can just repeat the steps you solved before, in order to assure no errors were made in the solution.

This method was difficult to implement with some students, especially for those who were resistant to something new like this. For others, in contrast, they really liked it and felt it empowered them more than they were before, with respect to problem solving, which is one of the hardest concepts to teach and learn. I drilled this for the first two or three weeks with all my classes, before I realized how much I could have used that time and needed it for other things. It is a great tool, without a doubt, but we have so many things to teach according to these state and national standards, and so little time; so this problem solving method is one of the hardest tools to implement with New Jersey students.

What I did the following years was to require students to complete one four square a week, out of the "do now" word problems that they started the class with every day. These do now's are from SAT and HSPA word problems, and it's not so daunting to complete one of these four squares a week, and it earns them pretty good credit. On the other hand, it can be very time consuming if not done properly; the point is not necessarily that students are going to solve every math word problem they come across with this method, though they may choose to use parts of it on different problems throughout their education careers and maybe even later in life. The point is to give tools they can use in solving problems, like drawing a picture to visualize the problem when at a loss for how to start. In another respect it opens their minds to seeing the problems in a different light, so they can view it from different angles, and hopefully come to new ideas, or original thoughts, that are often needed to solve problems.

Now, to get back to my situation where I almost left the wonderful field of education, here's a glimpse of how the education system works for the non-tenured. Firstly, people should understand that even when a teacher gets "tenure" it is not a guarantee that they have a job for the rest of their lives, sitting around ignoring students while reading the paper with no one looking over their shoulders, though that may have been the case in the past, and though it may occur in some schools. Teachers can still lose their jobs, no matter how tenured they are. When I lost my last job, as in the story I wrote where I found out three days before I was closing on my house that my contract wasn't getting renewed, the district was in straits, as was the entire state of New Jersey, and the district was not far from beginning to terminate tenured teachers. Whether they announced this fact to encourage some of the older teachers to retire, or things were as bad as they sounded, who knows? In their discussions with the whole group of employed teachers leading up to this point, they kept mentioning that they might even have to let tenured teachers go. What this showed plain and simple was that non-tenured teachers can be let go; there is no lock on the position with tenure, though it is harder to let tenured teachers go; regardless it is nowhere near impossible to do it, and I need to emphasize to the audience that it does not mean absolute job security, as the media leads people to believe. In this vein, and for this reason with respect to my teaching position and tenure, I am prepared for the worst, though I expect the best.

When the New Jersey government was teetering with respect to its budget and on the verge of collapse in 2010 or so, it was putting its fulcrum and blame square on the education system, and threatening massive budget cuts to an already decimated system. At that time our high school, which is in a pretty respectable town, still had holes in the roof for which buckets caught water when it rained, since we didn't have the money to fix the holes properly. How many of the readers can make that claim about their workplace? At that time, towns had to pass budgets by certain dates, and the schools didn't know their budgets until their towns passed their budgets, so our school district had to take the option of "non-renewing" non-tenured teachers' contracts. This author was a not-so-proud recipient of that option; but it should come as no surprise to anyone who knows me from reading about the character presented in the pages turned so far, that I am not one to sit around and wait for things to happen.

I got my resume in order instantly, got back online at www.NJhire.com which is the primo teacher job search site, and registered my resume with www.NJ.com which is the *Star Ledger* job site which has outstanding classifieds for New Jersey (and the teacher job section is great), and I got job-hunting. During that time, a job offer came through a yahoo group of which I am a member, which is for members of synagogues in West Orange and the surrounding areas. It was a position with Barnabas Health Care System, a hospital right here in West Orange, as a liaison between the hospital and the Jewish Community Center, also in West Orange. It was a newly created position, where the liaison was to create outreach programs for community members, using the JCC, and to implement preventative health programs, with the ultimate goal of getting these people to utilize the services offered at this hospital, instead of trekking into New York City for an allegedly higher level of services and doctors.

The job offer came through the wife of a guy I actually pray with regularly in synagogue, who works for the hospital, and the interesting thing about the offer was that in describing those who should apply, it asked for those who had experience as educators, along with those experienced in the medical field or marketing field, so I promptly applied. I went through two rounds of interviews, and they gave me a bit of the runaround, because, in the beginning, it was between another candidate and me, and towards the end, they kept having to go through more candidates. In hindsight, I guess that was a good lesson for me in how things work outside of education, and that's even in one of the noblest places, a hospital!

I didn't want to wait and find out if I was going to be rehired at my school, even though I had a feeling I would. I was expecting the best, figuring I would get that job back, but preparing for the worst, in case I didn't get the job back, so that I was already running when I hit the ground. To put this all in perspective, as a side note, I always had the dream of saving the world, or at least making it a better place, and for the majority of my life, I thought I could only accomplish that mission through the job and career in which I worked. I therefore saw, in my younger years, my best option to achieve this goal, in a position as an educator; hence my current career, despite more lucrative opportunities I could have sought elsewhere. Around 2005, after I sold my first house, I was living in Coos Bay, Oregon, and making ends meet. I had been through the grinder, (as an understatement), and I had taught some difficult and demanding classes, with at least one very bipolar student. During those days I would come home at times worn out, and nearly dreading going to school some of the other days. At that time I clearly remember making a conscious decision that I no longer needed to save the world, so to speak. It wasn't that I had given up on doing that saving, and I still wanted to save the world, but I didn't consider it an obligation. While I put in good time to the education system, it was starting to wear on me, and I always said to myself, and to others, that if I ever became one of those burnt out teachers who hated teaching, I would quit, and I felt myself approaching the point of being burnt on it. I didn't decide to quit at that point, I just decided that I could go into another field besides education at that point. The second part of that decision was that I had a new, simpler goal of keeping a roof over my dog's head (and mine). It was quite a burden lifted off my shoulders, to tell the truth, but I never burnt out, and look at me now!

Regardless, my abovementioned decision didn't require the world to immediately bend for me and supply me with such a position outside of the field of education, and it was another six years before this occasion would actually almost arise. When I was applying for this job as a liaison for Barnabas, (along with all the other various teaching positions for which I was applying through the aforementioned websites), an interesting turn of events took place. I asked someone at the school for a letter of recommendation as part of my interviewing process, as he knew the whole situation going on with non-tenured teachers not getting their contracts renewed, and he registered a surprised expression and responded as such. He was shocked because he didn't think my position was in any way at risk. On the contrary, this was the normal district way, to "non-contract" non-tenured teachers. He was sure the district wanted me back; he would talk to the principal to reassure me in this vein. The following morning, the principal of this school of 2200 students was at my door first thing when class started at 7:30 AM, asking to speak with me in the hallway. He said the same thing, assuring me I would be working there next year, and told me they liked me and that were impressed and gave a lot of nice compliments. The kids were funny when I came back in the class; they joked like I was in trouble for being pulled out by the principal. It was nice to tell them that in reality, quite the opposite was the case.

It was around this time I had to call my superintendent for something, not sure for what, but it was funny, because at the end of the conversation, he took me by surprise, asking me if they would be having me back next year. I was quick enough to say that I hoped so, but asked him when we were getting a contract. He said the board of education was supposed to meet the following Monday, and then hopefully the week after that we would know. It ended up being more like a month after we spoke, but that was fine with me; it seemed I had a job, (the town passed its budget; combined with that question from my superintendent, I was cautiously confident). Meanwhile I moved full speed ahead in applying with the Barnabas position, because I wasn't about to give up on it until they gave up on me, or unless I had to make a choice between the two jobs. I don't like making difficult choices, and Judaism teaches, (as taught to me by Rabbi Kasowitz), that a choice is not choice between a Ferrari and a Pinto. There is no choice: it's obvious which any of us would take. A real choice is when things are weighted pretty evenly, and it's a toss-up between or among choices, and these are the difficult choices to make.

This was the situation I was nearly finding myself in with regard to the job choices; I didn't want to put too much time, effort, and energy into the decision, as I had not officially been offered either position. On the other hand, I had to do some "background decision planning", because the clock was ticking, and I didn't know that I might get offered both positions simultaneously, and/or have to make a decision in a relatively short time frame, so I wanted to be prepared for such a situation. I had to be prepared for the worst but I was expecting the best; which is also, for the record, hoping for the best, as well. This was the point in my life at which I was closest to leaving education, and this was the time when I called up my union, and avoided a report to my district representative, as I explained before, and this is when I almost became a regular human, in a manner of speaking. I kept flashing back to the scene in *Superman 2*: after the man of steel gives up his super powers in order to have a relationship with the lovely Lois Lane, he is confronted by a bully in a diner, who whips Clark Kent, now devoid of super strength. It honestly felt like I would be giving up some super powers in going out into the regular world, doing a regular job, that doesn't require one to do super amazing things daily. I'm not implying that I'm amazing; I am stating that I have to try my best to be amazing, and I work hard at it. I hope I succeed.

Alas, or really, to the good, the Barnabas people did not offer me the job, and there were two things I saw that came out of that to be very positive immediately, and a third thing that I see now very positively. The first two positive things that came out of not getting hired were: firstly that I was going to have a much needed restful summer. The previous summer, while I was on vacation officially, was spent mainly looking for a job, which really puts a burden and a weight of negativity on a summer vacation. I had been meaning to go to Acadia National Park in Maine with my dog for that summer, since I had gone there two summers before, and had one of the best vacations of my life. I told myself back then that I could go back there every year for the next ten years and be happy, and now, G-d willing, I would be able to go again. More importantly though, in that first bonus of not getting hired by Barnabas, I got to relax, chill out, and do some more writing on this hopefully wonderful book.

The second bonus of not being hired was seemingly much less significant in general, but more relevant to my then-present state of mind and relaxation. It was this: I was not going to have to make that difficult decision, which bored down on my like a freight train in the distance; I really dislike making difficult decisions; maybe I don't trust myself with such big decisions. Sometimes I would rather flip a coin. I was more excited for this bonus than I was for having a summer vacation. The third winning bonus of my not getting hired by Barnabas, which I see more clearly now, is the fact of the superman complex. Teaching is truly wonderful work, and if you can do it, you should, because helping students and children grow, learn, and become better people is beyond a doubt one of the best things a person can do while walking this planet. The reward that comes from it is amazing, and I hope many get the chance to experience it. I was happy not to be going out into the real world; I didn't want to give up any super powers! Who would? I need to point out though that regardless of the outcomes, being prepared for any of the possible situations made the entire process a lot more enjoyable and generally stress free. Being prepared, but with a positive attitude, empowers people. It gives confidence, which in turn, helps a person to make the clearest, most logical decisions. It makes people smart and successful.

This next topic is one of my least favorite to write about. It is important, however, in understanding how to prepare for the worst while hoping for and expecting the best. The topic is labeled "third period's negative transition", and it reflects the fact that at a certain point of the year, in fact, for most of the first half of the year, third period was my favorite class. They were the smallest class, with only nine students, and had fun, and seemed to enjoy everything we did: learning, the games, all the activities, and class in general. Then, at a certain point, the dark elements of the class started taking over the vibe of the room, driving down the attitude, and brought the whole class down to the point that it became one of the worst classes. It may have been the worst class, technically, considering the obvious capability and potential of the class to do so well and achieve so greatly and how low it got. My senior class of that year never achieved their potential because they were busy making too many jokes that got old and stale fast; but at least I never saw their full potential at a high point from which there was a great fall: this something to lament that third period took the cake in, and that's no real prize.

What happened to this third period class, which had reached great heights, even where they were working well with each other, and helping each other, and learning from each other, was that they sank, and never really got back up to the heights they had reached; so it was pretty sad. They ended the year on a relatively decent note, and they never as a class fully revolted, but it is extremely disappointing considering the range of their potential, that they never came back close to it; and maybe the reason that I was not looking forward to writing this is that this is really the end of the story, and there is not much positive else to write. The only positive thing really to say is that I kept trying, and tried different reward methods, and believed in their potential, and hoped for the best, and sometimes, you hope higher than you achieve, and that's all right. It's better to be able to maintain high expectations and not let your hopes and expectations get crushed by one class or one student or by anyone for that matter.

How to go about teaching someone to be ready for anything? It goes hand in hand with being in control and staying cool, and most times it is advantageous not to be too surprised or to look too shocked. The way to do that is best illustrated by a story like the following. One day in West Orange High School, one of my students told us a story how in the South American country where she grew up, she would have cockroaches all over the house and they would crawl on her, and that it wasn't such a big deal for her: it didn't scare her or really bother her, and I couldn't believe it when she told me the story! That was a time it was OK, as far as I was concerned, to register a shocked expression, but that's not the point of the story. Her cockroach story led to a discussion about another girl, not in our Horizons Alternative program, who had taken a big piece of cake at somebody's birthday party in school. The student telling the story identified this girl with the big piece of cake as the "Jewish girl", and I didn't take to kindly to that, but I didn't want to show how upset I was, because I'd be giving up control of the situation.

I therefore asked the storyteller what this girl's being Jewish had to do with her taking a big piece of cake. The storyteller student replied that it didn't have anything to do with it, and that it was just the way they knew her and identified her. Another boy in class chimed in and proceeded to tell me something like, "You know, that is how we call each other, like we say 'he's the black one'." I've seen the kids do this before but it's usually by someone of that race or ethnicity identifying another member of their own race or ethnicity, which I don't consider it my business to correct. In this scenario, however, none of the people doing the story telling were Jewish, and I think I was the only Jew in the room. Remaining completely cool, however, and hoping for the best, I responded that that it fine in his case for him to identify someone as "the black kid", if that was his choice, because he was black, the same way it is my prerogative to identify someone as Jewish, because I'm Jewish. However, it's really not cool, when, in this story it's not in a positive and/or praising manner in which the "other" religion is being discussed: it wasn't a compliment that this girl took the biggest piece of cake. I told them that, in general, race or religion really shouldn't be used to identify someone, and I guess that goes for any other category people want to identify people by. That is how I find the rules of the game should be, and that is how I'm making it to be in my classroom, anyway, and I'm hoping for and expecting the best.

On another similar note, I'm not sure how my students first breached the topic, but one day, about halfway through the year, the students started asking me about my dating situations. To tell the truth, earlier in the year, this one boy in the front who was trying to be a wise guy, tried to ask me "if" I dated girls, trying to hint at me something negative, but that doesn't count. He was a troubled boy although after over three years with him he made some improvement. Regardless, at a certain point in the year, my students got more comfortable with me, the floodgates of their curiosity opened, and the questions came a-rolling.... The funny thing is that it really opened two sets of floodgates in one discussion; this was my first period geometry class which was the most lively and exciting. The students were dying to know two things about me: one, about my dating, and two, about my religion and religiosity. Mind you this is a high school class and everyone told me that when students ask questions, appropriately, it's OK to discuss. Both questions were tied up to each other and brought out in the same discussion. They would ask me these questions about both topics rapid fire, and the more students asked questions, the more other students shot their hands up with more questions; it was a total snowball effect.

It was funny with the dating questions because we would have these question and answer sessions, and even when it was a Friday and they would know I had an upcoming date on that Sunday, I assumed there would be no way they would remember about that date over the weekend, because students forget everything from and about school by Monday, and certainly about their teacher's social life. Then Monday would come, and sometime during the class, one of the students would remember about the discussion, and ask me how the date went! I was always amazed they cared enough to remember something from school that they weren't getting a grade for over the weekend. It warms me to know they have concern for others and gives me renewed hopes and expectations for them; it's sweet.

It was quite an art in the mastery of education to properly navigate those discussions, especially two years before I was tenured! It was risky even to have those discussions, but my supervisor told me that when the students asked questions about religion or personal stuff, I could answer them, and that's how I handled it. Still, it was a weird concept: on one hand these were high school students, generally asking the questions in an appropriate manner, and genuinely curious and wanting to know about things they didn't know about; and here I had an opportunity to impress them with proper manners and habits, as I have learned throughout life. What made this discussion especially funny, and I wish I had a recording of it, was that the kind of dating that I do, as an observant Jew, is called "Shomer Nogia". This basically means there is absolutely no physical contact whatsoever, (not even holding hands), until marriage. This fact actually made the discussions much more suitable and appropriate for the classroom; the worst that could happen was that they would ask off-color questions, which happened; but my answers were all very pure and innocent based on this type of dating which is modest, to say the least. When they did ask those kinds of questions, I simply didn't answer; or I would redirect or correct the asking of the question. The other funny part of the conversation came from the religion aspect; they usually got into this topic from the dating topic; that was when they learned how religious I really was, and got curious.

One day they were firing away questions about my religiosity; I was protective of my answers, to make sure I was not preaching to them or looking like I meant to indoctrinate them, (believe it or not, we are not a "converting" religion; we do not seek to convert more people to Judaism; we're not looking for more than we have already). This was despite the fact

I knew it was alright to answer questions when they asked, but I was still guarded, because even answers to questions can be problematic. At any rate, the questions were a-flying, and it was all about religion, and there was a boy who sat in the back, a little kid. I knew, from his other statements on other days in which he emphasized a certain axis of power connection from World War II that he did not seem to me the biggest fan of Judaism. He finally had enough of the discussion, and piped up with his question: "Mr. Miller, who's your savior?"

There's not too many ways to safely answer that question in a math class, but whatever, he popped it, and I'm game. The other students got annoyed at him because they knew what he was getting at, and one of them told him that it was a stupid question, but I was down to answer it. So I said, "G-d". The other students laughed and were like, "Good answer!" and were very cool and supportive about it, and that was as religious as our class got. I have to say for that boy's defense that he said the pledge of allegiance every day loudly and proudly and I credit him that. If you're calm and cool you'll be ready for whatever and while expecting the best you'll be prepared for the worst; and it won't phase you, and you won't get shocked by it, and you will give a level headed, cool response. You might even get a laugh!

Who would have thought these wild alternative methods would work in a mainstream high school in a suburban town seven miles from Newark New Jersey and fifteen miles from Manhattan? It's such a diverse mix of students we have in West Orange, by race, religion, ethnicity, culture, orientation. You name it, and it's in West Orange High School. Here was I trying to implement these alternative methods over my first two years at WOHS, and it looked like they would have me back for a third year. The students in WOHS, like other students I worked with, really came around a lot more after the first year, once they got to know me. We had a super great year and two extreme positives stand out, much like the female student from my first year I wrote about earlier, who did the fastest turnaround I ever saw. That student was with me for three years and did well, despite not having won the poetry contest she so ardently desired to win. She still had her days of testing things and people, but she never really tested me, other than that first few days. She stayed pretty solid. Anyway, back to the more recent students I wanted to talk about who really exceeded expectations, I should point out the following: each of these scenarios might not seem like much to the reader, but each scenario demonstrated a student rising to a performance level and a positivity level that I haven't really seen or experienced before in all my years teaching. That was mainly because these were some of the highest age students in some of the tougher circumstances I had; and I wasn't sure if they had the ability to change, to "rise above it" and to be superstars, really exceeding expectations. They proved they could and it is definitely noteworthy.

The first one who is pretty easy to see and understand is a boy who blew me away when he decided to take on the Great Stellated Dodecahedron, (pictured in the back in Appendix E). In geometry, later in my second year, in the fourth term, we were working on nets, which are fold-outs of three dimensional shapes. I printed up a couple of fold-outs and we spent a couple days making these fold-outs into shapes like cubes, pyramids, and icosahedrons. The students really got a kick out of it and enjoyed seeing the finished three dimensional shapes they produced. The hardest part, I told them when they were making these shapes, and the most important part, was for them not to get upset or frustrated, and to stick with it. If they could stay calm with these creations, they would enjoy, and they succeeded in the task. This boy, who was one of my top students ever, was very artistic, and he took a real liking to this activity; he kept doing it, fixing other people's shapes when they were having trouble, and making more shapes. I mentioned the Great Stellated Dodecahedron to him and told him how to start it, and he actually made two figures related to the Great Stellated Dodecahedron by the end of the year.

First, he made an icosahedron out of straws: a regular polyhedron with 20 identical equilateral triangular faces, (pictured in Appendix D). Then he went for the Great Stellated Dodecahedron. Here is the thing that makes this so above and beyond anything I had seen before: this boy already had a solid 95 average, which was not going to fall below an "A"; this was all after the last test of the fourth term, and the grades were pretty much locked. Accordingly, he did this purely for education, fun, challenge, etc. At one point, when he finished working on the dodecahedron part, which is really twelve linked pentagons, he brought it in to me, and it was very flimsy. When I looked at it I saw that he had done it right, and that it was tight, and I was trying to figure out what was wrong. I finally remembered back to the Great Stellated Dodecahedron days in Destinations Academy, and I realized it wouldn't gain solidity until he put the points or corners on it, which is really what makes it "stellated". In other words, when he connected the corners of the pentagons into points, those connections would strengthen the whole structure. He continued his work, and managed to finish the Great Stellated Dodecahedron; I am proud to have his icosahedron hanging in front of the class and his Great Stellated Dodecahedron sitting on top of the cabinet. I told him his work completely justified the entire program, especially if anyone every wants to challenge us about the existence and purpose of Horizons. My answer would be that here was a student who was able to freely explore, learn, and challenge himself, above and beyond anything state testing could measure. That, to me, aside from all the other benefits, justifies the program measurably.

The second example of a student rising above expectations will not seem as clear. It was a level of comfort and connection in the alternative environment that illustrates a positivity and change that might not happen in a standard high school classroom. This positivity and change proves the ability of these types of programs and these methodologies in bringing students over their own personal bars. This second student was such a pain my first year; she had a terrible attitude from about midway through the year until the end of the year, and it was extremely caustic and negative. She had latched on to some negative male elements in our program and ran with those elements, so to speak, in that wrong direction. She started off this second year, though, with a completely different attitude and seemed determined to change. True to her intention, she was possibly the most positive student I had that year. I even thought about creating a new award called by the name of the most positive student I had from my first year, the one who I recommended for my dad to mentor in his accounting profession. I would have this award yearly for the most positive upbeat student of the year, (though I haven't brought this idea to fruition as of yet). In my first year, the girl I recommended for my dad's mentor had no competition for the most positive student. While it might have been a close race in that second year, this girl I'm discussing with the improved positive determination would have ultimately taken the cake.

Without going into all of the fun and positive remarks, episodes, excitements that took place, I will say that this girl developed one of the most positive working partnerships I have seen as an educator, with another student in the class. She would always joke to this boy, to me, and to the class, how she and he were the best partners ever, and that they were such a great team; and when one of them was absent, you could sense the "missing-ness" in the class, and she would say she missed her partner when he wasn't there. Mind you, I never set up partner pairs in that class, though I allowed students to work together when it was successful. This one just formed on its own and had the strength of a generation.

Anyway, very close to the end of the year, when that class, which was one of the best classes of the year, was having a great day, I happened to notice that the boy and the girl, of the best pair ever, were dressed in the same theme colors: it was black, another color, and a hot pink accent; and it was totally by accident. The boy had these bright pink sneakers that were pretty cool. So I told them they should be a detective team, and their name would be "Punky and Pink Shoes". The girl asked why she was "Punky" and I reminded her she had shaved the side of her head. The boy turned about as red as he could when I named them as a pair, and it was pretty funny. They looked at each other and realized they were dressed very much alike, with the same colors, and could be such a detective team, fighting crimes. I said the boy would be the tough go-getter nuts-and-bolts engineering calculating guy and the girl would be the intuitive, positive, enthusiastic, "nothing-can-stop-us" partner, which truly reflected their attitudes and personalities. They got a real kick out of it and I even remember that there was another day when they came in dressed alike again, and I made sure to point it out to them! It was such a positive refreshing, pure experience, the likes of which I haven't seen in the high school arena before. High school students are usually so jaded, that they're not willing to imagine, to have a certain innocent fun, and to be so open and so positive, and that was what both of these experiences really brought out of the program. Those experiences brought greatly reinforced my having high hopes and expectations for the potential of my students, and seeing they could even exceed those hopes and expectations!

It's tough to come down from such a positive note, however, on the other hand, I'm still not sure if there are solutions for students, children, or people who are determined to be negative. There are really only two situations here that illustrate this point from this particular high school education experience, and I'm glad there's only two; I think both of them involve bipolar students. However, in the interest of positivity, I am posing the theory that these two students caught the tail end of negativity lingering from years before I was there, specifically of negative classes. In other words, sometimes an entire class (whole grade) is negative, and it's not easy to fix them; or requires the right circumstances. I am going to hope that the change going on in the program and the school grows stronger every year. With my first year in West Orange High School, for the seniors who had three high school years without me, and only one year with me, there was only a limited amount of change that I could effect. This depended on the students and how willing they were to grow and learn at that stage of the game. In my second year, with that last senior class gone and out of the picture, there was a new senior class. The senior class most strongly affects the whole program, and this new senior class, had half their high school years with me and half without. And really starting the program were then sophomores who, with their true welcome to Horizons program, knew only a program with Mr. Miller; it was easier to effect change. The following year, which was my third year, was even better. Each year it seemed that the effect I could have on the students, (hopefully it's positive), was stronger, as they were less tied to other learning patterns and can more easily directed to a positive direction. I expect greatly of them.

Now back to the discussion of these two students who really managed to stay negative, despite all effort, hope, and expectation. In my second year, these two students didn't succeed, as far as I would say. Now as a side discussion, when I saw high school graduation for West Orange, at the end of that second year, there was one girl graduating who was noticeably severely disabled, and she seemed to be mentally disabled as well. She was listening to a CD player, which seemed like the way she was able to cope with this situation of graduation, and it got me wondering what a high school diploma means? This girl was getting a diploma, and she was getting massive help throughout the whole high school process, and she probably didn't have to pass the standardized state tests which she didn't have to take since she was learning disabled; and she may have been on the crew of students who, for the majority of their day, picked up garbage around the school. They did that, since, in theory, I guess by the school's theory, it might be the only field they would be truly qualified to handle in life; and who's to say that they shouldn't get that kind of training while they could get it? This point, by the way, was stated clearly by one of my colder, often clowning and negative students, who made fun of everything, whose sister was this type of learning disabled. This same student said that his sister should get trained to do this kind of work, because it was the only work she was going to be able to do in the real world. It was the exact opposite of what I thought this student would say, and it made the point that much clearer. The question, however, still remains. What does a high school diploma mean; what does graduating mean?

This leads back to the point and question: what does it mean when I say that two of my students didn't succeed, from my point of view? It seems that the way the system is set up now, an important part of the high school process is learning how to play the game and navigate the system, in order to succeed in the world. The truth is that no one wants to hear that learning the game is the point of high school, or any school for that matter. The reality is that if a person goes into an interview and, (with some exception), asks the boss, "How's it going, bro?" we all know who's not getting the job. There's nothing officially wrong with asking that question in an interview, but it's not appropriate, respectful, or proper. In other words, it's not how you play the game. In the game of life, there are rules; and whether we understand them or not, agree with them not, or believe in them or not, they exist and they will probably exist throughout our lives. Consequently, we might as well know how the rules work, if we want to succeed, and we need to teach our children about the rules if we want them to succeed as well.

Therefore, when I say these two students didn't succeed, I mean that they never really got the message. This is something that even my seniors from my second year had gotten down by about May, (not that I should ever wish for a class like that again). They figured out how to be happy and get along with a boss that was going to make them follow rules they didn't want to follow, and do work they didn't want to do. In a nutshell, that might be the most important skill in high school, for the most part. Even if a student is a genius, or is going to be a business owner, or the President of the United States, he is always going to have people that he has to answer to. He's generally going to have to do some work that he doesn't want to do, and he's going to have to follow some rules that he doesn't want to follow.

So these two boys never got it. Even through the last days of school they were still miserable, and fighting against basics they had learned already, and getting angry at rules and me for enforcing them, which they learned and knew years ago. One of these students was the one who actually threw a tantrum at the auto shop teacher as discussed earlier. How do you throw a tantrum at an auto shop teacher? The other student who never got it, the sad thing is that he was so smart, and I haven't seen too many students with his degree of switching back and forth between top student in the class and worst student in the class. It is literally like two completely different people, like Dr. Jekyll and Mr. Hyde, and it would be nice if teachers had, instead of a lie detector, a disorder detector, so that we could instantly know when we have a student with some kind of mental or personality disorder. Just saying… That's what I mean about those students not having succeeded with me; they never really got it. They may go on to succeed in business or some aspect of life, but they didn't leave my class happy. With all the students I had over the years, most or all left happy; they didn't leave grumpy, excepting these two.

Along that line of thinking it is interesting how I ended up going to the high school graduation for West Orange that second year. It is right in line with the concepts of being prepared for the worst and expecting the best, and rolling with the punches and the game as it rolls, though I know I'm slightly in the wrong chapter for it. Sometime after January of my second year, when everyone was happy since we had passed the hardest, longest, darkest, slowest part of the year, my seniors, who, through that point, had been pretty cool, asked me if I was going to graduation. When I looked at the calendar, and realized it was AFTER the school year was officially ending, (and I'm on vacation), I started joking with them, saying I had to do laundry that day, or I was getting a haircut that day, till I ran out of excuses and finally put it in my calendar. Being in the midst of my summer vacation, I was not excited to go. Who wants to go to graduation when school is already out and we're on vacation? Now, while they had been better by far than my first year's seniors, this class still had their moments in which I wanted nothing to do with any of them, and/or regarding them as a whole class. So why would I want to give up my free personal time to work any more? They asked nicely and especially one boy who I could tell wanted me to be there asked especially nicely, though, so I said it was on my calendar and I was aiming for it.

Then time passed, and my seniors again changed from the angels they were to a different creature altogether. Note: I went to the singular with "creature" because the thing with classes is that they can develop an identity as a group. What happens is that someone leads the class in a direction, and the class can decide to follow that person, and a critical mass of followers develops. You can imagine it makes for an ugly situation in a class with seniors who have pretty fully developed wills, and enough intelligence to make things unpleasant if they aim for it. They also have enough boldness to go forward with ideas which don't sparkle in clarity or intelligence, just for the little laugh or attention they may get in the moment, and enough lack of care to do it. That happened with this senior class; they headed down the wrong path at high speed, and we had some days and weeks that were very unpleasant and, at a certain point, I decided I was not, at any cost, going to graduation. This class had already burned all their bridges to the point where I had barely written any letters of recommendation for them, and I was not being fun in the class. That's because, when a class is so negative, you can't really be fun while they're being so negative and out of control, lest they assume that their negative behavior and attitude must not be such a big deal, since the teacher is still in a good enough mood to joke around with them. At that point, the good news was that I was free for graduation and off the hook, and that was nice.

By the end of the year I still had the question in my mind of whether I was going to graduation, because the one student in that class had asked me, and she had always been nice, and never went up against me. She had a couple times when she came close, but never defied me. In fact, she listened so well, that the only thing I really ever had to come down on her for was this: once, when I was leaving school to go home for lunch, I happened to be behind her and another student, and she was smoking about 30 feet in front of me, and I actually breathed in some of her smoke. While students are not allowed to smoke on school property, there is another question of what the rules are whether they are eighteen years old or not. Aside from the procedural mess of reporting them, and how I'd go about reporting students I saw smoking, sometimes I didn't know their names. To top it off, if they decided to run, am I really in the shape to chase a teenager? The bigger point is, I had 42 minutes for lunch in which I had to go home, make lunch, eat lunch, and do the other necessaries I have in a short time window. I don't have time to go through that whole procedure in my little lunch break. On the other hand, I do not want to breathe smoke. So I told her if I ever breathe in her smoke again, I would write her up, period.

This girl was the one who asked me if I was going to high school graduation, and I knew she had worked very hard to make it there. I considered going on her behalf, (because I will go to great measures and do whatever is necessary, for the benefit of even only one student, who needs it, earned it, etc.). At this point I was probably 95% not going- there was a chance but it was slight. Then one day, after the class in which Punky and Pink Shoes were a pair, one of my other seniors in that class, a fifth year senior taking Algebra 2 again, asked me if I was going to graduation, and asked me in a very nice positive way, (this is generally a good way to get things done). I had forgotten she was a senior, being that she was in a class of juniors. Here is her story in a very brief summary, as she came through my classes. In my first year I taught her in Algebra 2, and she was the nicest student ever. I never saw her angry and only once saw her say something slightly sharp but highly warranted to another student. She was quite possibly the nicest student I ever had, but her attendance was horrendous. I hadn't seen attendance like this since my first years at Harding Learning Center in Oregon where students would be gone for days and weeks at a time, but that was due to meth, and I knew this was not the case here. I tried to come up with scenarios of why she might not be attending: maybe she had family in another country she had to visit or help. I told her she had to improve her attendance if she was going to pass for the year. I leaned far in her favor to pass her, but in the end, it wasn't enough, and she failed math for the year.

Right now the reader could be thinking a lot of things. One thought might be wondering how I leaned to her favor, or what that means. Let me start with the end of the story. Only after she failed math for the year, did I find out this student has cancer. For starters I now felt bad for failing her, because I could have leaned farther, but I never knew about her disease. More important is the question of how I didn't know this information. It's actually a very interesting ethical question because on one hand, every student has a right to privacy and may not want the world to know her problems. On the other hand, if I knew about her condition, there's no way she would have failed for the year. The question is who made the decision not to pass that information along to me; if it was the girl I understand her desire to keep her health private. It's possible that my superiors didn't think I should know, being that no one knew me well enough for that kind of information. I'm really not sure what caused the gap in information transmission, but it seems like I should have been informed. Then again, looking at the positive outcome, some students are so great, (and some people are so positive), that it's nice to have them in your class again, even if it means extra work, grading, re-teaching a concept when they've been absent so long, whatever the case, some people are really a pleasure having again; this girl was one of them.

Alas, there I was, going to graduation officially, due to this girl's asking me. Graduation was called to start at 8:00 PM but I wasn't about to sit through an hour of speeches just to hear one name called. I actually got there a little earlier than I originally intended and walked in the place a little before 9:00 PM. I found the teachers' section and sat down, wondering how, out of a graduating class of 500-600 students, I was going to find one girl and congratulate her, after the ceremony, when a couple thousand were all leaving the place at the same time. I have had bigger problems to solve, though, so I put off thinking about it, and listened to the speeches, without even looking at my IPhone once, (unlike the students, and for that matter, the parents). After everything was said and done, and I was walking out, as I actually exited the building, the two people, (students), right in front of me, had words for each other, where one of them was saying the other should step off, trying to disrespect him like that in front of his father. The one who had apparently disrespected the other was about to get into it, and there was almost a fight right in front of me as we were walking. The boy who had apparently disrespected the other was none other than the brother of the girl I was going to see! As his father stepped in to calm down the boys, I asked him where his daughter was, and he led me right to her. I congratulated her, and she was super-happy to see me; I even broke the Chassidic rule of not hugging women, (who aren't your wife), and told myself I make this exception for sick people (when she went to hug me; I would still in that situation never offer to hug a woman first, especially a student). This is generally true in the hospital as well: when I visit sick people there, if a woman offers to shake my hand, I generally shake it. I couldn't see G-d forbid making sick person's situation worse making them wonder why I didn't shake their hands or giving them some sense of rejection; I don't yet have that kind of strength.

Allow me to present a point that many might not think a teacher would say, and this is running lightly along the lines of the title of the chapter, but connected nonetheless. As a forerunner to the discussion, I should say I read an article yesterday, (it was the first time I got to read an actual newspaper in years, I believe), about a charter school in Newark, which is on the fritz. Now this charter school scenario, mind you, is what the state and federal governments have been banking their hopes on for the reform of education. Chris Christie especially has his hopes high on this, and this case might show how and why charter schools won't work as well as these people pipe dream they will. It was a Sanford Adelaide school, which I applied to; probably one of the dumping sites for the money big bill gates pumped into Newark for some half-baked education reform. The nearly hysterical thing about this school, as the article published it, was that the building where the school was alleged to be located, was empty! They were paying $450,000 in yearly rent and nothing was there: no classes, no desks, and no students. The administrators claimed they were using it for a gym and to make lunches, but that's an expensive gym and a more expensive bakery. The interesting thing was that the head of the school was also the head of a Women's Division of the Million Man March, an organization which, "coincidentally", was the owner of the building being rented for half a million. And, by the way, the rent jumped to $600,000 the following year. I guess this little oversight got overlooked; that's just one problem with charter schools: there's even less accountability and less ability to track progress, spending, and the reality of the school. In schools we strive to do the best with what we're given, and the regular public schools are generally positive, honest, and straight, to a pretty good extent. As teachers and parents it is our job to take these (limited) resources and use them the best we can, to prepare for the worst, but expect the best. Do it!

8
STRUCTURE IT

It's very important to set up the environment in the most efficient and effective manner possible; that's why this is the longest chapter. We do this order to avoid pitfalls and encourage success. Pitfalls will get in the way of success if the wrong turns are made, and there is no reason to put unnecessary obstacles in front of your students or children. Life is hard enough! While it's not absolutely essential to make a perfect environment for your class or home, and a teacher or parent can certainly succeed in an environment that is not set up in the ideal way, it certainly makes things easier and leaves students less traps to set off. One of the interview questions I memorized an answer to is, "How would you set up your classroom (to encourage success)?" My answer includes actions like setting up the desks in a way that facilitates easy maneuvering, setting my desk in a way that allows me view of and easy access to the entire classroom, and having an inbox for homework in a place that is easily seen, in student view, to make that part of the process easier for them, to avoid another difficulty. I try to make things as smooth as possible to encourage maximum success. Structuring the environment doesn't only mean functionality; it can mean including art, vibrancy, life, and more. For my class it also includes putting student work on the wall to foster pride and self confidence. This builds the idea that learning is a positive thing, that people should have a sense of self worth, and that they should care about the work they produce and turn in. This also includes posting the class and school rules in simple form around the classroom, so that students can read them easily and be reminded of them regularly. All of these things can easily be replicated in any classroom and in any home. I should have plants in my classroom, but I have enough trouble keeping my house plants alive; it's on the backburner of my mind for sure though!

To return to the days of Oregon, and specifically Coos Bay, the reader is about to see a lot of structure and a lot of structure, in description of the structuring of a program. One of the gaps we had in the Destinations Academy, which was also one of its advantages, was that there were so many different rooms and areas in which students could work. When I first went up to the Academy to teach there, I had to rearrange everything. I inherited a class which I cleaned out and literally threw out about twenty full size garbage bags (not kitchen garbage bags), of junk that had been cluttering the classroom for who knows how many years. I had to go and make the classroom more functional, useful, open, and positive, and this was not an easy task; but it paid off in the long run, and really, as soon as those trash bags were tossed out into the garbage where they belonged. One interesting note about the structure of that class was a privacy desk I inherited which had been there for a while. I wanted to get rid of that privacy desk, which is a desk that has three mini-walls attached to it: in the back and two sides of it, so that students are less distracted by all of the things around them. I was going with the idea that learning was meant to be a social endeavor with students interacting with each other, and this desk seemed to isolate students. Furthermore, it was an eyesore, it fit nowhere nicely, and it blocked my view of certain areas from certain perspectives; and as I mentioned earlier in this chapter, I always preferred to be able to view the entire classroom. This one classroom which was technically mine was actually part of three classrooms put together in one long triple classroom. My idea was that the teacher at the far classroom from my classroom might not be able to see things, (there was no teacher in the middle classroom, which just held a few computers). Or he might go out for something, and I wanted as much open view as possible, even across to the third classroom if need be. When I asked the custodian about moving it, he gave me a talk on why he thought it should stay, and that there might be students who would want the privacy provided by that special desk. I was against the idea but went with it, with the understanding that if I wanted it moved it would go. As it turned out at a certain point in the year, some students actually liked using it for the privacy and so it turned out to be a good move. Thanks Paul!

On the other hand, there was difficulty with so much space in Destinations. That triple classroom was one of at least three work places the students had available. The teen moms, (and their chosen friends), could work in the Teen Parent Program class which was staffed by that teacher most times (I think). Then there was also our meeting room, where we had our morning meetings, which didn't necessarily have a designated staff person there. It served as a nice afternoon work place for students, as long as a teacher was checking in on it regularly. At least one time that meeting room got closed off from student use for some reason, and it happened more than once. One time its lack of supervision had interesting results; nevertheless, I don't think any of the situations the students took advantage of were that bad compared to the potential possibilities. This one time the meeting room got closed was when some students complained the that rubber balls from inside the computer mouse had all disappeared: there were three computers in that room that students could use, and it was a favorite place to work because it was nice and quiet. The disappearance of the "mouse balls", was kind of funny, (though I didn't laugh out loud). At the end of the day, the computers were practically useless without a mouse, and I wasn't about to go ask for new ones, when they could and should easily be returned by those who took the rubber balls. So I closed off use of the meeting room for anything other than our large group meetings, when teachers were in there with students. Eventually, I'm not sure how, we got functioning mice; I think we re-opened up the lab for use, but the point was made and the parameters of use established.

The other case that took me by surprise with that meeting room was one day when I went in there in the morning, and I guess students had gotten to be in there for a while, and had been feeling creative. When I walked in there I was slightly shocked. The students had taken all of the desks and all of the chairs and built them into some kind of structure, which was pretty artistic, and pretty much reached all the way to the ceiling. It was quite amazing. I didn't even know how to react. The bigger part of me was impressed that they went to so much effort, and made something that was really cool, and must have worked together as a team, and did it in such a short time that they didn't get caught! The other part of me knew it was going to have to come down, and I think that after checking with my principal, we decided that if students would volunteer to help take it down under supervision, the room would still be available for use. It was one of those few things that I never found out who did it; I am curious!

The hardest part about this setup with Destinations working in so many places came in the afternoon, when we ran the CNN unit. This was part of the seven credits students could earn in a term just by being present, and these seven credits were the equivalent of about half a normal course load for one high school term. They would get one credit for the journal they did every morning in our large group meeting, (which, even for high school students, I felt it necessary and important to model, so this was the time I would write, and have other teachers walk around the classroom monitoring student progress). They got one credit for math, which I taught; one credit for English which was taught by another teacher; one credit for science, which I also taught; one credit for CNN, which another teacher and I led; one credit for the silent reading after the CNN; one or more credits for their projects which other teachers and I supervised. For the

CNN component we would watch a ten minute CNN Student News segment which had ten questions; students would answer the questions; then we discussed. I started reading a newspaper article or two daily to them with a discussion after. Sometimes we varied it and instead of the CNN segment we watched a Discovery Earth video, which they liked much more.

The CNN segment had advantages and disadvantages. It was difficult because we gathered everyone from the entire program back at the end of the day, and it was not easy having them all in pretty much one classroom at one time, (even though it was the big triple classroom: they could only be a certain distance away from the screen to see and hear the video). The advantage of this meeting at the end of the day was that we were able to dismiss them all at once, and I could take attendance to make sure everyone was there and no one left. This cured one of the programs earlier fallibilities, which was that students were apt to take off at some point during the day so that, by the end of the day, the program, which housed 70 students or so, would literally have five or eight students left. This solved that problem, and the students didn't like that too much. More importantly, I don't think they liked being in a more normal classroom setting with so many students in the same room, especially at the end of the day when they had been doing whatever they were doing till that point. Students would literally hide out in various classes throughout the program and I would do my afternoon "sweep" in which I went to all of our classrooms and attempted to gather them into my classroom where CNN was held; it was like herding cats and pulling teeth at once. The bigger picture was really assuring students stayed in school through the day; this seemed the most logical and easy to do that, so I used the structure; it worked.

This afternoon meeting served the same purpose as well as the morning meeting, in which I could take attendance. In the larger framework of this structure, it was necessary in forming an identity for the program and getting students to get to know one another, instead of staying limited to the people they knew and were comfortable with, in cliques. Aside from these two "bookend" meetings, we also ran a middle meeting which took place right after lunch, another time students were highly likely to disappear, as it was convenient for them to go outside after lunch downstairs in the basement in the cafeteria, where there was less supervision. These management structures all fall under the category of creating the best environment, which includes one of the most difficult aspects of an environment management, which is transition. This is not a physical part of the environment per se, in the respect of being able to locate a specific object or place, but even more challenging, because it involves moving from one environment to another, from one location to another, when the structure is the least stable.

These structures and security measures therefore need to be built into the system to anticipate and accommodate these gaps in the system, and that's really what all of these meetings were about. While there were probably other alternatives to accomplish this same goal, the systems we devised seemed to work well. The point of this structuring is to devise a system and to monitor it, and track it and your students or children, so you know, and they know, what they are supposed to be doing, and when and where they should be doing it; it makes for a much more functional and effective system for everybody, and the most productive positive scenario. It enables and fosters the greatest opportunities for success.

Aside from those given, the morning meeting had many other functions. In our school one of them was to track students in making sure they would learn the skills of being on time and prepared for an activity. It also built social skills, the students earned academic credit through their journal writing, as mentioned, and it built group identity and a sense of cohesion. These latter skills might not be so functional in a parenting situation but a meeting can be devised and adjusted according to each family's needs, and it could be set around the dinner table, and/or when children get home from school, one day on the weekend; there should be a series of meetings. One of the main points of a regular daily meeting is to establish routine, which children need, and another point of it, without sounding mushy, is to bond.

Especially for an alternative teacher, it is important to keep a clipboard or a chart of some kind during the day in the place where you keep your attendance. Keep a space around the edge of the paper on the clipboard or if you can use your grade book to mark more than just attendance, you should also have someplace special where you keep your announcements. This space, for me, served as a place to keep notes during the day of things that I wanted to announce the following day. I carried a clipboard with me pretty much wherever I went in Destinations, and it had the basics on it, including the attendance sheet, random announcements or upcoming events, and my most current grade percentages for students in math and science. When I would notice something or think of something I wanted to announce about the program, my class, something positive someone did, or anything in general, I would write a note in the margin of the attendance sheet and I guess I liked talking because those margins always filled up and overflowed. Somebody might say I like the sound of my own voice but it's not quite as melodic as I'd like it to be. I would make those announcements at the next meeting, or if they were very important I would wait till the AM meeting when I knew I would have the greatest attention and focus. Carrying that clipboard was very helpful, and having some system like that is essential, because for me, I always like to have relevant and current information available to me quickly; whether or not I share it with students is generally a function of their manner, persistence, and timing in requesting it from me. If they really want it they get the information, I am more apt to share it with them, but I'm also trying to get them to manage their own information, so I don't want to be too much of a crutch.

Nowadays, when I do my announcing, it's mostly organized through the Smart-board, which is super convenient. I am confident that parents would do well to have a bulletin board of sorts to connect with their kids for long term messages or as another means of communication. It's essential. Put one up, and if you don't know where to start, put one on the refrigerator if it's not already there. I carried that clipboard around with me so I could always be aware of what every student could be working on; they could never say they had nothing to do. You should do this during the day and get in the habit of keeping track of what is going on in the program and know what's going on in your house. Little things that people tell you, things that you read in your emails, or things you think of that need improvement, can go here as easy access for a regular routine; some reminders are worth posting in high traffic places.

If, perchance, there was nothing to announce because nothing bad happened, no one was in trouble, no bad behaviors were caught, etc., here is your first quiz question to see if you have really been paying attention and learning what I am trying to bring across. My question is, what do you say or announce, when there is nothing to announce? Please take thirty seconds or a minute to come up with an answer, and it is one of the most important things you can do for your students, and if you don't know, then take a guess. That's what we have to teach our children and students to do, even when they are unsure if they are right, (guess)! The answer is in the next paragraph so do not read that paragraph until you officially give up the game. When you teach it right, that is what learning becomes for students: a fun and exciting game where they want to continually challenge themselves to learn and enjoy the process of learning because it is dynamic, fresh, and invigorating. Instill that in them and you give a great gift.

Did you get the answer? Or did you give up? If you gave up I think you should skip this paragraph and come back to it another time; notice I am giving you another chance to try, learn, and remember, this is the behavior you want to model for your students all the time, even when they are not looking. I was on a ski lift once with a friend, (while I had become a teacher and he was becoming a doctor), and there were a couple kids on the lift with us. Some explicative or something came out of my mouth and my friend said something to me about being a teacher, and that I shouldn't use that kind of language around those kids, and I said, "I'm not teaching right now". He replied, "Larry, you are always a teacher." That stuck with me, especially since he is always on duty as a doctor, and I took the lesson, and also cleaned up my mouth for my own sake; I want to be perfect all the time because I am there in front of the kids as a model. I'm not going to say I don't think all people should be this way. Do it.

Look at how good I procrastinate giving an answer that I know someone can figure out. I guess you better not read this paragraph either if you gave up in the quest for the answer of the question: what to say when no announcement needs to be made. The following is the answer: when no announcement needs to be made because nothing is wrong with the program, then the students deserve **praise,** because everything is going great; they deserve a compliment and you owe it to them since you tell them what is wrong and needs improvement when things are wrong, you should tell them things are good give them praise and tell them so when things are good. Announcements can include any routine or topic that you want, and we integrated including a positive value, trait, or attribute of the week that we focused on, and a discussion of what that entailed. It serves to build character smoothly. This would be even more applicable and relevant in a home situation where parents could use this time to instill their values in their children, reminding children of the behavior, attitude, and character they expect.

The other interesting thing about morning meeting was also part of what I considered to be the Monday Morning Special and I cannot take credit for the originality of this activity, as it was borrowed from CE2, (Community Experience for Career Education), another program in our building, the Harding Learning Center, in Coos Bay, Oregon. This activity is the Monday Drawing, and it was one of my favorite activities; it was a little different from the drawing discussed earlier. It works better or worse with different programs and students. It works with some children as opposed to others, though I venture every child has *something* they would like to be in a drawing for, or something they would like to win. This drawing definitely worked for all the students in Destinations Academy: a little of the time for all of them, some of the time for most of them, and all of the time for some of them; it was a great motivator.

In order to do this activity properly and succeed in using it, you need to keep very good and accurate attendance records. You have to keep your attendance or records in a way that you can glance at it kind of easily for the week. On Monday morning, (or afternoon if you prefer to do at home; it's meant to be a week's summary, so you could choose the day), you go back over your attendance or records, and highlight everyone who was at every AM meeting and PM meeting on time, and write their names on slips of paper and put their names in the hat. Again, you could modify this activity to suit your needs, depending on what you are drawing to motivate. Then you draw out a name and the winner gets five dollars cash from the office or some prize you deem worthy for the effort. It was easy to give this prize away in Coos Bay, Oregon; I don't know if we'd have the same ease of distribution here in Dirty Jersey. Those names not selected out the hat stay in the hat for the following week's drawing, so the higher a person's attendance, the greater the likelihood over time of his eventually getting drawn. I usually let a student pick out a name because it was more fun and I get to lead everything else anyway. In general, the more authority you can give and delegate to students, (where there is little room for error on that particular activity), the more you are teaching students how to take authority and lead in a positive direction and to do things right. You need to give opportunities to succeed, if you expect to see success from students, and sometimes that means taking a risk, like letting them lead the show a little bit, (or in some cases, a lot!) There are not necessarily too many chances to get into the position of authority before one gets into a position of authority for a job, so we owe it to our students to put them there every safe chance we get and let them learn how to lead. Otherwise how will they learn to lead?

I usually ended the morning meetings with telling them to push in their chairs and have a great day or week or afternoon as the case might have been and when I told them to push in their chairs I added the word please for modeling sake. This model serves in any situation and in any house or classroom. It is proper manners we need to teach and these students and children these days do as you do and not necessarily as you say. For me, when I tell them to say "please", I want to be able to tell them that I say the word as well. It is not enough, in my book, to use the concept of "I'm the boss" in order to get respect; that's a last ditch effort used when you're exhausted or out of reasons, or just need to bail. Don't overuse "because I said so"; as far as I'm concerned that's like a "get out of jail free" card, and you only have a limited number of them available before you lose your audience. When it comes to general respect in teaching students to listen to me, I want respect because I give it and earn it, because that is the only real kind of respect there is. Everything else is just fear of authority or respect for the position, neither of which means so much to me. I think many of these students feel the same. I think it is right.

So all in all we held three main meetings a day in Destinations: one in the morning upon starting school, one right after lunch, and one in the afternoon at the end of the day. The afternoon meeting was in general much lighter than morning meeting. I can't emphasize enough the importance of tracking your students and children and knowing about their progress in academics and life; and that starts with attendance: knowing where they are. Though we never told the students that was the biggest part of our meetings, they may have figured it out, and that's OK; students can know that you need to know where they are, and that you care. It may stop them from making poor choices if they know they are being monitored. I knew this from my first teaching job in Coos Bay at IPASS, Interim Program for Academic and Social Skills, a credit recovery program to which students had been removed from the mainstream for mainly behavioral and academic reasons. These students had a tendency to try and disappear at the end of the day, and I needed to have some kind of final check-in at the end of the day where I could make sure everyone was present. I like to account for my students and it is important for teachers and parents to know where their kids are. Especially in Destinations, where there were five different rooms students could be working in, and different projects and teachers they could be working with, I needed unifying meetings where we all got together and we could assure we had everyone.

Afternoon post-lunch meetings happened at 12:20. Always underlying the current of that meeting and of the program in general, was the question of lateness. While we hit the target of timeliness regularly, and really brought the point home, for some students the issue was never really resolved. Now what is "late", you ask? If you're wondering how I could even ask such a question, since "late" means "not on time", in my telling parents their children were late for a class, I have had parents ask, "Well, how late was he?" I grew up with different values which don't ask the question of "how late"; there is only the question of being there on time or not. In the beginning of the year with Destinations, "late" was anytime after the bell rang. As the year went on, and I saw they had respect for the rule and were learning that part of the system, that you follow the boss's rules and get there on time, then I gave them a minute, even two minutes, because they were good students, and in the real world, if you do your job well, generally, and don't have an attitude, your boss usually won't fire you over an occasional minute.

In this afternoon meeting the main point was that we took attendance, and welcomed students back from lunch, and then one of the teachers started doing this fun activity where he put four words on the board, but there was only the first letter of each word, and all the words had to do with one concept. He gave hints: it was a neat game. I read trivia questions to them, like six questions from this little trivia foldout ringed card stack, which they liked, and we made any necessary announcements. Since the main purpose was attendance, I tried to make this meeting more fun and lighten up on the academics. I almost always talked during this time about people's projects, and reminded them who I needed to meet with and gave reminders to get projects going and check in with teachers. It was a cool meeting.

The second PM meeting, the third group meeting of the day, happened at 2:05, (school ended at 2:53), but it rarely started on time. There were usually several other things going on with other teachers, and students took a little bit of time to get to my classroom where the meeting was held. They lollygagged, and there weren't so many students who really wanted to do the meeting, or at least admit to it. Even I rarely got there on time, as I as busy with eight other things, and then leading this meeting, and usually had to do a sweep to gather the slackers. I think we had a pleasant understanding though, because no one really seemed to mind the meetings too much. We all worked really hard all day to make the program work; so if we were a little slow at the end of the day, hey, come on, I mean really; it is Coos Bay after all. You see, here is my theory on Coos Bay, (home of Steve Prefontaine, former holder of seven American running records, and inspiration for the founding of Nike footwear). The theory is: the United States is the freest country in the world, and Oregon is the most relaxed place in the country, and the south coast is the most laid back place in Oregon, Coos Bay being the center of it, and in Coos Bay, Harding Learning Center is the alternative center: the most chill place in town, and if you really want to get funky, come check out Destinations Academy in the Harding Learning Center. Catch my drift?

Every day, in that respect, in the beginning of the year, at 2:05, (truthfully we were pretty exact about the time requirement in the beginning of the year, now I recall), we all gathered in my classroom for CNN. On the CNN website, there's an education tab and within that page there is a ten minute news segment which comes with the ten questions. There is a printable transcript you could use for students or children to read if they couldn't listen. We never used the transcript, mainly because I wanted everyone to gather there, (as opposed to doing it on their own at some point in the day); also it is a social class and a social skill to work in a group, listen quietly to a speaker, answer questions and learn.

So we would gather there in my class, packed in like sardines, and I passed out the questions for the CNN Student News, which I always printed up earlier in the day, and streamed the video, and did the do. In the beginning of the year, I had to remind the students often not to ask their neighbors for the answers if they missed a question, since we were going to go over the questions at the end of the video, and they would get all the answers anyway. That was a hard habit to break not to ask neighbors for answers. After the news segment I usually took a survey to find out who got five questions right, seven, nine, and so on, and kept track of the stats on the board over the month, so students could actually see the class percentages improve. The fact is that the class percentage improved, which was exciting for me, since I told them the percentages would improve at the start of the year, and I was hoping I was not making an empty claim. The more percentages improved, the less likely students were to talk during the segment; but then again, news is a social activity and if they are talking about the news with their neighbor while the news is going on, who am I to stop them from talking, just to hear the news better? I mean, do I want them to devour the news without commenting about it? That's an edgy philosophical question I put forth about which I am not sure where I stand, but I lean to "listen now and discuss later".

Later on, as I mentioned, I also started including news article summaries in our news sessions after we had been doing the CNN segment for a couple months. I would read and highlight articles in the newspaper dealing with science, politics, social events, (often during the morning class meeting I would actually read and highlight the paper). Then, after we had the CNN discussion, I would read the article(s) to the class, asking questions along the way to the students, trying to incite discussion. Most of the time it was hard to keep them focused, because students did not want to go against the current of the class, and stand out as different in the eyes of the class; to show that they were really thinking, concerned, or interested in what was going on in the world; it wasn't that cool. It was kind of neat to me, that they valued each other's opinions so much, which for these students was a social skill, (these people did not get along with each other in the beginning of the year: the set of cliques mentioned earlier were pretty isolated, and by mid-year we had formed a pretty cohesive unit where everyone knew everyone and almost everyone got along). Sometimes, though, we got discussions that were opinionated and heated, and where a couple students really disagreed about things that were very important to them, which did not have to do with music, YouTube, or video games, and were relevant to the world; this happened as the year went on and students felt comfortable expressing their opinions and showing that they cared about the world and weren't so worried about how they looked through the eyes of others. Those discussions were some of my proudest teaching moments, especially to see one student disagreeing pretty much with everyone else in the program. I was so proud of that, aside from the obvious teacher reasons, because free speech is what this country is all about, and it takes real courage to stand against a group of peers, state an opinion that is different from all of the others, and not back down. That is the kind of social skill that we brought out of students who would not have spoken in other cases, and those are lifelong skills people keep which change fundamentally who they are; alternative education rocks.

At the end of the day, after the CNN news segment and news articles, we had SSR which is Silent Sustained Reading. This almost never got easy, as opposed to the other activities we did that generally got better throughout the year and as time went on. It's difficult to do in a large group and we learned the importance of this activity in my Master's program for any age student, and I strongly encourage parents to have a reading time for their children every day. If you don't do it already then start with a small amount, even five minutes, and build from there. The SSR activity certainly got good to the point where students could and would read quietly, but day to day or week to week, it would fluctuate and that is more understandable with this generation; I was honestly impressed that we did attain the silence pretty regularly and they were able to read well. Having a nice selection of magazines helped, as did modeling the reading for the students, so they could see that the teachers were reading too. I also tracked them by five minute intervals so they knew they were getting credit for this. The best way to run the SSR, when two teachers were there, was for both teachers to be modeling and take turns day to day with who would be the "shush-er" who had to remind students to read and redirect them to read. Then the other teacher would constantly be reading, as the model of how to read quietly.

That session was supposed to be about 10-15 minutes. So the second PM meeting would be 2:05-2:15 CNN video; 2:15-2:25 question review; 2:25-2:35 news article discussion; 2:35-2:50 SSR, and then dismiss students to put their chairs up and go to the lockers before the dismissal bell rang at 2:53. Parents can do this at home using rewards for a certain amount of reading done; Pizza Hut used to have a reading incentive program and I would think there are many still out there to inspire children to read, which are free. For our purposes in the program, those CNN credits earned within the program worked like this: forty CNN and/or Planet Earth daily assignments made one credit; I divided the credit accordingly so that twenty of those assignments made a half credit and so on down to quarter credits. I could have kept better track of their SSR time but I was busy keeping them reading and insuring a quiet reading environment. It could be worked out with some planning among teachers supervising the SSR.

In setting up Destinations we altered the fundamental structure of the program and that did wonders. There really was no structure when I came up there, so that might not be the right statement. It was like kids working all day on whatever they wanted and that included playing video-games on the television while sitting on the couch; if you want to call that work that's fine with me. When we decided to get rid of the couch and we put it in the cheer-leading room which was on the same floor as the program, the kids flipped when they saw it was gone, and asked where it was, to which I replied that it was gone, and it was gone out of our program. Why did they need to know it was 100 feet from where they sat? The cheerleading room was not part of our academy so it was truly gone from our program.

The plan we set up was under my principal's suggestion for a morning rotation of classes and an afternoon schedule of project-based learning time. It was difficult setting up the morning classes because there were only two full time Destinations teachers, and we were dividing the students into four groups. vSo the ideal worked as follows. There were four groups of students who traveled through classes together; I labeled mine A, B, C, and D, and they were in order of math skills, from high to low, which we never told the students, though they may have figured it out. Class A for me was from 8:30 to 9:10. Class B was from 9:10 to 9:50; there was a break from 9:50 to 10:00 and students had to remain in the building, which was a change from the year before, when they would go outside and smoke and often disappear for the rest of the morning or the rest of the day. For most of the year during this time I took students on a walk for fresh air, usually just around the block was all we could do by the time we gathered, but it was worth it. Students who walked regularly earned a quarter of a credit in Physical Education. Then Class C was 10:00 to 10:45, and Class D was 10:45 to 11:30, when lunch started.

I'll stick with the reorganizing of the structure first, before I get distracted talking about my classes, and how they were divided, and how they functioned. The same way I had four classes, every student had four classes in their AM schedule, but some of them had double periods. For example, the freshmen and sophomores were all enrolled in the English Teacher's "Read 180" program, a successful reading program involving learning centers, listening to books on tape, and answering questions on a computer. It is a great small group program that requires separation and isolation from the rest of the students for full effectiveness, so he taught this class in a separate room from the triple classroom, (the main classroom/work area of Destinations Academy) of which my classroom was part. This reading program left all the other students who might be in the "middle room" technically under my authority, but there were other teachers and assistants involved, so that lightened the load. That "Read 180" class happened from 8:30 to 9:50 and students could earn two credits for that class. Remember these credit systems are different from many other systems; one credit was what a student earned for a normal class over the whole year; so a student in Oregon needs between 22 and 24 credits to graduate high school.

The other double period class evolved later in the year when the English Teacher and the Life Skills/Resource Room Teacher, (who should rest in peace), joined forces to team teach the "Transition English" class, designed to teach relevant English and life skills, preparing students for the world after and outside of high school. That class took place from 10:00 to 11:30, and students could earn two credits or more through that class and they got two teachers for the price of one. Now it gets a little tricky to understand where all of the students were. Maybe it gets easier if you get structure well.

So the English teacher had all of classes C and D from 8:30 to 9:50, and I was responsible for classes A and B during that time. But you may see the issue here. Do you? When I taught Class A, where was Class B to be? The answer to that question which was never satisfactorily fulfilled for me, was on "Odysseyware", an on-line computer education program that our school building subscribed to, which got us about twenty licenses for the building, and could be used any time of the day or night by students with a computer. We did not get our money's worth, as far as I'm concerned, at least not in Destinations Academy. The students did not like using this program, except for a few of the kids. They complained that the program shut them out sometimes or lost work, (which I believe it did). One of my problems with it was that there wasn't enough supervision, which is really a generic problem in my opinion, with any computer education program, which is somewhat comforting to my career longevity. Computers really can't teach children; people teach children. For this Odysseyware program situation, there was an assistant supervising them but overall we had little success with that endeavor; so be it.

So I'm still trying to give an idea of the structure of the whole program to give the reader an idea of what a total alternative education program looks like. There were two places students were to be working on Odysseyware. One was between my room and the English Teacher's room, the middle room where our assistant worked, (but halfway through the year she got sick and never returned; the occasional substitutes we had never really got to know the students and never really had the connection or authority to monitor that area thoroughly). The other place the students could work, which is where I sent students who weren't working quietly on Odysseyware, since I was in that big triple room myself, was the Teen Parent Room, with the Teen Parent Teacher. This program was separate from Destinations Academy but part of it too. Many of the students in this program were taking classes in Destinations Academy, but they were enrolled in other programs within the Harding Learning Center as well. It was problematic because they sort of had a free pass to get away with less attendance, of which they sometimes took advantage. They had full and constant access to the Teen Parent Room, which other students did not have the same kind of access to, and especially at the end of the day, when CNN was starting, this was a place students would be found lingering and I never really found it fair that these students got this kind of advantage, since their babies were well taken care of in the main Teen Parent room downstairs. This main Teen Parent room downstairs was supervised by two teaching assistants, and always being watched by some of the teen parents who had that task as part of their responsibility in the Teen Parent Program. It was the cutest thing when there were fire drills, you would see these babies in wheel-able multi-baby cribs, coming down the hallway, a parade of babies in school!

Just when you thought you were beginning to understand Destinations, it gets more confusing, as do many alternative education programs when looked at from the outside. Here is how we managed to have four teachers involved in the Destinations program. Our special education teacher serviced the whole program by doing integrated classes that included special needs children, (so it definitely behooved us to have special education students in the program; otherwise there was no way to justify having a special education teacher teaching a whole class). In the beginning of the year, the Resource Teacher taught his own single period Transition English class, and that was one of the four classes students went to in their morning rotation, but only seniors could go to that class. I have no idea how we managed to work this out, but it took a lot of meetings and talking about all the students. Our Teen Parent Teacher was a certified teacher, (and is now an administrator, props to her), and her room was technically for teen parents, but it generally was open to the whole population of the Harding Learning Center, where our program, among other alternative programs, was housed. She had about ten computers there and that was the other place students could work on Odysseyware, as I mentioned.

Again, if they were working quietly in the middle class (next to my class), where there were about five computers, then that was fine with me. But I could not teach one class and simultaneously control noisy students in a separate room. I drew the line there. There was actually a third option where students who were not technically in a "teacher led class" learned on Odysseyware while the morning rotation was going on. This option was used when students were especially good and the program was running excellently, and in that option they uses the morning meeting room, which had four computers. When they worked there, no teacher was in the room, and they were technically in a completely separate room from anyone; but they were in earshot of the Teen Parent Teacher, and another assistant, (who was the best assistant ever), would check in on them so they got covered to make sure it was copacetic.

So those are really all the places students could be in the morning and it took students a little while, some longer than others, to figure out their schedules and where they were supposed to be at what time. There were students who never figured it out. And they probably didn't make it in the program. But in general, everyone got the picture and got by with a little help from their friends. Destinations became, and still is, a very positive place and students actually like to help each other out and point each other in the right direction. It's like this: **giving students opportunities to be leaders and to be successful is the best way for them to learn how to do those things correctly**. And our students really thrived as leaders, and I hope they continue to do so; they really need to gel, step up, and take the program's pride in their hands; they are the program. We have great leaders I have excellent belief in.

I pretty much divided the four classes in two broader levels and conveniently that division happened at the break. The two classes, Class A and Class B, which I had before the break, were the higher level classes and were pretty much all juniors and seniors. Class A was the fastest and smartest in math. There were two "division-makers" that got them into their respective classes. For every student I interviewed in the beginning of the year, before the program started, I asked them some algebra questions, gaging their abilities at single and double variable algebra, checking their abilities with basic multiplication, division, decimals and fractions. That was how I really divided the students into their classes. The Resource Teacher also gave them a test of math skills that had several pages and gave a number score and it all pretty much matched up, but my method was faster and I knew what I was going to be teaching, so I knew what skills were most essential for the different level classes.

Whenever we got new students during the year we interviewed them first, and I made a point to ask them about their math skills, so I always left the interview knowing what math group they would be in if we let them into Destinations. It usually matched up by their grade levels which made for a natural match for whether they were going to be in Read 180 or Transition English; so there were coherent groups by grade levels which had the same level English together, and the same level math together. This seems important in helping students to develop new friendships that are tied to academics. While it is great to have friendships based on hobbies, connections, sports, and the li, it is important to have a sense of camaraderie and positivity linked to academics and classes too. There were a couple students who did not quite fit the normal pattern, and we had small discussions amongst the teachers to make the best decisions we could about them. There were times we switched students to higher and lower groups throughout the year, after they had already been in the program, and this involved a joint decision between the English Teacher and me. Those decisions numbered less than five; it was usually the case that of a slipping student; or one whose grades were rising greatly in my class and in English.

So I had the four classes, who attended my classroom in order of their skills from most to least, so for the first class, the most advanced one, most of the assignments I just gave them I would ask them if they wanted some assistance, and guide them along the way. They always wanted to just go at it on their own, though occasionally they would ask for help or examples on the board. And there were times when I mandated that we were working on something together first, before they could work on it on their own, like standard direct instruction teaching. I kept a good balance of giving assignments and teaching; but when I gave assignments, I never went back to my desk and did work. I always stayed in the classroom with them and did the assignment myself, which was pretty fun. There were several benefits to this and they were essential to the success of this kind of work in this scenario, as follows.

First and foremost in importance was the modeling aspect, which I believe in strongly enough to make it a whole chapter of this book. Students saw I enjoyed doing the work, (or at least looked like I was enjoying it, though I always got myself to enjoy if I didn't enjoy it at first), and they saw I was dedicated to completing it. I varied whether I would let them use calculators based on the type of the assignment, the time of year, (more allowance for calculators in the beginning of the year and slowly transitioned them off of calculators as the year progressed), and their general attitude and skill level. I often awarded extra credit for work done without calculators, (less than half these students had cell phones at this point in time), or said certain sections had to be done without calculators, or every other problem with calculators. The point is that during the whole year, there was one assignment that I gave them that I used a calculator on when I did it myself, and that made it easy for me not have complaints about the difficulty of the work because whatever they were doing, I was doing, sans calculator.

The second benefit of being in there doing the work while they were working was that it was much easier for them to get my help and assistance. They knew that if I would have been back at my desk it would be an effort for me to get up and come over to work with them, and they probably wouldn't ask for help for that reason. It would be more noticeable and obvious that they were in need of help, and for some of them that may look like a weakness they seek to avoid portraying in themselves. Not to mention it is much easier for them to get distracted with each other and talking when the teacher is farther away from them; when the teacher is right there with them, he's part of them, and that's pretty exciting. So when they ask a question the teacher has the option to answer it right from where he is, plus if it's a new teacher, he probably just worked on the problem they are struggling with and may have the trick or clue they are looking for fresh in his mind since he just went through it on his own.

The best thing about working in there with them is that the teacher really gets to know them and build a bond with them. Working on assignments with students or even the same assignment in the same place is exciting: it's being in the space with them, being part of a team, and they feel that, and it feels electric when they ask something and in answering them with the help they need, they respond with something like, "yeah that's what I thought but I wasn't sure", thank goodness the teacher was there as that rock of stability and knowledge to encourage them to try and learn! What a great feeling! It is helping students gain confidence and courage, and it's great. For children who need confidence, it is good to have people on their team they can rely on, so they eventually get into solving the problems more on their own; they become solid and firm in their own skills and abilities; they become independent learners.

So, moving on, to quote Steven Colbert, (and by the way that is a great transition phrase for students and children), we have the assignment collection system. It is a pretty simple system. There is an inbox, and I still use this simple yet functional system today, and students need to know that is where they put assignments, and the assignments must be safe there, and the teacher must empty it regularly, and that doesn't mean emptying it to the trash bin. Well, in actuality, it's not so simple, because it is another of those evolving systems which changes as students change. The main part of the collection system that changed for me was deadlines. In the beginning of the year I was pretty loose with deadlines, in fact I didn't really give any. In the second term I started giving deadlines, the question is always whether you want to have a final deadline past which an assignment can be turned in or not. You have to realize, especially with teen moms like I had, and in general with alternative education, there are going to be some students whose attendance is horrible. Your decision is whether you want to be able to offer these students credit for work turned in late, or if you're going to cut them off at a certain point during the semester and say it is too late, and they can't get credit for whatever work they did. It's not easy.

To change the subject, pardon the pun, and to switch out of math for a while, (but staying with structure), I need to talk about science. I didn't necessarily feel qualified to teach science; nonetheless, it was assigned to me: I was to teach a math class and a science class, and how I structured the separation of them was up to me. Though I taught it as part of my mainstream sixth grade class back in Jefferson in my third year of teaching, (about 2003 for those keeping track), this was high school science I was going to teach, which I had really never taught to an entire class before. As an alternative teacher in prior years, I was required to teach the students a smattering of all subjects, and that mainly focused on math and English. Social studies concepts and ideas were pretty easy to weave into the curriculum; but science is pretty much its own subject and not as easy to integrate as social studies, so I would do an experiment here and there. All in all, though, of the core subjects, it was the one most left by the wayside in my teaching career; so there I was teaching high school science in Destinations Academy.

I created a curriculum of and from several key components. The first was from <u>Science World,</u> a student education magazine produced every two weeks. It comes with a work packet (with teacher's edition), and as many subscriptions as desired, and current science material which is interesting, relevant, and fun to read, along with activities that are engaging and exciting, and it even includes links to state and federal education standards. What more could a teacher ask for? The next component, and probably the crux of the science instruction, came from the Geo-kits which were giant binder like things with all kinds of cool color transparencies and copy-able materials, tests, quizzes, and all kinds of treats; and I would go into our book room, where the curriculum was stored, and pick out the two Geo-kits that looked most exciting and keep them on my shelf until we worked through them. Each geo-kit unit lasted about three weeks, and then we switched back to math, and so on. Things were looser in Oregon.

The third component of the science class was an array of projects and project-based learning which included individual projects, class projects, interdisciplinary projects, and theme projects; these are discussed in detail in the "Use Projects and Journals." chapter. There was still technically a fourth component of the program which I don't consider worthy to call a component in its own right. This part of the science program was definitely the least exciting, but made for a good activity for substitute when I had them in the classroom; it also helped build the students' skills in regular reading and learning from text, which is generally still part of most high school curricula, and arguably a necessary life skill. The assignments I gave out when I was absent for the day came from a textbook, <u>AGS Physical Science</u>. We got through almost the entire book in the year, and it was a lot to give the students, but I had to justify giving them a credit in math and one in science by really having me one period a day. In other words, most of the other classes in school, in a 45 minute period once a day, earned a credit for that class. Here I had the students for the same 45 minutes a day, but I was giving two credits for 45 minutes: one for math and one for science, as I split the class between math and science every couple weeks or so.

So I gave them overflow work that often students completed in the afternoons or at home. These assignments were usually about 20-30 pages at a time: I gave them one chapter from the science book each day I was gone, and they had to answer all the questions in the section reviews and the questions in the chapter reviews. Towards the end of the year I had them write all of the vocabulary terms in bold and their definitions on a separate sheet of paper. There was something better I could have done with that assignment but didn't know what it was. Maybe including it more in Jeopardy or having a quiz every so often would have been the solution, to have a quiz on the terms and key concepts at the end of that week, as a more valid form of assessment, but I was doing a whole lot here, and did my best!

There are so many facets of an alternative program's structure to take into account, that it's hard to structure the presentation of the structure! In taking attendance in my regular class rotation, (when I taught science and math), I wrote it in the standard red attendance book given out at the office at the beginning of the year. Now this was just for my class rotation, a different process was used for the group meetings discussed previously. In the class rotation, the groups were so small, (about fifteen students), that I could just take attendance as the students came in, mark with standard slash, "T" for tardy, "A" for absent. I prefer to this day, the crooked "T" because if a student has not shown up I can put the diagonal leg of the "T" coming up from the lower right corner to the center of the box, and then if they were absent, that same diagonal leg could turn to an "A" or if they came, it could turn to a "T". I offer that free to the world: the "crooked T", useless to some; I must have learned it from someone.

That was probably the easiest instruction I have written this entire paper. Doubt it will last long. This is where this is starting to get hard, trying to remember what I wrote already in this book about assignments I gave during the class rotation. I started the year with a crate in which I kept all the assignments, and I labeled each assignment, based on several criteria, and put them into a manila folder, which went into a hanging folder, which hung in the crate with all the other assignments I made. I ordered them by date, with oldest in front, and put the date at the top of the folder along with a title. Picking a title was a little tricky. Ideally you want to pick something that an assistant or student can find, (if you allow them to go in the crate, which I did). You want the title also to be mentally recognizable to you so when a student mentions the title, it comes right to mind. This was the first system I used back then, and things weren't as computer amazing for me in 2007 as they are now, but whatever you do, make sure it's an organized system that you and your students and/or children understand.

I think we are ready to begin talking more about the whole group instruction and organization, and the structure that was instituted in the program, which I think is the main reason I was brought up to Destinations from my position in AIMS/IPASS the year before, (also in the Harding Learning Center in Coos Bay). The first basic part of the structure was the meetings and attendance I explained. No matter what the situation, parent or teacher, however many kids you're dealing with, you have to have meetings. Everything else is icing, but you do not want to tell the students that; this is the glue that keeps the program together, knowing where your students are, that you care about that, and manage it.

So you should take attendance thrice daily if you're running or involved in a program like this. Maybe for parents this means checking in with your kids thrice daily to connect to them about different topics, in other words, connecting to them with intent; greeting them doesn't count! You should have a purpose in mind when you talk to them, whether it is to learn about their situation or to teach them something. There are several ways to take attendance for meetings and I usually used two. You could go alphabetically down the list but then when you're at the end of the list and Johnny Appleseed walks to class, in you lose your place. The easiest way is to pick a direction around the class, and go around the room marking everyone; that way, when someone comes in your really can't lose your place because you see the spot you were taking attendance, even if you have not had your first cup of coffee. Again, there are many systems but just try to cover the gaps. I took my time doing this task, to make sure I got it right, but keep your ears open also, for foul language or anything inappropriate, because if you don't catch it now it will grow into something big and ugly that I guarantee you will have to deal with in a much harder form and at that point it could grow beyond handling ability; so stay alert.

One thing to know about structure is that you may have to rearrange it, unless you get it perfect the first time; and even then it will probably need fine tuning and altering over time. It is important, however, to let the students know about changes in the structure as they occur or near that time. While we introduced students to the changes in the structure at the beginning of the year, I had really started "advertising" for the program the year before. I used to eat my lunch with some of the other staff in the student cafeteria in the Harding Learning Center. We weren't paid for this, but I felt bad: the cafeteria workers, (two or three of them at most), were down there alone with pretty much the entire school, (which was really about eight different alternative programs), at once, and no other assigned supervision. Since my fellow teachers who were also my friends ate down there for free and fun that time, and all seemed to go well, I ate down there also, and generally it was a no-problem situation.

Toward the end of my second year there, when I knew I was going to be moving upstairs to Destinations to restructure it the following year, a couple of the lead skater boys in Destinations asked me something about my moving up to Destinations next year, if it was true; and they seemed kind of excited about it, at which I was pleasantly surprised. I told them it was true, but I alerted them right then to the fact that there were going to be some changes coming and they should be ready for them; till that point I had mainly known these boys from the common "hack circles" with a hacky sack, which formed daily in the gym during shared Physical Education time; they got a kick out the fact, (pardon the pun), that a teacher could hack, and we had developed a relationship; but it was not a typical teacher-student relationship. Being that I was hacking with them, although much of the time it was my hacky sack being used, I let a few rules slide in terms of what they could say and what they could not say. Generally I drew the line at the f-bomb, which is not typical for me, as I don't allow any cussing, but like I said, it was good to establish a connection to them. That's because even then, when I was downstairs in AIMS/IPASS, I knew Destinations was a failing program, and I realized that their problems bled out to the rest of the school and became my problems, so, not being their official teachers, I let them slide a little with some of the lighter cusses. Interestingly, they didn't take as much advantage as I thought, and their language was generally pretty clean, as were their topics of discussion in the hack circle. I made sure, however, when it became clear that I was going to be their teacher in the following year, and they asked me in the cafeteria about it, that they knew that the relationships would change, as would the behavior and attitude, from what it had been in Destinations before I got up there. They smartly didn't argue.

So while I had this preface and warning for some of the students, for all of the students there was still another process which was implemented for them to enter the program, even if they had been in it the year before, they were not considered officially accepted. That application, interview, and acceptance process is discussed later. As to the beginning of the next school year, once the students had all been accepted and we actually began the program, there was certainly something better that could have happened with the "welcoming days" for the first week of school. Though our process was not half bad, I do not imagine too many people would handle well meeting with the amount of students I did and planning out forty projects in three days. Nor do I think students got the best project-planning services.

How these welcoming days worked was that we had half the students there for the first day, and half the students there for the second day, and then we went into regular school mode after that; I think we just split them up alphabetically for those first days. The first hour or so of those first days was mostly me lecturing them about things I had already told them were going to happen in Destinations (in the interview they sat through and signed off on). I reminded them of rules and consequences in the program, and how they could thrive or dive in this program, and I recommend that part of it again for every year, especially reminding them of the waiting list of people who wanted to get into the program; this was good motivation to succeed. The part of the day after that, though, needed to be revised. Students went through a rotation in seeing all the teachers. They went to the Teen Parent Teacher to plan out their course in Odysseyware, the English Teacher to choose a novel, the assistant to help select individual course work, and to the Resource Teacher to get tested in math using his placement test.

So we'll get into those other specialties which encompass the other beams in the support structure that made the program what it is and give students in Destinations a range of means to earn credits. Most boring, basic, and essential, in my eyes is the absolute last ditch backup plan of credit recovery through bookwork discussed earlier. We increased the number of pages necessary to earn a credit from 200 (which it had been before I got there) to 300 and included a mini-project of some sort to go with the 300 pages, (it could be cooking a dish, or an experiment, for example). There were complaints at first but students realized it was the new bar and stopped whining quickly. Students had difficulty with the mini-project that went with the 300 pages, and I don't even know if we had any mini-projects completed, because I offered as an alternative to that mini-project, fifty extra pages of book work instead and students constantly chose that option. I don't know that there's a use in varying this equation, but I made my best guess based on what I learned in my education program and teaching experience. Someone should have the task of checking out books to students from the book room and matching it up with credits they needed. Although usually students were aware of their credits, it is helpful to have a transcript present when doing this part of the process to make things faster and more efficient. The super-awesome assistant took over this job when the other assistant got sick, and not surprisingly did a fantastic job of organizing the books and keeping track of them; this is important if you want to keep the library or book room you have. It might be the kind of thing where you divide up students alphabetically and each teacher takes a quarter of the students as his responsibility for checking out their books.

In explaining how I got up to Destinations Academy, I need to travel back in time to the end of the 2007 school year, which was when I still worked downstairs with AIMS/IPASS students who had been removed from mainstream for behavioral problems. At that time, I had been asked by my principal if I was willing to teach in Destinations. This request is worth mentioning because it was one of the funnier discussions I ever really had. My principal, who is probably the best principal I have ever had, called me into her office and told me about some changes coming up. She said that I had done a really good job with AIMS and IPASS, which she had told me before. She then asked me my thoughts in that she was thinking of making some changes in the building; it was around May and I was closing year two with these students who were really the toughest students in the district, as far as I could tell.

She asked me if I would be interested in moving up to Destinations to teach the following year, and to restructure the program in a new direction from where it was. In its state at that time, students pretty much came and went as they pleased, literally. There were one or two classes that were taught, and the rest of the day was considered "independent study", which really consisted of whoever was left sitting, or I should say, lounging, around, (there were couches that had probably been there since the building went up), and literally playing video games all day. Students had no respect for teachers, cussed up a storm in the hallways and throughout the building, wandered in hordes throughout the building unsupervised, and lived only for the fifteen minute morning break they had to go out and smoke cigarettes on the corner. There were fights incessantly, and other teachers and students were petrified to go in the hallways and unceasingly complained to people, including myself, about the problems in Destinations and those kids and all the problems they had, and that was Destinations Academy. She wanted to move the current Destinations Math Teacher, who had been at Destinations for many years, down to the AIMS and IPASS program to give him a fresh renewed perspective on education that might have had too much time at the same position with the same type of students and little change.

Even though I was totally looking forward to year three of my position in AIMS/IPASS, as I had been making photocopies with plans and a mindset for the third year, (I would make enough copies to have left over for the following year), I was still excited. At this point in AIMS/IPASS, I had the routine down, and figured it would be my best year yet, but it was still quite an upward movement to be teaching in a program where students did not have to get thrown out of another school in order to get in, (which is how they got into AIMS/IPASS). That was really the criteria for admittance, although there was one intermediate program I supervised as well in that position as Teacher of AIMS/IPASS. That program was called ACE, Academic Curriculum for Education, which was designed for students who were on the verge of removal from mainstream or having trouble there, and those students could come to my classroom without getting thrown out, but that program was generally kept hush, because neither my principal nor I wanted my program to grow that fast. That is because we always knew that eventually during the year, we would meet our quota of students, and knowing my abilities for handling great loads, and my principal's generous and loving heart, we knew we would exceed that quota, so why hurry the process?

When I accepted the offer to move upstairs and teach at Destinations, we began to make plans of how we were going to change this program and make it work. Destinations Academy was in the toilet. As previously described discipline was non-existent and attendance was horrible; structure was not a word to be associated with the program; academics were a joke, and no student had ever passed the state achievement test in math. I aimed to change that. One of the things I stuck by was the interview. The Destinations teachers were still in the mindset of what my AIMS/IPASS class before was, which was really a dumping ground. But even in a dumping ground, there's no reason things can't be organized, and certain usable things salvaged, and value found, if proper time and attention are given. In Israel they are turning a former dump into a park which will be lit by methane fumes from the dump itself. How's that for ingenuity? It's called Ariel Sharon Park. Check it out and recognize innovation.

We had to transform ourselves into a newly imaged Academy. The first step of that process in my mind, which I refused to give any ground on, was in the application process, which till that point ceased to exist. Students would "transfer" down from Marshfield, the only high school of Coos Bay, (which was right up a hill, about 50 steep steps to the south). They would come to the Harding Learning Center with or without proper paperwork, and fill out an application in the same day they would start, for all intents and purposes. The teachers had no say about who started when; students would start at any point in the year, and there seemed to be no limit on how many students they could have in the program. In the very beginning of my time there at Coos Bay there had been a third teacher, who was a high ranking officer in one of the armed services, and he held the program together, if through nothing other than fear, it was enough; there was no one who would mess with him, and I think it was that fear of him that kept everything in line. But shortly after I arrived there he had to leave for service in Afghanistan, I believe it was, and then it was two teachers left to handle over 80 kids, which doesn't seem so bad, except these were all difficult students with very special situations. It was no easy task.

So we set a cap on the number of students, and established interviews. The cap was aimed to be 40 students though I had heard 50 mentioned once and knew that was well within our abilities, and thought we would be good if we kept to a pretty strict 50. That was an administrative task in terms of maintenance. Our principal did a very nice job on that and I think that kept teachers in a good place and kids feeling enough attention. The interviews were funny because they started at the end of the school year. The funny thing is that this was interviewing students who were already in the program! Which is a pretty funny concept, I mean how can you interview for something you're already accepted into? Except this was not your typical interview. Or maybe it was an informative interview. I can't believe I never recorded one of the interviews; I would love to hear what I had to say! Pretty much we sat with every one of about 30 students who decided they wanted to stay in the program for about 20 minutes, after being informed things were going to change toward the stricter side for the coming year.

The English teacher for Destinations, and the Teen Parent Program Teacher and I sat with each of those students, and it was mostly me talking the whole time. I had a two page list of things that the students needed to hear about what the new life was going to be like in Destinations Academy. I was coming in and dropping the hammer and I wanted them to know that ahead of time so they couldn't complain when the changes stuck and the work got harder. So I pretty much described to them what the year was going to look like, what the program was going to look like, what the structure was going to look like, what would be expected of them academically and in terms of attendance and behavior, and what kind of consequences they could expect for not living up to the expectations. I thought it important to tell them what they could get suspended and removed from the program for, and how many strikes they would get, (generally it was three, which was more than I would have told them up front if I was running the program myself, but others thought that too strict). I told them how requirements were changing for credit attainment. The biggest change in their mind, I saw their responses, was the change from getting one credit for every 200 pages they read in a textbook, (along with answering all the questions that went with the reading), to getting one credit for reading 300 pages plus a mini-project.

The other two teachers added reminders and nuggets of information to the students, and then we asked the students if they had any questions. Most of the students really liked the new structure and discipline that was coming into place and said they had been hoping it would change because it was really a joke and not a fun place to be. Then came the key part of the "interview" and that was me asking the student if he was willing to make the changes that were coming and to be a part of the change for the better. Almost all of the answers were enthusiastic and positive. I had one student who was on one hand one of the most laid back people I ever met and on the other hand, one of the angriest and most uptight people I ever knew. This was a student I had taught in IPASS and who had also been in CE2 and finally ended up in Destinations. He was generally calm, funny, and relaxed, but when he got angry, he was one of those I thought might take a swing at me. I didn't ever really think he would, except maybe once. Anyway when I asked him if he agreed to the terms of the new program he said something along the lines of "That sounds pretty cool". I guess I'm a little pushy but I want specifics and like I said, I didn't want to surprise anyone about how things were going to be, so I said, "I need to know a specific 'yes' or 'no' if you are part of this program or not," or something even stronger along those lines, and sure enough he responded in the affirmative. I knew he was going to be a piece of work for the year and really one of my bigger "projects" within Destinations Academy and I wasn't wrong on this.

In general, in questioning I also tried to get a feel of what the student might be interested in with respect to a project, and let them know an individual project and at least one class project would be expected of them within the year. They all nodded along and didn't realize what I was hitting them with at the end, when I asked them if they agreed to these changes and were willing to be in the program under these new guidelines, and I think we had them sign a contract. Interestingly, of all the students who had been in the Destinations Academy the year before I think there was really only one who got turned away, didn't even get to interview, but he was always big trouble anyway: funny kid, great in a hack circle, but couldn't get it together enough to maintain in the program toward the end of the year. He wanted it really bad too; he knew me from our hacking together and the lunchroom and he really liked me and wanted to have me as a teacher, and he even asked me if there was something I could do for his sake to get him in when it was too late, but there was nothing I could or would do at that point.

This kid incidentally had one of the funniest student questions I have come across; it was the beginning of my first year with Coos Bay Public Schools, when I was waiting to get some students for my class, (I had to wait till the middle school threw out any students from school, who would then to come to my class, so that was about a month or so into the school year. I spent most of my mornings planning the upcoming school year for my classroom, but at a certain point, there's only so much planning you can do with three hours a day without making yourself crazy). I would therefore spend my mornings upstairs in the Destinations Program helping the math teacher, who had interesting organization systems. The kids got to know me a little bit and I don't know how they found out I was Jewish but one day this same boy asked me if it was possible for anybody to be Jewish. I was a little on the defensive what with it being "Podunk" small town Oregon and

I being one of the only Jews known around. Plus I didn't know what he was getting at or where he was coming from. He was asking me weird things like how you become Jewish and I thought it was the lead up to some joke. Finally he asked me if anyone could be Jewish and I said that a person was kind of born Jewish. He then asked if someone who was Mexican could be Jewish and I finally understood where he was going with this and I was shocked. It was actually complimentary and I was probably so unaware of the direction because I had never experienced anything like it before. He was actually wondering if HE could be Jewish! I mean, I had class moms who wanted me to teach Judaism in class when I was a mainstream teacher, but that was different, that was coming from a parent, which, while nice and complimentary, was not necessarily so genuine. This was genuine. And it was based on his discovery of my being Jewish which meant I made an impression on him that he wanted to follow. So I told him absolutely there were Mexican Jews and people who were not born Jewish could convert. The funny thing is that I don't think he even really understood that Judaism is a religion. Maybe he wanted to convert; maybe he's a Jew now! That would be a hoot.

Interestingly or not, this affected my teaching for years. That's because it's not that I mind students knowing I'm Jewish, but I don't want them to think there are any more barriers than there already are between where they are and where I am, not that I'm so high up. In other words, if this boy wants to aspire to be like me, and this boy used to tell me how I was the coolest teacher. He would say he didn't know teachers who hacky-sacked or skated or snowboarded or were a deejay, etc. So why should I make him think there's a barrier to his attaining the life I have? Should he suppose he could never make it to where I was because he was not Jewish, and maybe Jews have some special power that he doesn't have? So for those days I was careful about wearing Jewish jewelry exposed for just that reason. Nowadays when I have a very long beard, and a yarmulke, it's kind of hard to hide the fact, but it's cool.

Now let's get back to meetings: after announcements I always ended the meeting with something positive like "Let's have a great day!", or "Break!" as a football coach might say; which I couldn't use too often as I knew it would get students maybe over-excited. The meetings were generally excellently toned. There were times when something pretty bad happened and we had to change things in the program or do some heavy talking to the students and the mood would be somber, but that was pretty rare and we were usually able to leave on a very positive note, feeling good about things, and it was easy to see students felt happy with the new program.

Students left the meetings looking more positive and feeling better, as I can best estimate, than when they came in. At 8:30 AM the meeting would be over and we went to the morning classes. And so began a typical day in the new Destinations Academy.

The afternoon meetings were generally for attendance purposes also, like I said earlier; though I never told the students this, I would think they figured it out. The kids came in a little slower to this meeting and sometimes there were students missing whom I then later had to track down, (or have an assistant do this). There usually weren't any announcements in this meeting, except me reminding them to work on projects and maybe telling them who I was going to meet with that afternoon to discuss their project. Actually those meetings were pretty fun and light. For most of the year I would ask them a handful of history trivia questions from this set of cards I had, and that wasn't even for credit, and they would still enjoy and answer! Then at one point the Resource Teacher came in with a fun activity, where he would write a bunch of clues about a word or topic on the board, and the students would have to guess the thing all the words had in common. The kids really liked it. They got a kick out of it and the teacher was very enthusiastic about the game; it was hard not to get involved and have fun. Plus he always gave some prize or points for his end-of-term shopping spree. We were all generally pretty mellow by this point in the day: we had made it through the morning, where the bulk of the hard work was, had eaten lunch, and knew that we really only had two hours left, so it was a chilled upbeat mood.

On the other hand, the final meeting, which was generally just referred to as "CNN", was not so easy to make happen. This is where I had to do the "sweep" I mentioned earlier, and I need to explain a little more detail here about the importance of this meeting with respect to structure. See the key in the structuring of any situation of students or children is to figure out where there are gaps, or where there could be gaps, and to come up with ways to avoid those gaps, bypass them, or overcome them. To me this was the easiest way to deal with this gap. We went through a bunch of phases with this program. First of all, there were two main purposes to this meeting. One of the biggest problems Destinations had the year before was students cutting out in the afternoon, and never coming back that day. There was no way to track them or know where they were; they could say they were downstairs or in the gym, and no one would know the difference. So we set up this late afternoon meeting to eradicate that problem, and it worked. Secondly, this was a good way to assure a relatively painless credit for students. I used this system the year before in IPASS and it worked wonderfully. Not that there weren't complaints there either, but it got the job done. All students had to do was sit and answer the questions set up by CNN to go along with their ten minute news segment created for and directed to students. I copied questions daily from CNN's website into a Word document with a few lines for them to answer.

The easy part, with which I gradually grew tougher, was that they really only had to do their best to listen. I went through the questions with them every day after the segment, and asked for volunteers for the answers to the questions. In the beginning of the year I was the only one who got all the answers, (I didn't screen the video first, so I was watching it along with them for the first time, to experience it fully with them). While I could have gotten the answers beforehand by reading online, I wanted to watch with the students, and my being able to get the answers was the litmus test for the volume in the classroom. If people were talking, I couldn't listen and if I couldn't pay attention and get the answers, it was going to be much harder for students who didn't have the same set of listening and learning skills I had. Actually this part wasn't so tough, because their attention was occupied with the CNN. As the year went on I added a little depth to this. I mentioned earlier, how I added a couple of articles from the newspaper once I saw students getting opinionated about the news and wanting to discuss it. I highlighted the articles beforehand and wrote some of my own questions in the margin, and then I would read the article highlights to students, and we would discuss. It was pretty exciting and heated, and at one point I offered for students to read instead of me and there were a couple who took me up on that. The point is, as the year went on, more and more students were getting all or most of the questions to the CNN segment answered correctly, and it was really great to see that improvement.

The harder part of this "meeting", which was really more of a class, was the Sustained Silent Reading component. I had to use a clipboard on this segment to keep track of who was reading. I would say, especially to get the reading started, "Mike is reading; John is on task", which is what they teach you you're supposed to do, as in rewarding the ones who are doing what they are supposed to do, with positive praise. Eventually the students all came around; it usually took a couple minutes to settle them all down. It was very difficult to get a large set of silent minutes to line up one after the other: there was usually some noise. But it was a good reading environment, and people generally enjoyed it.

This meeting and the day usually ended on a fun and upbeat note. I did a drawing every day, (unless dismayed with the program to such a point that the students really knew there was no drawing that day, which only happened a handful of times throughout the year). This drawing was based on the criteria that the students had perfect attendance at all three meetings for that day, and that they had not been disrespectful to any other students or staff. The prize was usually Dutch Brothers Dollars, which is a West Coast coffee chain, supplied by the principal I think by way of our program funds, which students loved because they could go get a coffee drink down the street; or Destination Dollars, which they could spend at the store in the office, which had snacks, drinks, and school supplies, which they also liked.

We generally drew out of a hat; it was fun even picking whose hat we would draw out of, and I always let one of the students pick out the names of two or three winners, depending how many names were in the drawing; up to ten great students for that day meant one name drawn; up to twenty great students meant two winners; up to thirty meant three winners. If we ever got up to forty names, I probably would have taken them all skydiving. The most fun way to pick for me was a way I invented in IPASS. I never came up with a name for it, but I would throw all the slips of paper with their names on them, up in the air, and then grab two of the slips of paper as they were falling through the air. That was cool, and I still do it to this day, and have as much fun, too! The kids thought that was the funniest thing; and I don't know if anyone else did or does drawings that way. It worked and it works. The very last thing I had kids do at the end of the day was put their chairs up before they left, and that was a request from the custodian, and I still had to remind them every day, they were so excited to get out of there.

The interesting thing about this meeting was that it was the hardest one to get students to come to. First of all we had the Teen Parents in their classroom, and they stayed there until aroused from whatever they were doing in there. I mandated that everyone would have to come to this meeting every day, and still it was a daily project to make it happen. See there were a couple parts to the difficulty. Besides the sweep I mentioned earlier, there was the problem of the other students who were already in the classroom waiting for CNN while I was looking for the slackers. The trick was that if I was gone too long from my own classroom, looking for others, students started getting restless wondering when CNN would start. On the other hand, if I didn't get those students who were hiding out, I would get complaints from the students who *were* there where they were supposed to be, about those students who *weren't* there and wondering why they got such special privileges of missing CNN, which apparently was the greatest thing that could happen to a student at Destinations Academy.

I had to strike a balance between finding and getting the students into the classroom, who were doing wrong by not being there, versus praising and rewarding the students who were already in the classroom for doing right. At the same time I needed to get the CNN rolling so that we could answer the questions; the English Teacher was there in the classroom, but mainly as a monitor to assure students remained where they were. Once we got CNN rolling it was actually pretty smooth. In the beginning, like I said, there were barely any students who could get all of the questions or even most of them, and even half of the questions. It was a little discouraging to students but I told them the same thing had happened the year before and with time and persistence and attention, we had gotten over the same hurdle and students had succeeded. So I started a funny count, kind of a survey. Every day right after the video I would ask how many got three answers, five answers, seven answer, etc. and I wrote it on the corner of the white board and kept an ongoing account of this. I noticed as the talking went down, and the focus increased, and time went by, that our numbers were steadily increasing. It was actually very cool to watch and I think the students also enjoyed watching their learning as a group increase, and seeing their skills improve. But the sweep.... oh the sweep.... I think that's where I got my first gray hairs.

It's such an interesting concept because the tone in the program of the day until that sweep was calm, and then it was like a hurricane tearing through the program, and often that hurricane was me. Things could sometimes be spread out and seemingly disorganized in Destinations. The most disorganized part of the day was also the most relaxed, and that was that afternoon after the lunch meeting and before the CNN meeting, we could run various activities by different teachers and have students working on individual projects, individual credits, and morning class work they needed to finish also. We would also offer different activities during that time like PE, an art class, and the like. But we were able to do all these different things because of the meetings, both because the meetings were where we could suggest new ideas, hear new ideas, and present new offerings to students; and because meetings brought us together and kept us in tune with each other so we knew where everyone was at. Meetings were the glue that really held things together in Destinations and kept us focused. I am still not sure how those meetings run these days and would like to know what goes on and what doesn't go on.

There are really so many topics to cover when dealing with structure, and they're all linked to each other in many ways that makes it hard to structure the teaching of the structuring of a program! In taking attendance, which I always did even if another teacher took their own attendance, I would note who was tardy and present and absent. I gave them a one minute window for tardiness, which is still really what I use today, but really, the way it went was that if they got there while I was taking attendance, they were on time, and it usually took me more than a minute as there were about 30 kids to go through. We had a drawing every Monday for five dollars cash, which was a lot of money in little old Coos Bay, Oregon. Every week, a person who had perfect attendance, (without any tardy inputs), at the morning meeting and the afternoon meeting, was entered into the drawing. If they didn't win that week their name stayed in the hat for the next week and hence students with better attendance had a better shot of winning as demonstrated by one girl who won more than anyone else, who had nearly perfect attendance. It was a solid system borrowed from another program, CE2, in the building.

After taking attendance came the announcements, and if there was nothing to announce, I would announce that the students of Destinations were doing great, because I had nothing to complain about. I repeat this because it's the hardest thing to remember, to compliment students and children when they are not doing anything wrong! That means they are doing things right and we have to remember that. I would then shower them with praise for doing good work, and being well behaved. It is one of the traps many teachers and parents fall into: forgetting to compliment when things are good. It is easy to find fault and correct and criticize, but it is harder to praise when things are good, and I'm well aware I'm in the wrong chapter right now, but this is key, that praise should be given when students are doing things well. In fact, really the best way they taught us to teach is to praise the ones who are doing right, and ignore the ones who are not doing things right, (to a point); because the ones doing things wrong are often doing those things because they crave attention, any kind of attention, even if it is negative. Generally, in school, the students causing problems are going to be the ones getting the attention. The system of rewarding those who are doing right works, and like a charm, and it was really the basis of the major behavioral changes we imposed in the program of Destinations. It may not be instant, but it is lasting. It instills pride in citizenship and a positive enthusiastic outlook.

But before the announcements happened, the students always wrote in their journals. There was one exception to this rule and that was Monday. I realized early in the year how stuck these students would get in weekend mode, in Coos Bay it's real easy to get into weekend mode; it happens almost the second you leave work or school; the air is made of it. They didn't even mean to cuss so badly, as far as I could tell, and every cuss I could imagine would pop up on Monday morning in their regular conversation; and I would have to correct them. So I began to remind them to put on their "Monday Mouth" so as not to dirty the class with the fresh lingo. I also offered up for anyone who wanted a Destination Dollar, the opportunity to make the announcement for me, since as I said, they had to listen to me all the time, maybe it would be better that they should listen to one of their friends. So generally every Monday a student would pop up, before I spoke, and it was usually this one boy, and say "Monday Mouth"; I made sure he said it loud and strong if he wanted the dollar. It was a fun system and I really liked the students telling each other the rules. That's the best way. Then I had a student in West Orange High School who did that same thing to other students completely of his own accord and completely in the right way. He wants to be an elementary school teacher when he's older and I'm trying to get him some practice. He's good!

Getting the students out of their comas in the morning was sometimes tricky, especially with that group. I would ask for their attention and the talking would reduce a lot, but in the beginning, there were a few remaining talkers. I just worked with my eyes. It's still a wonder what "the look" can do and it is a necessary tool for every parent and teacher unless your children are born angels and remain so for the entire time you have them. If they do, count your blessings. Wherever I heard sound I looked until I figured out who was talking and then I looked right at the person until they stopped talking, which was usually once they realized that I (and generally the whole class) was looking directly at them. Occasionally one was brazen enough to keep talking and ignore me, but I took care of that instantly. Sometimes I walked over to them, asked them if they wanted to share with the whole class, or whatever the situation required. There's always away to draw attention where you want it that's not so negative.

The different alternative programs I taught in were really as different from each other in many ways as night and day, and they all had such different structures, it's hard to compare and contrast because of the vastness of the difference. I hope the reader can glean ideas, strategies, and structures they might be able to implement into their own situation from seeing the different ways these programs ran and were set up. The first two hours of my teaching day in my first teaching job, in Jefferson, basically consisted of about fifteen students, grades five to ten in one classroom, and I was supposed to teach them everything. After the students dismissed at 3:00, (we started at 1:00), I walked or drove the half mile or so down the elementary school in Jefferson. Jefferson had one elementary school, one middle school, and one high school, all on or off Main Street. The after-school program started at 3:15, and ran till 5:00. I had a "lunch" break from 5:00 to 5:30, and then the evening program took place from 5:30 to 9:00, all in the elementary school. The evening program was a combination of an open computer lab for anyone in the community, which was free, and a high school evening credit recovery program. For this part of the program I mainly collected and assisted with class work. I turned in all work to my counterpart teacher for grading; she was the high school alternative teacher, and I returned it to students afterwards if they weren't in her class during the daytime; it was an easier task.

The programs in general went in order of most to least intense, which was great for my day. I generally knew that once I got through 3:00 without any major incidents, things were cooled out. Not that I would go to sleep, but there was generally a much lower level of worry about major incidents in the after-school program, because students were well behaved, were the "regular" students, and even in the evening, high school students are generally more calm anyway compared to their middle school counterparts. For the evening program it was pretty fun because every night it was never the same, and I had a different assistant there from my morning assistant, and she was younger than me and perky, and I worked with her in the afternoon program, and if things got slow I could go on the computer.

Students rarely stayed till 9:00 to study, and even though the attached computer lab was open till 9:00 to the public of Jefferson, people rarely stayed that late either. Usually if people left by 8:30 we were allowed to close the lab down and go home; when that happened it was sweet. This actually allowed me that much more time to go out in the evening, what with not have to get up until 11:00 AM the next day. There were rarely negative incidents in this part of the night, which made it so nice, in fact I think there was really only one, when a high school student wouldn't accept the fact that I was in charge. At that point in my career I dressed a little more casually or in style, though always with a collared shirt. This high school boy got angry when I set down the rules for him, and stomped into the hallway and through his books down on the floor. I never saw him again; the students didn't really have to come to that evening program, it was designed for their benefit to catch up on credits they had missed or failed, and it was a much quicker and generally less painful way of doing it. The thing was, the evening part of this alternative program was also the tutoring lab for elementary students. I actually had another assistant for that part of the program; so I think I was really supervising two assistants. Technically the other assistant was in charge of the computer lab; she stayed in there till 9:00; we hung out and kept the evening fun. My main assistant was an older woman who had been a full teacher in the Philippines but lost her licensure when she moved here, so she really knew how to work with the elementary school kids and she did most of their teaching and tutoring when they came in for assistance during that time.

So that leaves the middle of the day, from 3:15 to 5:00 to discuss, and in a later chapter, I will finally be able to get to tell about the qualities of a good mentoring program, like the one which blossomed within this session. During these hours, I was officially in charge of the whole after school program which supervised 80 to 90 children daily, from Kindergarten through fourth grade. Available to the students were: a supervised computer lab where a teacher and assistant worked, and then an arts and crafts program, supervised by some women who I think were mothers from the school, and an outdoor recreation program, which is where I usually stayed and played; I actually played with the games and even swung with them on the swings. I was hard to defeat in tether ball; I had a slight advantage. There were different mothers working outside as well. It was a great program and students got to choose which activities they would do daily, and it was very positive, productive, and especially nice, it was free.

Structure and consistency work, any which way you turn the compass. Students need to know what to expect in the class, in the home, in any program, and in life, and they need to know what the rules and expectations are if they are expected to succeed. The rules need to be clear and consistent, and the structure needs to be sure and solid; the second you slip and allow an exception to your rule, this generation of kids will be all over you, without regard for those who benefitted from the situation, arguing only that they got the short end of the stick another time. They'll say it's not fair, they should be allowed the same exception, and then they're asking for a further slip of the rules, and an inch becomes a yard faster than you can measure it with a ruler. So it's just easier to be consistent, and like I said earlier, it's easier to let up later than to gather them in later. Start strict and loosen the lines once you know your students and children well, and they know what you're about, and you trust them. I found certain routines in place kept things paced and charged. Students became used to Fridays for Math Jeopardy and regularly requested to play. I could have given more quizzes and pop quizzes; I guess if that's one area I would improve or change, that is it. But in my earlier years I didn't have enough time to make them, in later years I've gotten better at the assessment piece, and that helps a lot too.

So as it seems, I was wondering the other day, if I should be tougher or softer in the upcoming year, and with respect to grading as well. And the conclusion I came to is that I was just about right. At the end of my first year in West Orange I was doing final grades, and it was the first time I had to convert my grades to a four point scale: it was kind of confusing at first; then I got the hang of it. It's funny with grades, you really have so much control; someone asked me once if I slam a kid with grades because he was a jerk or whatever. My answer was that I look to their positive sides, attributes, and participation in order to weigh a grade to the positive or in their favor, but I do not detract from their score for negative attitudes, etcetera, regardless of how negative they may have been or how negative they are, and how deserving of such demarcation they may seem to be, (though I admit it is not easy at times)!

In completing grades for the school year, there were a million emails that went out from administration to the teachers in regards to closing up the year and five times as many things to do about closing up the year, this many emails about one subject I haven't seen before. A high school is an unbelievable bureaucracy with forty people for twenty jobs and another thirty you have to respond to about what you did in doing that job. Our high school has 2200 students, 130 faculty, and 22 administrators. Insert your own comment here. In closing up the grades there were many forms and what not to be filled out. One of these forms was the "final failure form", a list of students who failed the class for the whole year, and it had to be completed on the day the final was given, so that the guidance counselors could figure out who they were putting in summer school. What that meant for the teachers was that we had to grade the finals of and calculate the grades of anyone who might possibly fail the class for the year, on the day the final was given! That's a lot of work, but this is one case when being a math teacher might have been a little easier than subjects like English or Social Studies, which usually involve grading essays.

As it turned out I was able to complete this amazing feat and it worked out that I had one student failing for the year in each class, except for one class which had two students failing for the year, (my class size about fifteen). This is a pretty good percentage of students passing, in my book, and there were a couple of the failing students who were sweet kids, who it was tough to dole those grades out to since they were such nice people in general. Regardless, I was really trying to be fair, so I let the math speak for itself. Just so I would have that information handy, since it seemed like pretty important information, to be affecting a year of a person's life, I memorized those students who were failing. Sure enough, during that period, after I had given my finals, the administrators asked me who was failing for the year. So I said who were the students that were failing, and after I gave the list, they said, "Oh, Mikey, that's rough, did you call his mother? "; and "oh, Jane, it'll be hard for her, she's failing so many other classes." I said something along the lines of "well, I can look at the math and see how close it is, and I'm good with whatever." They told me to look it over and get back to them about it tomorrow. Ha! I saw it as a victory, a crack in the wall, mercy in the official system. So I double failed them all!! Just kidding: I did some correctional math like my father probably does in his job daily as a CPA in the New York City garment district, and behold, the students passed! The power of the keyboard is an amazing thing. The whole grading system was very weird, surprising, and seemingly uncontrolled and free. Midterms and finals were a perfect example, in that this was the first year that the school decided there would even be mandatory unified midterms, (all Algebra 2 classes would take the exact same midterm, excepting honors classes and special needs classes), and it was the first year we had those midterms given, as opposed to waiting a year to make the midterms, then giving them the next year. What was so difficult was the lateness and lack of preparedness that came with this whole situation.

The midterm review I got was pretty good, but I only got it for one of the three different classes I teach, (Geometry, Algebra 2, and Selected Math Topics; Topics is a senior "mish-mosh" class of topics like trigonometry, statistics, and sequence/series). When we got close to the midterm for one of my classes, and the other teachers found out I taught this class (Selected Math Topics), they realized they hadn't included me in the preparation and creation of the test. This resulted in the fact that everything I taught in the first half of the year was pretty much everything that they would be covering in the second half of the year (the different math topics didn't necessarily need to go in a specific order). Everything they were testing in the midterm, was what I was going to teach in the second half of the year. As a result, I had to make up my own midterm and final, which really turned out to be alright, so we got to keep a little of the autonomy in Horizons that is slightly getting stripped from all of this unification and standardization, (here he goes on the soapbox again!) It's not too easy to keep it alternative while standardizing everything, but it keeps me on my A-game and keeps us moving forward so I'm not really complaining. I think I shouldn't really have been included in this whole "unified midterm final" situation, as Horizons is supposed to be its own entity, a small learning community, slightly independent of the rest of school which gives it its charm, appeal, comfort and success; but things are what they are!

The final was not much better in the preparation aspect, and it came on pretty fast, but I guess that's inevitable when you do something like this in the first year and it happens pretty fast. Looking back it went a lot better than it could have and there was pretty much enough staff development time with the math department to get it all done, so that was cool. On the other hand, they never really told me what to cover and more importantly, what not to cover. For that reason, by the end of the year in my main two classes, I was pretty far behind, and had to rush to catch up to get the students the necessary material to be up to par for a final that was created independent of yours truly. A large portion of this final had not been covered during the year, putting my students at a distinct disadvantage, which I tried to make up for in review. So later (as I did on the midterm), I made up for this deficiency with the curve, which may not be something I should share, as the teachers tried to come up with a unified curve as well, a curve for Geometry, a curve for Algebra II, etc. I didn't think it fair to my students that they had such a disadvantage, so this was where I took advantage of the fact that Horizons was supposed to be a separate entity, and so I created a separate curve. I proportioned it, to be fair, to the effect of the strength of effort that each particular class put forth toward their success, regardless of the disadvantage they had. Now that I know what will be on the finals and the midterms, it looks better for planning each year, especially since most of the material is created already now, and I get to edit it, as opposed to starting from scratch. From another perspective, this concept falls under the category of "backward design", which is a trend in education in which we create an assessment based on what we want students to learn, and then gear our teaching and their learning toward those goals, so that works.

This was also the first year the school finally implemented the Parent Portal, which it had been trying to do for a while. It was funny because it's going to affect education in a neat way, and already does, in many places. The parent portal allows parents access to their students grades, assignments, and I suppose, attendance, by computer and really gives them access to view the computer grade book in real time into which teachers enter student grades and assignments. This only works for teachers who are already using the electronic grading system that the school offers, which brings up an interesting legal contractual question, since, (as an administrator informed me), we are not under any obligation to use the electronic grading system, therefore we cannot really be obligated to offer the parent portal to our students. This is apparently a mostly moot point, nonetheless, since of the 130 teachers in the high school, I think there were only four not using the electronic grading system, and I think they will be retiring soon. It's actually pretty efficient and much more so than the paper grade book of old.

So the difficult thing is it seems like parents would be looking over a teacher's shoulder to evaluate them. In reality, it turns out nice, because it's a lot easier to handle the few parents who try (and usually succeed) to get their students free passes for turning in late work or redoing tests when the students slough off the responsibility. The parent suddenly figures that out, and the teacher has to bend the rules because of parent pressure, which translates to administrative pressure, which really isn't fair, and which I generally don't mind doing when parents are nice and polite about it. All of my parents were nice and polite about that these years, and I didn't mind doing the extra work so much, but there was one parent who tried to get snotty with me, and I had to look back at my saved emails to show her where she was wrong and where she hadn't responded to my email. In terms of organization, I have an organization system for my school email which is much like my personal email account in which I have over 70 folders to organize all my emails, as in I almost never throw emails away, but rather file them in the appropriate spot, as it only takes an extra second. In my school email I don't have 70 folders but I do have about 30, and one of them is called "parent" where I put any emails from parents so I can easily retrieve them for situations like the one above; and even if I only use it a few times in a few years, it's worth it to have the answer at my finger tips, and to be correct. I don't like making mistakes.

It was nice having the parent portal later in the year when that parent tried the same routine about asking me which assignments her child was missing, and I was able to return a reply, by asking her if she had signed up for parent portal, which of course, she hadn't. After that she was able to see everything that her son was missing and when it was due, and all I had to do was give him the assignments a few at a time, (as long as it was within a reasonable time frame), and I didn't have to get involved in discussions that might border on who is responsible for turning in work and who is not.

Now as it turns out the New Jersey teaching system is pretty funny and you can't figure that to be a surprise. It's pretty strict, tight, and crazy, but I have found there are ways to maneuver through it. When I left my last teaching job I heard lots about getting "highly qualified" which I still don't really understand what it means, though I am highly qualified in a few things as an educator. I had to go through the process and jump through the hoops to do that, and I did that well because I connected to a very helpful person in NJ Department of Education down in our beautiful state capital of Trenton. One of the unbelievably useful things I found out from that amazing connection in Trenton was that, in order to become highly qualified, I had to fill out paperwork from the job that I was leaving, before

I left, in order to be highly qualified as a teacher of, for example, High School Math. So I got that form filled out before I left my last position working for the Union County Educational Commission, where I taught in Roselle Catholic High School. With this form signed by my previous administrator, I was suddenly highly qualified. Combined with my seven years alternative education experience, and nine years math teaching experience, I was allowed to become a high school math teacher, which was pretty cool.

As my second year in West Orange High School started, human resources contacted me to tell me I would have to have a mentor since I did not have a Teacher of Mathematics Certificate. This mentor was a girl ten years my junior! I would have to pay $50 a month for that! Oh well, even though after paying her for several months we had one meeting which was for three minutes standing in the hallway, I was happier when they finally decided I didn't need a mentor after ten years public school teaching experience. Sometime during the year the district figured out they made a mistake, with an administrator's help, who explained how I was highly qualified, and that I taught math at the high school level for years beforehand, and they refunded me the money and I didn't have to pay her not to teach me anything anymore. Along with this mentor came my application for a Teacher of Mathematics Certificate, which I apparently should have had, since I was a high school teacher of mathematics.

I applied for this certificate in the beginning of the year, and jumped through whatever hoops they wanted me to, and at the end of the year the principal called me down to his office to tell me that I had to apply for this license. I really didn't know what he was talking about, and pretty much forgot that I had applied, and the short of it was, they rejected my license application, and I then had to take 26 college level mathematics credits, of which 12 credits needed to be at the 300 or 400 level. For the record, now, I have completed 17 of those credits and I am planning to take the other 9 at Thomas Edison State College, online, and complete them by May of 2014. Also for the record I was able to get 10 of those credits by taking CLEP exams, which allow you to get credit for a class you can already pass based on prior knowledge, and these exams replaced three of those college courses, saving me time and money. And that, my friends, is one branch in navigating the system; I hope it can help you get through.

Every organization, school, parent, and teacher, will have their different methods of organizing and structuring their classroom, home, or location, whatever the case may be. It is useful to learn from others and to know the different types of structures out there and available, because you never know what bits and pieces might be able to integrate into your own little world. It's also useful just to understand how the world works for those of us who are trying to make it a better place! I discovered a peculiar discrepancy between private education and public education in my working in both arenas, which, for whatever sake you decide, I would like to elucidate. This was when I was working for Union County Educational Services Commission. My official position was Supplemental Instructor, so I taught small groups of students, but only aided the curriculum given by other teachers. I wasn't responsible to give my own curriculum, homework, or tests. This position took place in a Roselle Catholic High School, and that's when I discovered the interesting discrepancy in structure. Both types of schools, public and private, are eligible for and receive special education services, and those are available freely and seemingly fairly in both arenas. Compensatory Education is offered in private schools and it is almost like special needs; it helps students who aren't performing up to par. It comes into play in Section 504 in legal codes which provides assistance to people who have any kind of disability, no matter what arena or field it is in, and they don't have to limit the assistance to school scenarios. It's very thick to understand but the relevant matter here is the following. As I experienced, all students took a certain standardized test towards the end of the year in math and English. Students who scored below a certain number, around 40, (though not out of 100), were eligible for my services as a Supplemental Instructor.

This was the main way I got students into my program and classroom, (through that test and the test scores), besides the students who came to me with Individual Student Profiles, or ISP's. An ISP is the private school equivalent of an Individualized Education Profile, or IEP. An IEP is given to Special Education students, and this document explains their difficulties, needs, and modifications required for their success in the classroom and at school. After giving the test at the end of the previous year, which got them into the program, when I would see students for the first time at the beginning of the year, I would administer another test to double check that they needed the services and warranted them. If they scored below that score, or got a certain number wrong on a certain line of problems, they were given services. I didn't really understand why I had to give them the test again when they had already been given the test before but that was the policy so I did it. Then these students had my services available every week, once a week, (or twice depending if it was math *and* English), and got help in very small groups; the largest group I had was six students; it was much more common to have two to four.

Many students came all the time; they really used the services and appreciated them; they generally had to miss gym which they didn't like, but they seemed to know they were truly benefitting from the small group help. I got to learn high school math curriculums very well, which was nice after being in isolated alternative programs for seven years out in Oregon. Out there, I, alone determined the curriculum, without necessary connection to anything that anyone else in the town, state or country was doing in their classrooms. So this was a big benefit for me, and it set me up amazingly for what I would do the following year in teaching real full year math classes in West Orange High School. In teaching in these small groups at the private school as a Supplemental Instructor, I was definitely able to bring across the concepts in a way that students understood, and I know they appreciated that, which is all well and good. The discrepancy I have been edging toward, though, is this: I never saw, in any of the public schools I worked at, any such programs or services available to students who were lacking basic skills of this, (not counting special education, which requires an entire legal document and process, which is also available in private schools). I worked in a lot of public schools, and was involved in many of the different programs in the school, and I am aware of what is available for students, and I have gotten a good taste of what is going on. So if there were these programs in the public schools, I would probably have known about it, especially since my kids in the types of programs I taught would have needed this kind of help the most! The problem with this discrepancy is that my job was funded by government money. I assure the reader that most of the students I taught in all of my alternative scenarios would have failed if I gave those tests to them, and they hence would have been eligible for these small group learning environments. This would benefit them greatly. My question is: why are these services only available in private schools to those students, and not available in public schools, to these students?

In closing this chapter which has really been quite the "doozy", the structure is going to be and must be related to the goals of the parent, teacher, or program. It is important to have those goals in mind when you are structuring your classroom, home, program, environment, or scenario. What the goals are of alternative education is a constant question and must be at the forefront of the parent or educator's mind; the same is true for the goals of regular education. This is really the point of backward design, which is a concept worth looking up, and I don't have enough time to explain in detail here. The goals will certainly vary from person to person, student to student, and child to child, and as educators we seek to make our students educated and productive citizens, at the least. Different programs will have different goals, or no goals, or lose sight of their goals, and we must have goals clearly in mind so we know what we are trying to accomplish. Our program at West Orange High School is interesting because it has as one of its goals, the gradual reintegration of the student into the mainstream, and it has a clear, well defined process for doing this, and this process has shown continual success over the years. In their freshmen year students are in the program for the four main subjects of math, science, social studies and English, and by senior year, generally, the only subject in which they were still in the program, (if they did things right), is math. In other programs, like Destinations Academy, for example, there was not necessarily the goal of reintegration, though that did happen occasionally. Destinations Academy had its own graduation and so the main goal of the program was to graduate students from high school.

In the end, most structures and strategies, if well planned out, will endure. I have included in Appendix B my original "EARN" sheet, (it has a front and back side, which should be double-sided). This sheet can easily be modified to use at home or really for any situation. EARN stands for Evaluate, Achieve, Reward, Notify, and it is designed for alternative students who need structure, self-confidence, and success-building. The sheet allows them to monitor their own behavior and learning daily, while developing pride in achieving goals. The rewards are determined by parent or teacher, and at higher levels, they can input or even suggest and/or create their own. They can be physical rewards like food and/or games, or they can be responsibility and freedom awards allowing them access to greater choice in study, research, movement about the environment, access to trips, and computers. The list for reward possibilities is limitless. Find our what the student or child wants, likes or appreciates, and then incorporate that into the rewards structure, and you will get them involved and make them owners of their education and growth and the success rate will climb dramatically. Believe me: this really works.

9
BE COOL

Stay in control and calm. Breathe. Think. Relax. Chill. Focus. It was tough to decide whether to name this chapter "Be in control" or the title it received, and the reason I chose this winning title is: being cool, which is great in the Arthur Fonzarelli, (Fonzie, or "The Fonz") sense, really encapsulates being in control, and adds more. You can be in control while fuming inside, but that's not being cool. When you are cool, you are also in control, and not fuming inside. And while it is possible to manage your kids or a classroom while freaking out inside or outside, it is not the best method for your health or for theirs. Of course you should be in control of yourself, and of the classroom; even if you are running a student-led classroom, ultimately, you are behind the scenes, running it, and therefore, truly in control. But you should be more than in control, because that's really the minimum of your state of mind and emotions; in the maximum and ultimate state, you are cool, and really, cool like the Fonz. Make the jukebox go on.

You should get in the habit of thinking for a few seconds before speaking. Decide what you want to say before you say it. Then, when you really need to think for a few seconds before you speak, it won't seem out of character for you to take that time, and it won't even seem like you're fazed, though you might be! What I have found most effective is to say the word "Chill" or "Relax" to myself. Truth to be told, I sometimes say to myself, or in my head, "Ch-ch-ch-ch-ch-chill". Maybe I have heard that in a rap song somewhere. Whatever the case it gets the feeling in my head and has a rhythm that tricks me into relaxing. Yes, I even trick myself, it is not only my students I pull these stunts on, believe it. I need a clear mind when I have important stuff to do! There will be time for other feelings later; in the present, I am focused on achieving the goals at hand and that requires a clear mind so I do what's necessary.

There are other techniques that work for many people, and I recommend these techniques as well. Counting to ten or some other number is helpful, (counting backwards seems to work for my students even more than counting forwards). Taking deep breaths also works. I stretch and do yoga when I have the time, and of course fun hobbies are useful and relaxing. My brother, he should rest in peace, told me good advice as well that sticks with me. He said to smile at least once a day, even if you do not feel like it. I try to do that, and it works. It makes me think of him, too, which is nice. I might not remember every day to do it. On other working techniques, when I am not feeling my best, I usually need something that is fast and effective. Maybe I feel too busy or I do not take the time to remember these other techniques. For me, the "Ch-ch-ch-ch-ch-chill" statement works wonders and I use it because it is also pretty fun and gets you kind of singing. Other times even just thinking "chill" works even better.

For those completely opposed to anything rap-related, pick a song you like with relaxing qualities. It should be something you connect to and love which has words that you know will relax you and bring you peace. Say it anytime you start to feel "not great" and I think you will see some great happiness coming your way. Remember, however, to give yourself time to recognize, accept, and deal with the issues that are underlying the difficulty later on. A good example of this is illustrated later in this chapter with the cases of two students who I consider not to have really succeeded with me in my second year at West Orange High School; they show the example of negativity not dealt with well; it must be addressed.

When you are a parent or a teacher, it's pretty much a guarantee that there are going to be situations that test you, push you, and challenge your frustration levels. It's important in that type of situation to be calmly bold in a clear minded fashion. Students are going to push the limits and want to see how the boundaries respond. Many adults do it too, and if they can get a rise of excitement out of pushing boundaries, that's more exciting than reading a book for them, and it will get them some attention too. It gets fun for these people to try and make that excitement happen again as well. It is a challenge. So the key is to respond controlled-like to these stimuli. It is very difficult not to fall into the trap of engaging it and getting wrapped in it. One must separate himself from the situation at hand in order to remain aware of the various forces, emotions, and goals of the people involved, while connected enough to decide what is best for the parties at hand. One must stay clear minded enough to say the right thing (or not say a thing) at the right time to get the behavior to continue or cease, depending on the desired effect, and that is truly an art, which should get better and better with practice.

The most important rule here is to maintain clarity of mind and focus of thought. I felt I always wanted to maintain a place of peace in my mind along with all of the other activity up there. I think I found that in my doing fun and cool activities outside of school, that gave me peace of mind in school. But I also worked hard for all of my life to achieve a certain calm clarity and I think that is important to maintain in an education setting, especially with alternative students. Of course drifting off to never-never land or not paying attention is not the answer either. A person should be totally distracted or even distracted at all. But there should be a place of peace in your mind and if you don't have it, the students will find the way to your unpleasant place very quickly, and make you unpleasant. So keep the place of peace forefront in your mind. One of the other chill phrases I tell myself is "focus" and at times "relax". All of these were done at first purposely and then often they come as a peaceful voice when things get hectic, reminding me to stay clear, focused, and calm; in other words, stay relaxed so you can think clearly.

Part of the art of teaching is learning while you teach, learning on the fly, so to speak. As a great teacher or parent one must be constantly alert, reactive and active in the moment and able to change complete views as quickly as possible as new information is constantly taken in. If one can adjust the worldview to new information that may rattle it and shake it to its foundations, so much the better will the teacher or parent be. One of the things students and children like to do, if they find themselves opposing a teacher, is to get under the teacher's skin, to irritate them, to make them lose control, whatever will throw the teacher off balance and make the student appear the victor in what the student has decided is a battle. There are many options on how to handle these types of battles and hopefully some of those methods are gleaned from this work. Sometimes the students really have something to teach even in this type of situation, and it is best if a person can take a lesson from this type of situation. The more a person is aware that these are normal, or at least regular patterns they will see in the classroom, or possibly in their home, the more they will be prepared with techniques and strategies to avoid falling prey to these traps that are really just that: traps, and avoidable ones at that as well. So get ready!

Now to get to the stories of the two students who didn't really succeed with me; they demonstrate the traits of sadness and negativity. One of the two students had a certain method of response whenever he was in doubt about a discussion or argument he felt he might be losing. I say this because he used this technique with other students as well. He would say, "Chill; chill; chill; chill; chill" anywhere from three to ten times; please note the irony in the similarity to my use of a similar phrase to calm myself down. Now on the other hand, if a person wants to know a surefire method for getting a person who is upset to become more upset, here it is: tell them aggressively and/or uncaringly, "calm down", or, as this student did, tell them strongly to chill. The first time or two this boy did this to me, I noticed I got more upset internally; though I think, as usual, I managed not to let that internal combustion be exposed. I thought about his statement, however, in the times between the classes in which he made the statement, and realized it could be a useful tool for me, if I could respond to it properly. So I adjusted my worldview and integrated the new information, and changed my through process ever so slightly, enough to adapt to the new information. I made it part of my own frame of mind; it worked.

The next few times he said that phrase to me, I responded, "I am TOTALLY chill." I said it in such a strong and clear tone, that the other students were taken aback and registered a slight shock at both my sense of chill and the way in which the situation suddenly turned around. As time went on and he kept going on with his "chill" instruction, I upped the ante and told him that he was the one that needed to chill, as he was the one that was raising his voice. This method worked; he stopped telling me to chill. As a matter of fact, what I found, at certain times, (not even in school, like, for example if I was driving), and I found myself "heating up", I started using that phrase in my head to cool myself off and, believe it or not, it worked. It worked to the point that now I recommend it as a way to calm yourself down, in this book. So maybe that student did succeed. Whether he knows it or not, will be a function of whether or not he reads this book, I suppose. That's pretty interesting in my world; I hope he reads it.

Adaptability may be the most important tool in a teacher's work bench, and I hope my work bench is at least as good as my father's work bench when I was growing up. He built it himself and it had everything; it was completely organized and had everything he needed to do all the jobs he wanted to do and even the ones he didn't want to do. That's the kind of teacher's work bench you need, and better the parent you'll be if you have that kind of work bench too. And back to adaptability, it's learning on the fly and applying on the berm. Interestingly, as a side note to the story, "chill-instructing" student had been using this strategy on other students, as well. And I think this is where I got the idea to turn it around on him: one day, after he had used it on a girl a few days earlier, she turned it around on him, and told him to "Chill. Chill. Chill. Chill. Chill" He didn't like that very much and said something along the lines of her using his own expression on him and that it was his expression. I thought to myself at that point he must have gotten the expression from someone else, or a song. But I think that's where the idea germinated in my mind to use it on him as well, I mean, if another student can turn it around on him, then most certainly can I. Both turnarounds were greatly successful on all counts.

Now I need to relate one more "negative" story of the two "non-succeeding students" before I plan to close up this chapter, which sadly, though the coolest chapter, is probably not as long as everyone wants it to be, and I think some of the root of being cool will be revealed more subtly in some of the books which, with G-d's help, will follow this one. Being cool is a state of mind, and you just have to keep pressing with it, and focus on it, and want it, and you will get it. Anyhow, the other student who didn't make the grade for my second year at West Orange High School, had an interesting story of ups and downs, and may have been battling some bigger forces than he could handle. During the height of his attempted overthrow of the government, (the government being yours truly), he purposely tried to drag, openly, and without any attempt at hiding this deed, another student down into the mire with him. He did this in front of the eyes of myself and the other students, sans remorse. He got thrown out of my class one day for something obnoxious, and in his obnoxious battle, another boy came to his defense, and got slightly involved. I basically told the other boy to stay out of it, and probably asked him if he was his lawyer or something, and the other boy listened to me so he was relatively off the hook; at least he wasn't getting thrown out of my class for anything. The first boy, who I had thrown out, called to the second boy, as he was leaving, to come with him. The second boy was walking out the door with the first boy, (the second boy confidently drinking his 96 ounce Mountain Dew), and as the second boy walked out, I told him that he would be getting a cut for leaving, (throwing some water on their passionate and dramatic exiting fire). He responded shocked-like, "You're going to give me a cut for throwing me out?!" I calmly responded, "I'm not throwing you out. He's getting thrown out. You're still here." The first boy then went on to do what I had yet to see in my education career, the attempted "drag-down", and failed. He said, "C'mon, just curse him out and get thrown out." I don't remember how the second boy answered the first, but he took the high road and stayed. That was a good move on his part. That second boy managed to make it through the year by the skin of his teeth; the first: meh.

That second boy and I had a couple of interesting conversations. He was really one of my smartest math students if he would have applied himself. I'm guessing in my nickel store psychology analysis, and based on my own experience being a smart-kid in class, he couldn't hold the balance between being smart and cool, and much more wanted to be the funny cool kid than have anything to do with being smart or perceived as smart in an academic sense. That is a sad loss, but alas, life goes on. Regardless, we had some very fun conversations, even if they were very short. He worked like 40 hours a week at various restaurants till all hours of the night and then would drink these 96 ounce Mountain Dews from corner stores to keep him awake, and then he'd be wired for hours with no idea what to do with his extra energy, and he certainly wasn't about to apply it academically. One time he asked me, toward the end of the period, if he could go catch a bus to get to work, and it was one of the first times he was doing this, and I couldn't officially give him permission to go. On the other hand, I understood his obligations, and I knew that if he committed to learning something, he could learn in five minutes what the rest of the class would learn in 30 minutes. I kept trying to tell him on the down-low that I couldn't give him permission to leave; but if he left and was gone for less than twenty minutes I didn't have to write him up for a cut. We went through this discussion three or four times before another student finally told him the clue I was telling him: that he could go, but I couldn't give him official permission to go; it was like a great comedy routine, and I would love to watch the playback of that conversation.

I have to tell a quick funny story about this same boy to end this chapter in a cool way, being that it is all about being cool. It was towards the end of the year, with the same student who did not succeed with me, who had tried to drag this boy into cussing me out. This student who did not succeed with me had been suspended for cussing out the auto-shop teacher, because the auto shop teacher refused to work on his car, which suddenly needed a major repair; he then got the car in an accident. Mind you, this was the car he'd been dreaming of his whole life, and he had told me about it years before he ever got it. With respect to his desire to have the auto shop teacher fix it, however, as far as I learned, he had not done the written class assignments, or something, and the teacher was refusing to work on the car, and the boy flipped and got suspended for a few days. This boy and the other boy were friends, and it was obvious that the other boy was otherwise a pretty happy person. He could, however be easily led in the wrong direction, so that when the auto-shop cuss boy was gone, this boy had a pretty good few days.

So to finish off this story, or to tell it, and to close this chapter, here's what happened. And for the record this might be the shortest story for the book; and interestingly, (or not, depending on your point of view which will probably decide whether you enjoy reading this book or make it a paperweight), this story sheds some interesting perspectives on the different interpretations of what makes something cool or not. One day, just after the auto shop boy had been suspended, the other boy said something to me about his friend being suspended, and how it was cool to not have to go to school. I responded along the lines that while it might be fun to miss school, this was like the worst part of school to miss, at this time of year, which was the end of the school year. After all, everyone is in a good mood because there are only like two weeks of school left, and who would really want to miss school then? This boy thought that was funny and realized I had a good point. He then went on to take it further though, and said something like, if he knew he could have cussed me out in the beginning of the year and gotten away with it, he might have had a little more fun back then. It was a good call on my part, because when he said how cool it was that his friend got to miss school, I didn't lecture everyone like many teachers might, on how bad it would be to cuss out a teacher. I pointed out that he did it at the wrong time and that he ended up missing the best part of school. This student though an interesting point like maybe he should have cussed me out earlier in the year, and it was a good chuckle for the whole class!

10
USE THE SHELL; ACT WELL

This is one of the most advanced chapters in the book, and possibly the most so, but its advantage is ease of explanation. And while it may be easy to understand, it is in no way easy to apply. This skill, using the "shell", is a specific method, and really requires as a prerequisite the mastering of the art of being cool and in control. It is for that reason that its position right after the cool chapter. However, for many, this skill may be the prerequisite to mastering those skills, so if you are game, give it a try. There are several steps involved in applying this method, and the good news is that it is not an all or nothing situation. A teacher, parent, or anyone, can apply any one, a combination, or all of the steps of this method to improve their interaction and direction skills. It will be a benefit to the personality for sure.

The main focus of this method is dealing with negative energy in the most positive and effective manner. Redirecting negative energy is a key strategy and has many methods and solutions, without one clear answer, and the best solution or method often falls in the category of "thinking on the spot". A teacher or parent must always stay positive and optimistic and hope for the best, (or at the least, try to do so), and that is a great tool in redirecting the negative. When the negative comes at you, it's tempting to take a lot of wrong routes and responses. Being that the trigger emotional response to the negativity is usually anger or frustration, it's important to overcome that emotion, so as to be able to think and function clearly, and not to be blinded by these misleading responses. The way I can best describe it is having and using a shell, so to speak. This is not the typical shell a person thinks of in this situation, in terms of psychology, where people develop walls, layers, and protections for themselves to defend against attacks; though that is an important byproduct of this method. It should be noted that some walls and protection layers are positive and enhancing, and some are negative and destructive, and I hope to clarify the difference in explaining this particular shell. Using this shell will involve some practice. If you notice, when you get really mad, you probably get a sudden swelling feeling in your chest, like blood rushing there; I believe it's the fight-or-flight syndrome, as they describe it. This is NOT the impulse to act on. But it is useful to take notice of the symptoms and be aware of them.

This is where another strategy comes into play, and I'm aware I haven't really explained the shell yet, but have patience, please. Here's the other simpler strategy: if you can do nothing else to calm down, then, before speaking or acting, when your child, student, or person infuriates you, then do this one thing: take a long, slow, deep breath. This is where it gets tricky to separate the shell from the act of being cool, calm, and in control. The shell is really an advanced form of those three states of mind, (being cool, calm, and in control), and if you can use the shell regularly, you are really taking care of the "being in control" part of your personality. It's never a completely finished battle in dealing with anger impulses as a parent or a teacher, at least not for me. For the superstars who never have to deal with those impulses, I commend you. For the rest of us normal people, there are anger impulses or responses to deal with. If you act on the anger impulse first, you're not acting rationally, and believe it or not, your emotions are not as intelligent as your intelligence; that's why it's called intelligence. Now here is what you should really do, if you can manage a long-term strategy other than the breathing/chilling strategy, which, while a good strategy, is not the best strategy for truly trying situations, like my never-ending sentences. The best strategy is the shell, and following details how it works, and the practice you'll need to implement it to make it more natural and make it stick.

The way the shell works is like this: in general, as I've written, in teaching school, one of the best ways to reach students is through positive rewards, praise, and encouragement, which do work, for many and most students. The problem is that when you get a student or a few students who go down the wrong path, they lead these reward-seeking students away from the right rewards, and they get everyone to seek the wrong thing, which is negative attention. My first theory in education was that everything really revolves around attention, and that everyone is trying to get or avoid attention in one way or another. I don't hold so much to that theory alone anymore, but attention is a mighty powerful instrument. The ideal is that we should be leaning to the kindness aspect of our personalities when dealing with our children and students; and we should try to avoid the use of the strict side of our personalities if possible. This is the ideal in a perfect world. I say this without trying to contradict that concept, in recognition of the fact that there are times when we will need to put on this shell and toughen up. If we can do it out of love though, and with a feeling of love and kindness inside, then we are truly in control and truly giving the education for the right reason and from the right perspective.

That is the point: it is a shell we put on, like a garment or a jacket, and we must be aware that we are putting it on when we don it. If we just let go with our true anger and frustration on our students and children when they do what we don't want them to, or don't do what we want them to, we are not doing the best service for ourselves and them. I wrote, "Ourselves", first in the previous sentence, because I think we lose out the most. In the end, though, this will probably hurt our children worse. If one is a really good "actor", when giving off the attribute of discipline to students and children, the student may never know the difference of when you are wearing the shell or when you are truly angry, (unless you have a really bad temper). On the other hand, our bodies, minds, souls, and selves know the difference when we let go with true anger or frustration. There's little to be done to correct that damage to ourselves once it's done. The truth is that the students will know when you've lost control and flipped out, and some of them might feel a sense of victory, some a sense of loss at their faith in you and your ability to manage things, and some will sadly learn that when things get hairy, it's OK to flip.

The answer to all of these quandaries is the shell. When the anger hits, you take a breath, and wait, and realize that you're not mad at these students, because they are only kids, and they shouldn't have the ability to get under your skin. You recognize that everything is OK, and you are healthy, and have family and friends, and that life is generally good. You become conscious of the fact that you really have a lot to be thankful for, and there's very little that's truly worth getting terribly angry over, and surely not furious over, that this is a job, (almost) like other jobs, or a responsibility, and that you are a calm human being. These are just a few ideas of thoughts to have in your head when you get to that point of flipping. There are tons of philosophies or thoughts that I have conjured to calm myself down. Whatever the positive thoughts are that you want to be thinking when you get to the frustration or breaking point, you should have them clearly memorized. You should practice reciting them in your mind when you are walking or driving around, and I try to remind myself of my positive thoughts every day before school, especially if it's a particularly difficult time of the year or a difficult class I'm dealing with. You don't want to find out in that moment of frustration, when you're brain is at it's least intelligible, that you now have to struggle to figure out and remember your positive thoughts, because in that moment, you really don't have a moment to lose. I will tell you one of my best positive thoughts that I use regularly, though I hope to need to use it less and less as I become calmer and calmer. It comes from a former Israeli commando soldier, who had experience running heavy ops in enemy territory with high risk of being caught and undergoing torture, so they have great ideas to battle stress.

He teaches a class in educating people on dealing with stressful situations, and how to function the best in these pressure situations. It goes like this: when you are going into that difficult moment, or the heat is on you, or you are about to freak out, or you are freaking out, or in a stressful situation, this is the three part method he uses. It's so simple, amazing and easy to remember, that I remembered it as the BeST, (he didn't call it this). The real letters are B, S, T, and it means "Breathe; Smile; it's a Test." The first step is the easiest and it is probably the most important, if you are only going to do one, and it's the easiest step to calming yourself which I mentioned a couple paragraphs ago. Take a long, slow, deep breath. This act forces you to chill, calm down, relax, and think. It delays the anger and puts it aside at least for that time. Try it the next time you are mad; the longer and slower the breath, the harder it is to be mad while you're doing it. Then, naturally, once you're done taking the breath, you feel calmer.

You can then proceed to the next step, which, to me, is the most fun and the weirdest step. I think I had gotten very good at using the shell and I hadn't really been using the "smile" phase of this commando method, and I told my brother about it the method while he was staying over my house for a week. We got in an argument over something, and he challenged me about the fact that I was getting heated up and showing frustration and wondering where this method was that I had just told him about; I seemed a little on edge during our "discussion". Now, given that this was not in a classroom, (and specifically MY classroom where I get to make the rules, which gives me a little advantage, I suppose), I wondered if I could separate my true self from so my teacher self so easily. I was definitely more emotionally attached to this situation with my brother than I would be in a classroom situation, especially since my brother and I almost NEVER fight. So I was definitely heated, and he challenged me that I had just told him about this method, and here I was not demonstrating it; how was he supposed to recognize the validity of the method? It was a very good point. I respected that and his ability to call back to something so relevant, recent, and pertinent, and bring it into the context of a real current argument.

Right in the middle of the heat of the argument, (and it was heated, though both of us were respectful to each other enough to allow the other to complete his entire thought before responding), while I was speaking, and I was heated and angry, I noticed it, and I told him I was going to do the method right then. So I took a deep breath, and then I smiled, and I have to say, that might have been the most awkward smile I ever smiled; then I said out loud that this is just a test that G-d was placing before me to see how much I could handle. Then I proceeded with what I was saying, and was definitely a lot calmer. The method works for sure, and it takes time and practice like anything else. Like I said though, that smile is awkward and weird, and when you're with students, and probably with children to a certain degree, you don't necessarily have the luxury of saying this all out loud, which may lessen the effect of its success, but it will still be ace nonetheless. So again I say, give it a try. There's little to lose.

Now, for a little information about the third step which I touched briefly on in the previous paragraph, and this is probably the hardest step, because it involves thinking about something clearly, logically, and rationally, while in the heat of the moment and in the middle of anger, rage, fury, frustration, or all of the above. This may be getting a little religious, but the method is so good, simple, and effective, I would be doing you a disservice if I didn't tell you about it, so here goes. I can tell you from experience that, while I am very religious, and believe wholeheartedly in G-d's plans for the world and for me, that during the moment of anger or frustration, it is one of the hardest times to see and believe with clarity in G-d's plan, but I believe it strengthens my belief and faith. Basically, the point is that G-d gives us tests throughout life to challenge us and make us stronger. In truth, He never gives us more than we can handle, so when the moment of passion comes, recognize it is some kind of test from G-d, and if you're not religious, you can suppose it is a challenge from something greater than yourself, or that it is a challenge to you to become something greater than you are. One simple benefit of this process is that it forces you into logical thought: to have a rational conversation in your head about the severity of the situation, or lack thereof. This will also give you an appreciation of something greater than yourself. It also helps to move you emotionally out of the situation so you can use your intellect and reason, which moves you in a more successful direction than anger. Even that benefit is worth the little effort it takes.

Mind you, if you can't do all of these strategies, doing two is better than doing one, and doing one is better than doing none, so do what you can, and eventually you will be able to do all three steps. A good idea is to write them down somewhere you have them handy when you are likely to get in that situation of frustration or anger. For some people that place might be a wallet, but I never carry my wallet in school, (for one reason, so that I don't have to feel bad about not having money to lend students when they ask, because otherwise it will turn into one more distraction from education when they keep coming to me asking for money; for another reason, who needs it?). Some might post the reminder it in their car; or at work, like I do, taped inside my right desk drawer, written in a nice, cool-written style very clearly so that I can look at it and read it, in case I ever forget. I also have it typed on my phone somewhere but I almost never look at it there. Make sure to have it in a handy place you can get it when you need it, and more importantly, whatever your phrase for calming yourself down is, assure that it's burned in your brain for easy retrieval. It will make you a better, calmer, happier person.

Once you have this clarity of focus before you speak, you can then don the shell. So really, this is all really a preparation for the real work. Here comes the true work. You must put on this garment of discipline, force, or as a better term, strictness. If you can manage to act angry, or strict, or strong against the action that needs to be corrected, you will be keeping the anger out of the situation, and it will be a much healthier outcome for everybody. The way to practice is very simple, and I tell people about it; sometimes I even tell my students. I'll look at an eraser on the chalkboard, for example, and with all seriousness, strictness, and alleged anger, I'll say, "That eraser better not move from its spot," or something of the like. Obviously, I don't care if the eraser moves or not, and more obviously, I know the eraser cannot move of its own accord, so there's no harm to be done by my practicing this skill with the eraser. It strengthens my ability to "act strict", without having the anger inside going along with the strictness. Otherwise, it is difficult to separate and distinguish the act and the emotion. The best part is, there's no need to worry about hurting the eraser's feelings. You can try this with anything; some people might think to try it with pets or animals; being a pet-lover, be careful; I didn't really practice that with my dog; I think inanimate objects are the best for this activity, at least until you're an expert.

The important thing to take note of with these activities, as far as I can tell, is that they don't seem to be the kind of methods which, after you learn them, that's it and you got it done. Check it off on the list of teacher and parent skills because now you have it down pat, and you can just repeat as necessary. On the contrary, it seems to me, the stronger, calmer, and better you get at it, there will always be new situations which will test you, and you always have to be ready and practiced. That is because it's very easy to slip into old habits or forget for just a second, especially when you're mad, and the emotions flood you, and you can easily forget everything you knew and learned, and forget all of these steps. I don't think that's abnormal for a teacher and I assume for a parent, as well. That's why I plan to always have it written in my desk and, at some point, probably in permanent marker somewhere even easier to read, like on my desk, but I suppose that should wait another year, G-d willing, till after I get tenure.

I need to give some clarity on the shell concept about things people might be wondering. When people first read the statement they should use a "shell", and act well, it seems to be a metaphor for lying, or doing something negative. The titles I used here are meant to catch attention, and sometimes, to point out the contradiction to what people might think is not acceptable or usable. In this case, the profile of the method I present is meant to illustrate how to use a shell in a positive fashion that brings more positivity to a situation, and brings control to emotions, clarity to thought, and peace to the person. What follows in the next few paragraphs, to distinguish the good way from the bad way, is an example of the way NOT for a shell to be used. I do not mean for a person to alter their personality in this way, as in lying, or doing something negative, or hiding their total self to the point that they forget who they are, and lose track of the truth. This type of personality skill can be used for good or bad. So the following is an example of the negative use of a shell, when a person builds a wall or fortress that is thick and fortified. It is so thick and fortified, that he blocks out the truth, along with the majority of people, only allowing a select few in to a shadow of his former self. He loses sight of the fact that it is a wall or fortress that he has built, and this becomes who he is, so that he is really shielded from himself. He forgets who he was or means to be. Good luck to all of my psychologist readers on this discussion!

There is a group of student I need to describe here, who are a specific type or group of students, and I have given them a group name. This is an original title which I will not trademark, use it freely. I call them the Dark Riders. In certain perspectives they are the ultimate alternative students; you might call them Ultra-Alternative, and that would be the more PC term, I suppose. The typical Dark Rider, if such a term can even be used, because really there is no typical Dark Rider, is as follows: each is his own complicated story. This one boy I am about to describe and discuss, call him Captain, was, for me, the most poignant example of a Dark Rider. It was out in Coos Bay, Oregon. There were a trio of Dark Riders that made up this very tight knit group, and I watched them form over the years. Of the three, this boy had the least connection to the mainstream world. Of the other two, one was pretty good looking, and tall, and in good shape, and had a job working with a contractor; his uncle owned a business that he hoped to go into later in life, so he was connected to the mainstream world in those ways. The third, while he had health problems, was smart, gifted with computers, very funny, and very well liked by the majority of students and people he knew, other than when he was in a certain emotional phase and he intentionally antagonized people. But even that was obviously forced and you could always see the bright nature of Barnacle Bill, as we'll call him, behind the darkness, along with a goofy smile hoping to come out. So he was connected to the mainstream world in those respects.

But Captain was different; while playing guitar finally gave him a sense of pride and place in the world, music and art are generally not accepted as fitting or accomplished until one is in a band and playing in front of others, or successful, or having a strong sense of self-confidence. For all the time I knew him, I never knew this to be the case for Captain. He wasn't big, he was skinny, and just didn't really fit in with anyone. In fact, the fact that he had the Dark Riders and friends in them was a relatively new development in the life of Captain. In the years before those Dark Rider years, when I had him in my classroom, there was one boy who he was kind of friends with, who started him on playing guitar, but even that was sporadic and not lasting. So it was when he found these two boys as friends, it was like a small band of people who he could relate to, and with whom he knew he could mostly be himself.

To everyone else outside the group there was generally a very strong shell up and this is specifically the type of shell I mean not to use when I discuss this concept. This shell consisted of snide remarks aimed at others, generally meant too deter attention away from him, if I was going to guess a quick psychology of the situation. It was a successful method too; it is hard to get made fun of when you are making fun of others or other things all the time; it puts everyone else in the defensive position. Now as a relevant side note, in general, when one, especially a teacher, asks a Dark Rider a question, the answer gets averted, and one must always expect a team discussion if one disagrees with a Dark Rider. This took place several times with Captain, when he saw one of his compatriots getting what he considered a raw deal. He could never let the person handle it themselves and he regularly came to their aid in the name of what he saw as justice. I could see his point, motivation and goals; they were sometimes noble, but more often they were really just for a good fight. But I never let it ripen anyway for several reasons.

To answer the question that might be on people's minds, about why not to let students fight for each other against the teacher, here goes. First of all it is not the business of one student to be discussing the business of another, and it is not my right as a teacher to discuss the business of one student with another. In fact there are laws against it: if you say the wrong thing to the wrong person about another student's business, as a teacher, you are liable for that, and I'm not about to risk that for somebody's desire to argue. I am supposed to keep matters confidential, even if students are friends with each other. Secondly, this student doesn't necessarily know what's in the other best interest, even if he has a good point, there are generally more aspects to the situation than a student can grasp. And he could be making the situation worse for the other student, especially with other teachers who might see this as a team attack and launch a punishment on both students for something the "lawyer" said.

Thirdly, and my favorite reason of all, is that he deprives the other student of the right to learn to speak for himself. And in this situation, when he was going to defend his friend Barnacle Bill about something, Captain might say that Barnacle Bill is afraid to speak for himself. Well then he must know that it is only after being given the opportunity to speak for himself repeatedly that Barnacle Bill might learn to do so. And if Barnacle Bill knows that Captain is going to come to his aid every time something goes astray, then Barnacle Bill will never be required to and hence never learn to speak up for himself. Not that I would purposely rebuke Barnacle Bill in order to force him to stand up for himself. Quite the contrary, and really the most important point is: I have been doing this teaching thing for a long time, I have a deeper understanding of the whole situation than Captain does, and that is why they have me doing this job. The final point on this matter, which is less philosophical and more practical, is that it is not reasonable to have a discussion, disagreement, or argument with more than one person at a time, and certainly not more than one alternative education high school student, and especially a Dark Rider! I could do it, but I don't think they would keep up. The argument would never end; it would be pointless.

The Dark Riders are such an interesting concept and an important element to comprehend in order to understand a lot of what's going on with our children and with our American society, so here's a bit more on them: they are almost never satisfied. They always want more. They have a bottomless pit of desire and attention. There is some kind of void or vacuum inside of them that is never full, and they always need interaction and energy from others. This sounds contradictory to what I was writing before about them being anti-social in certain respects, but it is really not. There's a lack of original thought. Most thought, action, and speech from them is only responsive, and it is combative. So I think they are operating much on the animal energy level. They like to drink, party, and entertain themselves with music and movies, (not that people that do these things are therefore Dark Riders; I'm just trying to give a picture of them in general). That seems to fill the void of whatever is lacking in them, while the entertainment is happening. Absent those stimuli, the people around them are used as entertainment for them. And if they don't suffice for entertainment, then the Dark Riders engage others and try to get a rise out of them. That's about all the Dark Rider talk this writer will allow for his readers at once. Let's get back to the matter at hand, which is using the shell, and acting well. It means acting the right way!

Using the shell often falls under the category of staying cool and in control, but this next story illustrates how I prefer to act calm in certain situations. Even when I know I'm right, sometimes I'd rather not let someone who hates me get the satisfaction of knowing they upset me or angered me, because most of the time, that's what they are really aiming to do. At times, even if I could maintain complete calm inside and don the shell to give a perspective of disapproval, I prefer to display no disturbance at all, because sometimes that's all people want to see, (disturbance). Knowing when to know the difference is an art that comes with experience and practice. Hopefully hearing some of my experience helps someone tell the difference between the two scenarios; so check it. I was working in Jefferson, Oregon, in a mainstream sixth middle school grade class; things had gotten pretty comfortable for me there, and I had let a side of myself that will be discussed in the third novel express itself. It was the spring when I dyed my hair blue, and I got to enjoy a couple of months in the glory of going to school like that: pretty cool. There were really only three restaurants in Jefferson that I ate at; there may have been four altogether. One of them wasn't even a restaurant; it was a coffee shop with bagels, sandwiches, Danishes and pastries, and since the time I had working in alternative education, I had been going there for coffee in the morning on my way to school. The owner knew me for a long time and I enjoyed going there: it was a cute little shop. On one of the last days of school, it may have even been the last day of school, (I believe there were no student), all of the teachers and I went to the coffee shop for lunch.

There was a line of all of the teachers and I was right around the middle of that line, and I was friends with all the teachers in the school. The teacher in front of me ordered, I still remember who it was before me, too, and then it was my turn. Until that point the owner's daughter was taking orders, because as I came to the counter he said to her, "I'll take over for orders". I told him what I wanted, and he said to me straight-faced, "You can turn around and walk out of here." I thought he was kidding but I think

I knew he wasn't, so I said, "Are you serious?" to which he replied in the affirmative; OK...

I have made stinks in my life but this was not the time for it and I smartly turned around, walked out of the shop, and went back to school without saying a word. None of the teachers even realized what happened and later, when I was talking to the principal, she said the teachers said that if they knew what happened, they would have left and eaten somewhere else. I had ideas of what had happened to cause the whole situation. Those ideas included but weren't limited to the ruckus I was raising in the town by being the only blue-haired person in that town, and especially being in a position of influence with their children. I didn't know if any of the townspeople knew I was Jewish, but I think I was the only one of those people too. The teachers later all decided to boycott that place. Mysteriously, a few days later, someone tagged up the placard in front of his store, (I always suspected my ever loyal though ever battling alternative students); and a couple weeks after that he went out of business. This guy's story, though, that he came up with, was that he had seen me stealing change from his tip jar. This comes from the fact that I used to buy a pop in the elementary school in the evening which cost 50 cents, and occasionally I would put a dollar in the tip jar and take 50 cents out so I could buy a pop, but still leave him a tip. I wonder I should have left him no tip instead, but then the truth might not have been exposed. What is the truth? I think it's that some people think that some kinds of people are mean and hard to fix, but that's a universal truth, applicable far outside of rural Jefferson, Oregon.

Now to return to the topic of the shell and acting well, remember there is a point to all this methodology, and that is to change behavior. When a student is doing something they are not supposed to be doing, I need to correct it. Depending on the level of disrespect, disregarding of the rules, disruption, or danger it is my duty to respond accordingly. I have a bit of a triage perspective on deciding the strength of the negativity of the action of the student. It's like this: if the student is disrupting his own learning and only his own learning, that's the lightest level, he is really only hurting himself. If he is disrupting others while he is learning, at least he's still learning; sometimes he doesn't even realize he's disrupting others. The worst level of the situation is when a student is not learning, and he is disrupting others; that really grinds my gears, so to speak. The aspect I focus on here, however, is when the behavior must be stopped immediately, regardless of the triage level. For example, in one scenario, a student throws a paper in the garbage; it seems harmless, but opens the path to students throwing pens or pencils to each other, and I won't get into the horrible story I heard about that. It was bad enough to warrant my reacting very strongly to any kind of throwing situation.

In closing this chapter I would like to point out, without getting into the fineries of which situations require immediate stopping, there are in general, certain situations with require immediate halting and correction. We can go further and imagine that there are certain situations which require immediate correction, in which students are not responding to proper, calm, polite correction, and the behavior continues, thereby endangering the students themselves or others. It is this situation with which I am concerned. As an observant Jew, and really as a person in general, and specifically as a teacher, I should not be flying into uncontrolled rages to get these behaviors to stop. I heard a story of a teacher who set up the garbage can behind her door on the first day of school, and then flew into a rage at her students, acting like the students had set up the garbage can to make her a fool! That's another example of using a shell in the totally wrong way, and while this strategy may have been effective, and makes for a funny story, it has many consequences, including demonstrating the effective success of anger as a tool to get what one wants. We cannot advocate, therefore, this strategy as the best for behavior correction.

In addition, it is not healthy for the teacher himself to run through emotions like these. Doctors can cite the dangers of elevated blood pressure and the ill effects of anger. Nevertheless, the behavior needs to be corrected and ended immediately, and the question is: how is a teacher to do that without getting angry? This may be the critical point of this book. The art is to have that shell of the personality on top of the inner personality. Within the skin, there must be peace, focus, and determination, a higher thinking being guiding the course of the correction, regardless of what is being portrayed to students or teachers on the outside. The top and highest attributes of the personality are those of the mind, and they are what, more than anything, separate us from the animal kingdom. Below those attributes are the qualities of emotion; the former should govern the latter, which does not in any way rule out or invalidate the use and feeling of emotions. That is simply because we look at the mind as being above, guiding, and governing the emotions. So at these times we have to give an appearance of discipline and strictness, which might look like anger, but which is very different from it, while internally being focused on being chill and guided by the mind. Whether the students perceive all of this or not is not as important as the truth, because a class being run only by fear of anger and punishment will not have the lasting impact in the long run that the teacher may desire. If the fear is only of a specific teacher, it will probably only function to make the class work that year. Our goal is bigger: we need to make an impact on the students that affects their entire education and personality in the positive, and lasts a lifetime.

11
KEEP IT FRESH

Without a doubt, stability encourages success, and that is probably the reason that the chapters on boundaries and structure are two of the longest chapters in this work. Students and children greatly appreciate boundaries, but they are also dealing with a fluctuating and unstable world that is changing all around them, rapidly in their own lives. The new information they are constantly bombarded with only serves to make the children themselves more shifting, which is all the more reason why I spent so much time talking about boundaries and structure. On the other hand, we do need to recognize the truth of their (and our) changing world, and encourage their ability to adapt to that change and succeed in it. Not to mention the fact which many, (including myself), don't like to deal with: that due to this overstimulation of change and transformation of the world, and rapidly varying stimuli and information, we get bored. As teachers and parents, it is our job to figure out the proper balance between structure, boundaries, flexibility, and innovation. We need to introduce new concepts, ideas, methods, strategies, and everything else that can be innovated, to prepare students and children for the changing world and get them better at adapting to it, while encouraging them to build and foster stability in their own lives. Even when I was in public school as a student, they told us we should expect to change careers or jobs seven times in our lives; the world is obviously a rapidly changing and evolving place. We have to prepare our students and children for that reality; we have to make them comfortable with change and stability, and able to thrive in a situation that includes and encompasses both of those aspects of life.

Classroom approach, in a manner of speaking, first and foremost includes manners and tone. In the old model of the standard classroom, the teacher was the boss and spoke to students like a factory owner might speak to his workers. This worked in the majority of cases because most students sought or seek the prizes and the reward that the teacher holds access to, which are grades and credits, (also corporal punishment was used, and there wasn't really much other choice by students). Teachers also hold the reward of positive affirmation which most people seek; most people feel they need this positive affirmation received from the people in charge of and responsible for them. But we get a unique population in alternative education especially that either sees through the veil, or just does not care. As time goes on, many children and students lose interest in this standard model. In any case, the fact of the matter is that speaking from the perspective of fairness and justice, the teacher does not pay his students, and therefore does not have the right to treat them as paid workers. The fact that the teacher does and can get away with it, in many cases, does not justify this practice. It may be effective and necessary at times, but should really not be the only model of relating to students.

In alternative education, many of the students come to this environment, by choice or otherwise, for that very reason, that they saw the flaws in this type of system and were able to exploit them or else they just lost interest in the system and bailed on it. What I find consequently is that many of the alternative students I get are of a higher moral caliber than the typical student. On Kohlberg's scale, which is a scale of morality rating people from levels one through six, they have seen past the stage of obeying rules simply because they come from an authority figure, and they are seeking a higher moral ground. Maybe the same is the case with a child in general. Of course there are certain cases, no matter what, where the teacher or parent gives a rule and it must be obeyed without question, the "because I said so" rule, if you will, but we should try to keep this to a minimum and last resort.

Hence we have a group of students who have not bought into this old school philosophy of education. Some figured it out as false, some could not make the grade, and some just were not even paying attention to the game enough to know that there was a game going on. Whatever the case, it is our responsibility to reintegrate them into the stream of life and reality as we know it. Doing this involves two tasks, in my philosophy: task one is acquainting them with the rules of the game of the real world and reality, and this is where solid structure, consistency, and predictability are essential. Task two of this philosophy stems from one of the first reasons I got into education and one of my main purposes in life. That task is to change the world so that it is fair and right. So that means implementing and using a parenting and teaching system which shifts balance like the trends of the real world, linked with ways to change the world, streamed with teachings, ideals, and philosophies of how the world should be.

It is tricky to present these types of ideas, concepts, and philosophies in a class without preaching, and I try to do it mostly with quotes. Although this is very difficult to do or justify in my current position as Math Teacher, I haven't ruled out the possibility. It just takes some time and creativity. In all my other positions teaching, I always had a quote of the day on the board, which I got from some interesting quote books, and students would have to respond to it in a journal, about what they thought it meant, whether they liked it, what it made them think. Then I would go over the quote with them and this activity gave me the opportunity to inject some philosophy, idealism, and positive thought into the program, which I think is essential to alternative education. Most students need to connect with a leader or a teacher, especially if they don't have that connection at home. This helps them in creating significant, personal learning memories - between the educator and the student or child, who will inspire him or her for a lifetime. I was blessed with such teachers, and I hope everyone else becomes a parent and or teacher who can do the same for their children and students; it means the world to us.

Keeping it fresh, in general, as compared to structure and boundary, is much harder to teach, and there is no real rule book for it. It is very difficult to teach someone to have new, original, creative ideas. I will point out, however, that having a structure within which to work, allows much more freely for the generation of these types of ideas. The more time I spend teaching the same material, the more creative I get. This has made things challenging for me, because I have never had the exact same teaching position more than two years, until this past year, but now my position is changing again! This forced me to learn to become a better teacher, and also forced me to become much more structured, which for me, was my biggest weakness. Now I got structure pouring out of my class under the door, and it's giving me a real opportunity to get creative. The ideas come from different places; some of these ideas came up through listening to students, looking around, being open minded, and being willing to try something new, even if there were seemingly risks involved. The ideas also come from having a positive, creative environment, and from being happy and relaxed, which allows the mind the freedom to create. I recently saw a post on the website of one of the best teachers I have ever known in my teaching career; she wrote a book on education the same time I did. She called the idea of being controlled in trying something new, "Taking Responsible Risks", (http://jaquiforney.weebly.com/). It's a good motto for allowing oneself to try new ideas, and I'm sure there are other applications for it as well. If you would like to read more, contact her on her site and she can get you a copy of her book!

So I will try to show a few variations and ideas that have popped up throughout my career that I think are pretty neat, and which come from just trying to keep things fresh. They may not be the most amazing ideas ever, but, hey, I'm still working on it and not keeping it stale. If I keep writing all the new ideas that come up I may never finish this book, because it will just keep going on and on. In terms of the CNN meeting that happened at the end of the day in Coos Bay, I would always have variations to try to keep things interesting and fresh and keep the students' attention. To that end, I made sure to change it up and do new things they might like and find interest in; even if all the students didn't find interest, I figured some would, and sometimes that's the only way to get to everyone, because people have varied interests! There were three variations to be noted, as follow in the next couple paragraphs.

One variation was that sometimes at the end of the day, (actually almost every day unless it was a bad day and I did not feel they earned it), I would do a lottery drawing, which I discussed earlier; (nobody had to pay for the drawing so it was legal!). I described the drawing process before, but I should note that I varied what the prize would be to keep things interesting, and sometimes that was random, which was usually influenced by how good the kids were, better prizes being awarded for overall better days and program behavior. Besides the coffee bucks from Dutch Brothers, a local coffee store, we had pizza bucks for a five dollar pizza from Abby's Pizza. The kids loved those and they really enjoyed the drawing, as did yours truly, for the fun of it. It kept things light while reminding them we were looking for good behavior, and had a system that would track it which inspired them to work harder to attain success.

Another of the three variations was the hangman alternative, which was probably my favorite. Sometimes the day was just so great, there was not really enough time left to read in Silent Sustained Reading. Sometimes the reading went so well it was just a nice reward. Sometimes, someone would ask for this alternative and I knew as well as they did that they had earned the right to play hangman, (also, I was happy that high school students would ask for something fun, light and positive, that didn't even earn them official credit). So I would come up with some clever statement, quote, a fact or whatever; it was never just one word, and it was always a sentence, and usually a long one, and believe it or not, even in high school, kids still like playing hangman. Don't you like playing hangman? Wouldn't you play if I put it up on the board right now? If your answer seems "no", think harder or loosen up.

The third variation came around the second term, when the English teacher came across the <u>Planet Earth</u> video series by National Geographic, which was lent to him by one of the other teachers in the building. I knew when we started these videos that it would make CNN that much worse, meaning

CNN would be much less interesting and desirable, and it would be that much more of a struggle to get the kids to watch CNN and answer questions on it. Who wants to watch the news of current events, when they can watch killer whales chomping baby whales in Alaska? The kids always used to complain about CNN, but I was always able to tell them that each and every one of them was told in their interview, in the beginning of the year, before entering Destinations, that this was part of the curriculum and a mandatory routine for everyone in the program, and that they should get used to it, because it was here to stay. But after they finally got used to it and accepted it, then we came across <u>Planet Earth,</u> and we were able to lighten things a little. Therefore we set up and instituted a rotation where Monday, Wednesday, and Friday were CNN, and Tuesday and Thursday were <u>Planet Earth</u>, and in third term we exchanged the days of that rotation, which the kids really loved, as they got more <u>Planet Earth</u>. I showed the other teacher how to quickly watch and scan the <u>Planet Earth</u> video and write questions for it, to help the students focus and direct their attention in watching and learning, and he took that on.

Now along the lines of keeping it fresh, I need to ask myself a question out loud, and that is, exactly how did my version of Jeopardy start? It started way back in my first alternative education class, and I am not sure where I got the idea, I believe it was back when www.metacrawler.com was the dominant search engine, and Al Gore had just invented the internets. I used that website to find some interesting lesson plans, (I believe for an upcoming observation), when I had my first teaching assignment in 2000. I found the plans for Math Jeopardy and created categories out of colored card stock, each card being about twelve inches by four inches, with different categories having different colors, and I stuck them to the chalkboard with tape; I think back then we would play boys against girls. And I think I used that cardstock because I found it laying around. Nowadays everyone uses the computer version which is easier and faster but there's something to be said for the physical reward of a prize feeling, of being handed the card, which the kids liked. Maybe using Monopoly money or something like that would give that hands on feel that the kids enjoy. But all that really takes a lot of time which is probably why nowadays I just use the computer version and sometimes give out physical real prizes to the winners. The kids even get excited for glow bracelets, and you can get 20 of them for a dollar in the Dollar Store.

The other nice thing with the computer format of Math Jeopardy is that it is easy to keep updating it and add new material to the game from recently studied curriculum, and this makes a nice review process. Ideally we play

Math Jeopardy every other week and test or quiz on the opposite weeks, but sometimes it comes out to more like once a month, especially as we have more standardized testing. It is a great end of the week activity. The best parts of the game are the building of confidence and learning the will to take a risk and guess. It has continuous and thorough success, coast to coast, fifth grade to twelfth grade, (I'm sure it works with younger kids too), alternative and mainstream, special needs and not. This is the most consistent successful aspect of my teaching career that I could vouch for and say, "This works well everywhere with everyone". It's cool to have something that I can say that about. The trick for me, still to this day, is to find the balance of when to give rewards for the winners, and when to play without rewards, for two reasons. Firstly, I need to give the less successful students motivation to play. If the motivation is only for a prize that is given solely to the winner or the winners, and these students know they won't win, then they may never want to play, and I've seen that happen before.

For a proper response to the difficulty of students unmotivated by winner rewards because they know they won't win, we come to an original idea generated from the writing of this novel, and that is the "Daily Surprise", which I already started using, (successfully) at the end of this year. This bonus means that certain questions will automatically guarantee a prize for the player, and it could be one kind where they get the answer correct or another kind where they just get a prize for picking the right question. You can also give extra credit points just for answering questions. There are lots of ways to vary it up. You can give two points per question answered, (even if it's wrong, which will encourage participation), and four points per question answered correctly, (which rewards success). The possibilities are limitless and you should be creative. The second reason for which I have to be careful about the prizes given is that I want students to develop and/or strengthen the love for learning for its own sake, and not only for the rewards brought. While in the real world very few people work for free (I guess that's considered "volunteering", which is different from working); nevertheless it is important to develop the desire to learn, so we groom life-long learners, which is a very "in" term these days, as it should be. A person who loves to learn will generally find happiness, success, and his place in the world. So it is alright that children like getting rewards, and like playing the game for rewards; that is a normal part of life; but I think it important to vary it up, like at least every fourth game should be played without any prizes.

Keeping it fresh also means varying the assignments or tasks you give your students and children. At home this can mean having a daily responsibility, along with a weekly and monthly responsibility, and changing them up from time to time, as long as it doesn't disrupt structure too much. In class, I have always had an array and variety of assignments for students, and I try to use clever names for assignments if possible. I also vary by day and week by week. So I have them do a "do-now" journal every day, and of those do-now's, they have to do a "four square" every week, which I discussed earlier. We have homework from Tuesday through Thursday, and quizzes and tests, and for advanced students, I have projects assigned to be completed at home. I also allow students to make up work from various books we have throughout the classroom; they can look up the topic we're doing and find problems similar to those and work out of the book at home; I come up with a related amount of problems.

With many of the assignments I give in my math classes, I include a darkened box that has refresher instructions on how to do the assignment. I make the assignments look cool and easy to read, and I think that's important. With most of the math assignments I did in earlier years, when I wasn't doing "do-now's", and not under so much curriculum pressure, I included something interesting, like a single page word problem from the workbook, Thought Provokers, (listed in the Appendix I. These problems are fun, solvable, and got the brain going. So I always included one of the Thought Provokers on packets of work, that were more of the regular math skills and life skills, which students need to learn. And if the math packet was on measuring backyards to figure out the length of fencing, I looked for a problem that started with the letter "m" or "b" or "f", so one packet was called "Homes and Hypocycloids", for example; this kind of thing is fun to alternative students and really all students and people. But any system you come up with is great. The reason I did this with the alphabetizing, was that I had a feeling I might get to a point where I let students go into the assignment bin with my permission. I therefore wanted it labeled easier for their sake, and it made my life better when I had to search less through those files. That's because as many times as you give assignments out, you better make extra copies, because there's always going to be a few that are lost, and it's time consuming to make more copies.

The other math assignment that has been a regular in all of my math classes was those coming from this book: When in the world are we going to use this? (Appendix I). It is a great workbook that I used constantly and it has a few extra special benefits. First of all, as a math teacher, this has to be the most commonly asked question I get, year after year, class after class. There are plenty of answers I have ready at the tip of my tongue when the question is popped, but this is a much more visual way for students to see the answers themselves. The book is divided into the different strands of math, like algebra, geometry, percentage and decimals, to name a few. Then within each of those strands are about 30 to 50 different careers, and word problems that would be solved in that career. I have to rave about this book for a bit: first of all it gives them practice in problem solving, which is an important math skill and an important life skill, and this will transfer to other areas of their life, when they get comfortable looking at, analyzing, and trying different methods to solve a problem. It also covers all the strands of math that we are required to and should study, including probability and statistics, algebra, geometry, measurement, calculations and estimations, and of course problem solving.

Probably the best part of this book, which is really a bonus for a math class, is that it gives them exposure to a range of careers they might not otherwise know about. It gives them ideas of what people in these careers do. So in doing these problems, they might think to themselves that they like solving the kinds of problems that an airplane technician solves, and it might be a good career for them, or that they hate it, and they never want to be an airplane technician in their life. The coolest thing about this book, also, was how much improvement I was able to see in students and how much confidence they gained in solving these problems. This is where it is essential to be in there with them, and solving the problems, so that if they have questions, you can help them. Especially with the slower classes, I was able to see positive changes throughout the year, to the point where they were solving the problems on their own; compared to the beginning of the year where they absolutely needed my help from the board at pretty much every step of the problem. So aside from getting an answer to the original question of when they are going to use this math skill in life, and aside from getting practice within these necessary math strands, and aside from career exposure, they get practice with word problems, of which I am a big fan. The other nice basic about the book is that they get practice with math skills and used to the routine and format of these problems. I recommend this book for parents at home, as well as math or career teachers as early as possible, even starting with one problem a week. It will make your children better problem solvers and expose them to the realities of different careers. It's great.

While it's a little diversion from the topic, nevertheless, I want to give a heads up on the question of students going into the homework bin or not. In many classes this won't even matter, as teachers may not have a bin or receptacle students can into on their own. Regardless, when I was in Coos Bay, I got into a regular routine where I planned out the week ahead of time on every Sunday, when I came in for a couple hours; sometimes when I got ambitious or I got a planning day I was able to go a couple or even a few weeks ahead. Now there is a balance between giving assignments that involve a little teaching versus assignments that involve lots of teaching. If students go into the bin without your permission they may want to go in and get a bunch of assignments to get ahead so they can have a bunch of time to relax in the future. And that is totally up to you. I wasn't really for this system and idea, because I wanted my work to be done in my class. That was because if they get done early with the work, they could go work on any of the independent projects that every student had to work on. I only had two students, part of the "Dark Rider crew", who wanted to go into the bin and get ahead, and that was the first time I had to point out the fact that it was by permission only that they were to go in the bin. Before that, students just assumed they were not permitted to go into the bin, but the Dark Riders always pushed the limits. After that, I am pretty sure no one ever went into the bin without permission or stealthily; I do not think they wanted extra work that badly that they were willing to get rebuked for trying to get ahead of the class. Either way while it was still by permission, it was still another nice flexibility and a fresh option that students, if they wanted, could work on assignments at their own pace.

What else works in keeping it fresh? "Do now's" as I mentioned earlier are solid. I never called them by that name; I called them "Problem of the Day" or "Journal", though now I'm flexible with all three names. Whatever the name, there was always a choice of two problems or more for students, (they only had to do one problem), and so they have less to complain about. I get the problems from various places, like general word problems sites; as the years went on, I got them from SAT word problem websites, and then I was getting them from HSPA, (High School Proficiency Assessment) word problem sites as well. The difficulty with HSPA problems is that they are often long, involved, and complicated, and can rarely be solved in the 5-10 minutes I allot for this activity. I get an email every other day from an SAT site called The Official SAT Question of the Day, (http://sat.collegeboard.org/practice/sat-question-of-the-day). In the beginning of the year the kids usually complain and sometimes ask about not having done "do now's" since fifth grade, but as time goes on and they get the routine, they stop complaining and I see a lot of success with students, as well as a sense of accomplishment from solving original thought problems. I am a firm believer in teaching problem solving in math, and really in all subjects, and in life; math is really the only one that has it ingrained though, so it's more natural.

So here's an interesting look at how NOT to keep it fresh. In looking back through the book, one of the topics that was only semi-covered, and which I meant to cover, was the "laugher" juniors on their last day. This is the class of juniors from my first year in West Orange High School that was never serious, never got focused, and eventually got stale. In the beginning when I had them they were kind of funny, at least they laughed a lot, and weren't really dirty or too negative; but their jokes never evolved, and they never got down fully to the business of learning, and I called them on it. On the last day of school they were cracking old jokes that they had been making all year, (I think the joke was "you look like a _____" where they would try to come up with something funny to say the other person looked like). It got old and boring, so I told them their style was stale. It really threw them for a loop; one of them asked me if I just said their style was stale; I affirmed. They asked me, if their style was stale, then what was something that wasn't stale? I said that was my style, and we got in an argument about it for like fifteen minutes. We got a little off-topic but generally stuck to the theme. My point was that they were stale because they weren't generating new ideas, because they weren't learning. I'm not sure what their point was, I just wanted to let them know they should get into gear for next year. They almost did.

Keeping it fresh in one respect means having the ability to change things up and be flexible. To that end, one of the hardest things for me to adjust to was giving quizzes and tests. Creating tests and quizzes means you are going to have to work towards them in instruction which means a much greater degree of organization and sometimes less flexibility and innovation. Now they call that Backwards Design, which as mentioned briefly, basically meaning you decide what you want to assess, create the assessment, and teach toward that end or goal. It seems awfully close to "teaching to the test" as far as I am concerned, but I don't know anybody made that point. As I think about it now, I don't think I really gave high school tests before I was in West Orange High School. In the alternative situations I taught before that, students might have to complete the tests at the end of the book, but that was with the book, and on their own time and pace. In middle school when I was in AIMS/IPASS in Coos Bay, I gave a vocabulary quiz every week, upon suggestion from my assistant, but the high school students didn't have that quiz. There were too many students working on too many subjects and projects at the same time, and too many attendance issues, to have that weekly regularity of routine. I think when I was a mainstream middle school teacher in Jefferson, Oregon, I must have given tests; I think there were vocabulary tests and there must have been other tests, but I don't remember that so much and so well. So in West Orange High School the last few years, was the first time I really had to make up quizzes and tests and give them and grade them. It was pretty intense in the beginning: it was difficult for me to write the tests and quizzes, and it was difficult to grade them. Surprisingly, those who seemed to appreciate the tests the most were the students. I guess they like the structure and routine they are used to and getting their minds in gear to excel towards a goal. They also like knowing whether or not they "got it" and getting proof of that fact. I think they also like the positive feeling of meeting their own expectations. Since creating all or most of the tests over the first two years, it was nicer to edit and refine them rather than working without a clue from scratch to create them, in the third year.

One final note I would like to include in this chapter really involves two aspects of music, which has been a big part of my life and which I have generally tried to include in my classrooms as much as possible. One of my best classes in West Orange High School, which included the girl who was my most positive student ever, who almost got me to create a positivity award named after her, earned the "808 reward". To explain that reward I need to give some background on the musical events leading up to it. One of the activities I created was what I consider to be (in my mind) nearly legendary, the original "Beats per minute" lesson and tracking sheet, included in Appendix H, designed to teach proportions and give students a better understanding of proportions. I used this lesson coast to coast and this is the second aspect of teaching that I can say with assurance works fantastically, fifth grade through twelfth. The basic concept of the lesson is that you want to figure out the tempo or beats per minute (BPM) of a song. To simplify this process, instead of counting the beats for a whole minute, you count for 30 seconds and double your answer; or you can count for 15 seconds and multiply your answer by four, and so on. It's a class favorite and I enjoy teaching it greatly. In getting into this lesson, I explain to students the fact that a deejay who uses vinyl, (which I have), needs to have his records categorized by BPM, and in discussing the activities of a deejay, they often inquire after my gear. My Roland 808 sound processor is the coolest piece of my deejay equipment I have; I told the classes that if they got it together I would be happy to bring it in and play with them. In my other schools I think I brought in my turntables once, maybe twice, and it was always kind of messy, as in managing the excitement over it without worrying about my equipment getting damaged. Till that point I had never brought in the 808, because it was too valuable to me, and I hadn't trusted my classes enough. But times changed, and I got better classes that I connected to and trusted more. Despite that fact, I knew the chaos and excitement that would be generated by this thing, so a class had to be in tip top shape in order to merit the 808, because I'm not about to jeopardize it or my situation by making things too exciting that they can't handle it, (it's $600).

I did the BPM activity with all five classes in my first year at West Orange High School, and of all those classes, only the fifth period, which was the coolest, (which had the super-positive girl) got to have the 808 brought in to play. It was funny because they seemed almost afraid of it! I was trying to get them to use the different parts of it and it was a first for me to see, that high school students were reserved and shy, but I know how it is, really, making music in front of other people. Those who think that using electronics like turntables and processors to make music is not a form of music making, should see how students act around it, in that they were afraid to perform poorly, and then they will know the truth: this is a form of making music (the 808, that is, in certain forms; I don't vouch for all synthetic forms). And that's how to end a lesson on keeping it fresh, with a lesson on 808's and synthetic music, y'all.

12
BE BOLD; BE BRAVE

Being bold and brave is difficult to teach. The closest idea I can give will sound like it belongs in my hopefully upcoming book about exciting exploits in the life of a public school alternative teacher. That idea is of jumping off a bridge or a cliff, which may not be the smartest thing to recommend to readers; in fact, I officially do not endorse it. Do not attempt this at home or near your home. On the topic, if a reader is considering the bridge or the cliff, I will inform that the former is safer, believe it or not, as far as I am concerned, presuming you find a bridge that people are already jumping off of regularly, (and swimming away from afterwards!). The reason it's generally safer to jump off a bridge than a cliff, (though, again, not safe enough for my students and/or readers to try), as I have learned, is that with a cliff, you never really know how the cliff slopes under the water, and where and how deep it slopes by which part of the cliff. Once upon a time we were cliff jumping in Lebanon, Oregon; I jumped off and, when I went under water, my foot skimmed the side of the cliff. I realized if I had jumped a little differently, G-d forbid, it might not have been such a pretty landing. A bridge, on the other hand, is usually jumped off of from the middle of the bridge, which is in the middle of the lake, where it is the deepest, and you don't have to worry about hitting anything, (as long as a check is made for upcoming boats). The point is of this seemingly long side story is, at the moment you are getting ready to jump, in order to make the jump, for me at least, at times, I have to stop my brain from thinking and just go.

That really is the crux, in my mind, of what bravery is often about: it's about defying the odds and going up against something that might logically be greater than yourself, or bigger than yourself, and more difficult or scary than you think you can handle. You really have to put that fact aside, to trick your brain into ignoring the fear, difficulty or danger, and into doing what must be done. In the gym of the Harding Learning Center in Coos Bay, at times we would have multiple programs going on in the gym at once. Sometimes things would get a little hairy; there would be all types of sports balls flying in all types of directions and I was always amazed how people rarely got hurt for as much chaos as was going on there. One of those times, one of my high school students was getting into it near fighting with one of the other program's students; these were both big boys; my student was a farm boy and he was probably 6'3 and about 240 pounds. The other boy was a little skinnier but tougher. I saw it erupting as it was happening: they had squared up and were face to face, and I went over to them, and stood between them, and put one hand on each chest and pushed them apart. I literally had to reach up to do this, it felt like being a little guy between giants, (I guess that's what it was), and I don't remember what I said to them, but it made them separate. I didn't know if it would work when I did it, but I tried and I made like I meant it. The funny thing was that another student came up to me afterwards and told me I should have let them go at it, because that was the only way they would know who was tougher, and they would have gone at it anyway somewhere else. I think they ended up fighting after school a few days later, and that's fine; there's little that can be done if they are determined, but not on my watch!

I don't know whether the next examples fall in the category of bravery or stupidity, but there is often a fine line between those categories. As a teacher, I have found that some of my braver moments were not necessarily in the classroom with students, but were with co-workers. One of my braver moments isn't a glamorous story, but was when I was Jefferson, as a teacher in the mainstream middle school. There was an old teacher there, who had been there since time eternal, and who was very much from the old school and he was staying that way; there was no flexibility or discussion about it. He seemed unenthusiastic about teaching and was pretty negative about the students and it bothered me, but I was still a third year teacher there, and I wasn't necessarily ready to start a ruckus. Nonetheless, in a staff meeting, he was being very negative about the students and the new methods of education that were being discussed and he mentioned something about the good old days when you could corporal punish kids, and things worked much better back then, and it crossed the line for me, so I spoke up. I told him something like he needed to get with the times and the old days were different and they were gone, and he better adjust and start trying new things if he wanted to succeed in education. It was one of those moments where everything was pin-drop silent after I spoke, and then things continued. I guess I broke the rule of respecting elders when I spoke to him that way, but I am pretty sure it needed to be done.

The other case was even earlier in my career, and I think it was my first year teaching. It starts like this: when I decided I was going into the field of education I wanted to prove to myself that I was still a rebel and wild, and still against the system or something like that, so, for the second time in my life, I got my tongue pierced. Somehow, I managed to hide the fact from my boss and the other teachers in the school, but the kids knew the first day, and I think they dropped a hint to the effect that my assistant knew. She was cool, though, and didn't drop the dime, and that was going real nicely. I had a good racket there, teaching during the day with my tongue pierced, and being a deejay at night in various locales. One day, I remember very clearly walking with my boss down the hallway at the elementary school during the second part of my school day, and she was discussing one of our students who had, in sixth grade, just gotten his tongue pierced. I was walking next to her and she was telling me how disgusting it was, and she didn't understand how anyone could do that, and her true disgust was so obvious that I knew she meant it. Tongue in cheek, I managed a reply, and I probably had to bite my tongue to keep from laughing, but I kept a straight face. That night I figured I had taken it far enough and gotten away with more than enough, and I took it out. That tongue piercing seemed brave to me.

Being brave will form one of the largest chapters in the book and it may be the most important part of being a teacher, because there will always be difficult decisions to make, tough situations to handle, and challenging people to face unfalteringly. Bravery is essential for all these situations. To the end that people don't get the idea that teachers' unions or general unions have difficulties, I should describe my intimate involvement with one of the other unions in which I was involved, namely the Jefferson School District Teachers' Union in Oregon. When I was leading my double exciting life as a second year alternative education teacher during the day and deejay at night, I had a lot of action going on, and was involved in a lot of action, and the stories of that action are the meat of the yet-unwritten book. Suffice it to say I was pushing a lot of boundaries. When, towards the end of my second teaching school year, I went to back out of my parking spot at the end of the school day, a white mini-van pulled up perpendicular to my rear, I thought my deejay life had caught up to my teaching life and something big was about to go down. Fortunately, I was wrong. It was actually the other alternative teacher in the program, (she taught the high school component of the program). She was stopping to ask me if I wanted to be a union representative for the next year. I told her I would think about it. I decided to go for it. Though in my youth I stayed as far from politics as possible, as I had a certain enmity for them, I thought this would be a good experience.

ALTERNATIVE EDUCATION FOR PARENTS AND TEACHERS

It was pretty interesting going to the meetings and learning about the whole process of what goes on behind the scenes to get teachers' salaries, health, and benefits; and learning how the system really worked, or at least a part of it. It got more interesting and exciting as the year went on and we got further and further from settling our contract with the Board of Education. This was a contract negotiation year, which meant that we had to re-negotiate our contract with the Board, and try to reach a settlement for a new contract which would probably last for another three years, till it had to be re-negotiated. That process was very educational in learning the business world, (which I had strongly avoided as well), and how these types of negotiations and processes take place. Two particular stories stand out, one of which felt like one of my braver moments, and one of which was enlightening as to the way of the world, boards of educations, and government systems. We'll get to that story shortly, since it is not only irrelevant to bravery, but on the contrary, is quite the opposite of it, as far as I am concerned.

In the heat of the whole negotiations, it was obvious that things weren't going anywhere. It was right around the time when we were getting ready to go on strike, and teachers, I think, by this point, had started marching up and down the main road, (during off-school hours), carrying signs to the effect of our needs for negotiation, and there was some kind of board meeting. I don't remember if it was a regular board meeting or a special session called for discussion on the topic of negotiation, but it was a public meeting, and a lot of people came out. The room was full, and I, being a middle school teacher, (mainstream at this point), had been asked by the team to speak to the board, which I was happy to do.

I had written out my speech, or the main points I had wanted to make, and I recall that one of the points was about attention, and along the lines of needing to have good teachers to get classroom attention and direct it, manage it, and focus it in order to bring about the desired education goals. The board consisted of about ten members, and I noticed while I was talking that I had the attention of the whole board and the whole room. It was silent, and all eyes were on me, with the exception of one pair of eyes. I had already spoken to thousands at my high school graduation, and thousands more as a deejay, and so I had a good command of public speaking, honed further by teaching, and I saw that it was one particular board member, who had his eyes down, and was reading something. As far as I could make out, he was completely ignoring me, a point to which I did not take well. This may not have been my smartest move, but it was one of my boldest: as I finished a statement that ended something like, "in order to make sure you have their attention", I stopped cold, and looked directly at him, and waited, and every pair of eyes in the room turned to him. He looked up, realized he had been caught not paying attention to something that the entire town was paying attention to for its own best interest, and he might have been slightly embarrassed. I don't think he had a great fondness for me after that.

The other event that stood out during the same time frame, and which was enlightening in a different way, was in negotiating with the Superintendent, who is in general the highest member of the Board of Education. Interestingly he still answers to the board, and he is really the most powerful person in a school district, and in many respects, one of the most powerful people around. When I was first hired to Jefferson School District, the Superintendent was a great man, who doubled his duties as the Middle School Principal as well. He was excellent in both positions, and as far as I could tell, everybody loved him, and as I knew him, he was a super sweet guy who loved kids and did his best in all arenas; he was making people very happy in the district, from kids to parents to teachers to principals; he rocked.

A reminder for background about the components of my position during this time: I would get to school at 12:00 and have "prep" till 1:00, during which I would go over to the teachers' lounge in the middle school in order to connect with the teachers there. I did this since I realized the students I would be getting came from their classes, and if I was sending them back to mainstream, they would be going to those teachers' classes. I figured it would be useful to exchange and share information for our sakes and for the students' sakes. I also had in mind the possibility of moving into the mainstream and thought that would be a good way to make those necessary connections. Then I would teach my main class, which consisted of five to fifteen students, grades five to ten, from 1:00 to 3:00. I taught them math, English, social skills, and sometimes science, social studies, art, and PE. That took place in a building which was separate from the middle school though on the same grounds, in what used to be the wood and metal shop. My classroom shared a bathroom with the high school students, and in the shop which was entered through another door leading out of the classroom, was my supervisor's office, where I could sometimes send students if they were unruly, as you might say.

I then went to the elementary school down the street, and ran the after school program for elementary school students from 3:15 to 5:00; there were about 80 students in this program from kindergarten through fifth grade, and there were several parts to it, over which I was in charge: arts and crafts, computers, games, and outdoor play. I then had "lunch" from 5:00 to 5:45 or so, and then the evening part of the alternative program would kick in, along with the computer lab, which was open for free to anyone in the town, till 9:00, at which time my work day was done. The evening alternative program had an aid, as did my daytime alternative classroom, to help the high school students who came in at night in order to make up credits they were missing. The whole point of this story was to inform that in one meeting I had with a student who had gotten in trouble with at the elementary after school program, I got to meet the principal of the elementary school who, in the meeting, said some very nice and appropriate things to the student, and seemed to me to be a very sweet and genuine man.

Fast forward a year or so to the former super superintendent's retirement, which was the end of my first year there, and the restructuring of the district, which has been a process I have seen over and over again in my teaching career. The district also hired a new principal for the middle school, who might make a chapter or so in another more risky book, I suppose, and the new superintendent hired was the very principal I sat in that meeting with at the elementary school. I thought that was a great move, especially since I knew him already. Like I said, he seemed very sweet and genuine, and I was happy to have him running the ship. Fast forward further to our negotiations for the union during that contract year, and fast forward even more specifically to the night the negotiating team slept in the school, to try to reach a last ditch settlement before the teachers were to go on strike the following day I think it was.

That process itself was an entirely interesting experience. I forget how the negotiating started for the evening, and who went first, but basically the pattern was something like this: first, the board of education would make a proposal, and we would respond. We always responded very quickly, as we wanted the process to move along, which was not the smartest strategy. Then, the mediator would bring our proposal and response to the board. For their reply, they would always take a very long time, (sometimes more than an hour, and amazingly we never recognized this pattern nor changed our habit). They would come back with their proposal, and this back and forth tedious and slow negotiation game went on through the night, (we brought sleeping bags and all of our night essentials in anticipation of staying over). We had a guy with us named Roger Trawick, he should rest in peace, who was a cowboy poet; he lived in Eastern Oregon, and had been involved for a long time with unions and negotiations, and was there for support and help. Throughout the night, he recited cowboy poetry, which helped keep us motivated and inspired, and kept us from losing our cool during this crazy process.

One point to make in this is that from every angle and experience I could see, the union was completely legitimate and righteous and doing what was in the teachers' best interest with proper teacher input and response. It checked progress and thoughts with teachers throughout the whole process, and responded to their desires and needs, and that's how a union should be, as far as I am concerned. It was completely and fairly representative of the teachers, in every manner I could observe, not to mention the fact that dues there were a lot cheaper than in New Jersey, but that's no surprise! Now back to the point, at some crazy hour in the night, when we were all locked in the building, for all intents and purposes, I was going to the bathroom, and as I was walking, I noticed a man in front of me who I could not discern. I say this because I knew everyone in the building who was there for that negotiation. There was our union negotiating team, who I obviously knew, and the members of the Board's team, who I had met in the first meeting of the night, (there were only about five or six members of each team), and then there was the mediator. And here was a tall gentleman, walking with good stature, pretty much strolling down the hallways with complete confidence, (I could only see him from behind), and I had no idea who he was. I was perplexed.

It wasn't until after he turned the corner that I realized this was the very superintendent who I had known since he was an elementary school principal. Till that point in my education career with the district, I had only seen him carry himself in a completely different way, namely, hunched over which a very sweet smile. You could trust him just on the look he gave and the way he carried himself; he seemed very sweet, reserved, innocent, and harmless. Here I saw him as he apparently was; I had never seen him carry himself this way and it woke me up to the fact that some people like this have two dispositions, if that is the right word. This person aimed to establish trust with those below him, and it was to his advantage to appear sweet, meek, and kind, in order to make the kind of moves he made, without upsetting or uprising the students, teachers, parents, or board. Now that, my friends, according to what I have seen in the last few years, is what makes a superintendent last for at least a couple years; though I haven't seen the follow up evidence to prove this strategy works in the long run. In fact on the contrary, I am starting to see that not only does strategy this not work in the long run, but the crowd is starting to wake up to the trick earlier in the game and call it quits early for these types of shenanigans.

Not too far off the mark from the aforementioned story in my dealings with politics was my visit to the Oregon State Legislature. I think it shows some bravery in the respect that I was going into something I had no idea about and into a game that was much bigger and higher than any I had been in before, and I had to make sure I minded my "p's and q's" if I wanted to succeed in the mission my class and I set for myself. I was definitely venturing out of my standard comfort zone, to new and unchartered territories. During this time of my educational political activity, I was informed by my fellow union leaders that we would be spearheading a trip to the Oregon Legislature to lobby for better funding for education, which seemed to me to be a logical thing to ask for and take part in. Prior to the trip, being that I sought to make my students into informed, productive citizens of the state and country, I told them about my upcoming venture. I asked them about ideas, questions, or thoughts they might like me to present to any legislators, should I get the opportunity to actually meet with them; at this point I had no idea whether I would be able to accomplish this task, but I had it set in my sights. They had some great ideas; so I wrote them all down and prepared them, in case I had the chance to present them to one of our fine legislators. I don't remember who came up with the idea of an invitation, whether it was a student or I, but we included, at the end of the list of suggestions, (which, as I recall, included allowing students to continue to say the Pledge of Allegiance in its full form: a student idea), an invitation to an "Education Celebration" that we would be holding later in the year, if the legislator would be able to attend.

When I went to Salem, the capital of Oregon, for this education rally, it was a pretty exciting and informative day. I got to sit in with a few other educators, (I believe only two), and a State Senator, Senator Frank Morse, as we presented ideas and requests for him which the union and teachers had, such as the idea of getting more money into the school systems, and ideas we had of ways to spend it to the best advantage of the students. This meeting was held in his office, and in that meeting, I spoke very little. I considered myself fortunate to be able to attend, so I did not think it was the time to present my class's requests; this was a meeting about securing funds. Also, Senator Morse was not the coolest guy I have ever met; it kind of surprised and then annoyed me, that he wasn't really listening to anything we said, as evidenced by his asking a question at one point which we had just answered two minutes earlier, and he kept rejecting us for everything. I had, however, spoken to someone there at the capitol building earlier, and found out who was the appropriate House Representative connected to our town and district with whom I might be able to speak about our student requests and petitions. I apparently asked the right people in the limited time I had in the Legislature and found out that the Republican Representative Lane Shetterly was in some kind of joint committee meeting. If I could get the attention of a certain secretary in that meeting, she could pass on my request to him for a meeting.

I went to this committee meeting which he was sitting at, and amazingly, somehow found the right person, gave my request to that secretary, who then passed it to Representative Shetterly, who was sitting up on the dais leading that meeting, and as soon as the meeting was over, he came to me and we met for a few minutes in a large empty legislature room of some sort. I presented all of the student ideas, pleas, and suggestions and at the end of this meeting, gave him our invitation for the Education Celebration, and he said he would get back to me on it. Even more amazingly, I got a response shortly after that day from his office that he would be attending! We put together this whole celebration, and there were parents in attendance, and the Superintendent, and it was only right after Representative Shetterly arrived, that I realized I had forgotten to invite our principal! Fortunately, as it turned out, Representative Shetterly is a former Public School Teacher, and was very comfortable running the class while I went to the office to "invite" our principal, which was one of the more embarrassing moments of my life. She had dressed extra nicely, and I knew she meant to come, and she came down to my classroom with me, and it was a very sweet celebration, and very positive, other than the fact that a few parents took advantage of their children's educations to voice their own political opinions to Representative Shetterly, but he handled that well. So to me, that all was a success in a brave endeavor.

So it is difficult to say that politics and unions, teachers and principals, superintendents and Boards of Education, are all bad or good. Like students, these people, bodies, and organizations run the gamut of good and not-so-good, smart and not-so, positive and otherwise. They all need to be handled in different ways and with different approaches in order to get the best success out of them and with them, and in order to help them towards their greatest potential and our greatest potential, and that is our jobs as parents and teachers. We work a multi-leveled and multi-layered institution which is connected to many others of the same structure and organization, and it requires constant refinement and fine tuning to achieve success. The hardest thing to do might be to sit still and let the system work when you finally have something going well, though monitoring the system is important to assure it is still functioning as you think it should. There are times when you are doing things right, and it is important to recognize that things are working. It is equally important to praise those involved and performing properly during that time to encourage continued success. This is the best way to assure sustained success while it occurs, although it will probably seem awkward when you praise this positivity at first. It may even continue to feel awkward; nevertheless, it is essential to continue this positive praise, unless you want to end up making only negative corrections when your student or child does something wrong. Therefore tell them that they are doing things right, WHILE they are doing right.

We return to alternative education specifically: one of the things that is going to determine the angle of success in alternative education is the way that schools are accredited and the way teachers are licensed. I think it interesting to point out two very different cases of what I imply. In Oregon, when I was hired for my alternative education position in Coos Bay in 2005, I really didn't understand what the position entailed and how it worked until I got into the school, and saw what was going on and how the school worked; my principal explained to me this would happen when she hired me. Let me tell a bit more about the beginning of that job. In the beginning, there were no students, and I was alone in my classroom. Literally, the rest of the schools had started and I had no one, because as mentioned no one had been thrown out of the middle school on the first day of school, and the case was to be expected that no one would be thrown out for a while. Any teacher would look weak, who threw out a student in the first month of school. So for those first glory days in Coos Bay, after I got my classroom set up and prepared as well as I could, for a position teaching students yet to arrive, I could not fathom or understand. I was therefore invited to help out in the Destinations Academy, which is how I first got to know that academy. They said it would be most useful to help in the morning when they had their "classes" and I could just go up and assist the other teacher as needed. That was the math teacher I would be assisting, who two years later, would be taking my position downstairs, as I took his.

So when I would go up to Destinations, to the three-room jointly connected classroom, all of the students' tables were set up against the window wall, in rows: there were about seven tables. Then in the front of the class was a rarely used podium. On the opposite wall from the windows, there were books in the floor to ceiling bookshelf interestingly arranged; I'm not sure how they were categorized or organized. There were random tables with piles and piles of papers and books, and the teachers desk nestled behind it all, right next to the entrance to the door. It was kind a maze to walk through that classroom. The actual period was about an hour long, but I couldn't really tell when it started, when it ended, when it was on pause, and when the students were supposed to be working independently on assigned tasks. There was a schedule on the board; I didn't really get how it worked, which was OK.

Those students were pretty funny and pretty cool. This particular student, who I told the story about asking if a Mexican person could be Jewish, was one of the ringleaders of the program and the crew in Destinations. I think he was the only student who got rejected before his interview from attending Destinations two years later when I went upstairs to restructure it and we readmitted students based on that screening and interview process. I believe there was a grade point average entry requirement for admittance as well, which he was well below. Interestingly, this student, along with one of my later students, who was my first IPASS student, and was very cool, was the first (and only) student to ever show me the infamous "Crip-Walk". It was actually pretty cool the way they did it. I don't know how strong their gang affiliations were or were no. I think they just thought it was cool. Who knows?

So the kids up there were fun, and I got to actually teach them sometimes. The main math teacher would ask me if I wanted to teach a lesson or something, usually that morning when I got up there, and I always went for it; the kids seemed to get it, and it was good practice. Those were truly the glory days; one Friday morning I remember had been a particularly good week and our principal sponsored a spontaneous Destinations Academy trip down to Dairy Queen. All fifty or so of us walked down there and got Blizzards, which, in blue collar Coos Bay, was the next best thing to whatever the best thing is. They loved it! There were such wild kids in that class in the beginning of that program when I was a guest there: hard core surfers, musicians, and some kids with tempers I didn't get to see so much. But I can tell one student who I made a lasting impression on, though it may not have been the best one.

I was in Destinations teaching, really as a guest, and it was my school and responsibility as far as I was concerned while I was up there. I therefore acted accordingly: if I caught someone cussing or doing something inappropriate, I corrected them. Generally the students were responsive, and did not cause a fuss. But one female student, who ended up later getting a front tooth knocked out for calling out the wrong person in the hallway, (she had quite the mouth up till this point), did not accept my authority, as Cartman from "South Park" might say. After I corrected her she said got real heated up and said something along the lines of I wasn't a real Teacher and had no right to yell at her. I said I was a real Teacher and she would have to listen to me and that was the end of that, as far as I was concerned.

She held a grudge for two and a half years! I would see her in the hallway and she would completely ignore me; or when I was up in Destinations she would just glare at me which was fine; I just never saw a grudge kept longer! In fact when I came up to Destinations as a teacher two years later, she was still mad at me, and refused to be in any of my math classes for the first half of the year! Finally some time during the year the ice began to thaw and she began to talk to me and get comfortable with me. I think she had some major difficulties with men in life and saw a pattern that she just totally reacted to and turning off completely was her defense. I am not sure what the case was; but I was glad that she finally came around. She saw that there was nothing personal and that I treated all students with the same disciplinary code; there was nothing in particular I had against her, which I think is what she realized.

Anyway they were generally good times up there and it was actually really relaxed. I mean, I worked up there for a couple hours in the morning with another teacher, which made things great, because two teachers can really take care of things a lot better than one; it makes a world of difference. After lunch I would go down to my class and at that point, I had one IPASS student. That student was my first Coos Bay student I met; on one of the first days of school, before students even came back from summer vacation, my principal came down to my classroom with two students, and introduced two boys me and told me one of them had been in IPASS before and was thinking of coming back, but wanted to meet the teacher. The other boy, incidentally, was the one who would later ask me about Mexicans being Jewish.

The main boy who was examining the program, or more accurately, scrutinizing yours truly, apparently had major differences with the teacher from the previous year in IPASS, and wanted to "check me out" to see if I was cool or whatever the case might be. It was real funny the way he checked me out too; posed, head cocked slightly to the side, obviously examining me to try and see what I was made of. He was a great person though. I have never been interviewed by a student before or since, but it was one to chalk up to experience. Needless to say, I made the grade and he became the first IPASS student for me and for the first month of school, I had one student in the afternoon and he was it! We got a lot done and did a lot of talking too. His dad was out of the picture and I really think he needed an adult male to connect with, which is something I have mentioned is a necessity for some students, having a role model to connect with, it does wonders. We had a great time and he learned a lot and I learned a lot about him and Coos Bay. It was just that boy until I got my first AIMS student. And even when I got the new boy, it was still pretty smooth sailing for a while. The new boy was probably the student I got to know the most and developed the strongest relationship with. That does not, for sure, imply it was a good relationship; I hope I benefited him; what he did for me is another story altogether. The point of this all is being bold and brave; to do this you have to stay cool and positive in every situation, whether it's a student interviewing you, someone asking you personal questions, dealing with difficult and negative students, being in surprise new situations and dealing with totally new scenarios, you have to be optimistic, hope for the best, and allow yourself to be creative, and not fear. With those ingredients together, and if you can ignore the fear if it's there, you turn it off and do what must be done: bravery.

Now along those lines, and in trying to explain how to be bold, we need to take a short detour from Coos Bay because this reminds me of a great example of on the job training, and that is how I learned the proper methods of restraining a student. I had never taken any kind of course in this feat before, as I hadn't imagined it a part of teacher education, nor did they include or offer it in my Master's program! When I was teaching alternative education in Jefferson, Oregon, the interior exits to the high school alternative teacher's class and my class opened to a vestibule which held doors to a set of male and female bathrooms, and this foyer exited to the main shop, which also held my boss's office. My boss, the supervisor of the entire 21st Century Learning Grant that supported the program, was in her office most of the time. When this occurred she was not in her office. Bravery is doing what must be done.

If I remembered every event of every student getting set off I don't think I would function normally. I was probably trying to get one of our new students to do work. I knew there was a little extra something to worry about with this new student who had come in because there had been no problems with him; he was too quiet. I had learned that lesson the first time with our ever famous arm-biter. That boy, who is still not the main point of the story, was like a real live Bart Simpson, but with more talent, charm, and skill. I heard about him before he got to our class. He came as a fifth grader and his classic story was that once he got mad at his (yes) kindergarten teacher; he bit onto her arm and held on for I don't know how long. When he showed up to our class I was wondering what all the fuss was about. I was still pretty new at this teaching game and only had a few students by this point; this was my first year as a teacher. All of these students I had until this point, made a big stink as soon as they set foot in the classroom, or very shortly thereafter. The arm-biter, when he came into the class, was cool as a cucumber. He gave me no problems, didn't act up, did his work pretty well, and then about a week into it all these other problems erupted simultaneously, and upon untangling them and pulling them apart, I came to realize it was the brilliant and destructive work of possibly the most alternative student to ever come under my tutelage. I learned my lesson from him: be the most careful when students come in calmly and cause no problems; that is when the guard must be the tightest!

So to return to the main detour about the boy who taught me how to restrain students, this other new student came in a similar quiet and eerily uneventful manner, but he didn't have the same social skills or energy of the arm-biter; he was much quieter and really did not interact with the other students. He didn't put up to much resistance, though, and would work at an average pace. I guess on this particular day this boy didn't want to do his work, and I wanted him to do his work, and I put a little pressure on, and he didn't like that very much. I am not sure if he asked to go to the bathroom or if he asked to spend some time in the hallway, which was a good option of choice before having to go to my boss's office or the high school classroom; but either way he was in that vestibule, and I heard a banging noise.

I went out to see what it was and saw the new boy was banging his head on the wall, which was cement. I told him stop, and he continued, and told him again, and still he went on. So I grabbed him and restrained him however seemed most logical; he wasn't very big; he was a fifth grader. I was probably using some wrestling techniques I had learned in high school. The high school alternative teacher heard the ruckus and came out, and fortunately, she had been trained in proper techniques for restraining students. At that point the boy and I were sitting on the floor and I was sitting behind him with my arms wrapped around his arms and chest. The first and most important point I learned was to move my head to the side. Till that point I had my head behind his and if he had been smart and mean enough he could have swung his head back and broke my nose, and I would have remembered all the details of the story from having to tell it so many times. Thank G-d I don't remember the details. The second point of the restraint was to wrap my legs around his legs so he couldn't flail them. That was logical and that's all the lesson I remember, and I hope to never have to use any of those practices again, and Thank G-d I have not had to use them since then. That was one of my least favorite teaching moments.

It says something interesting about my teaching experience that this event is not obviously the clear cut winner. Oh well.

This first teaching position had a lot of interesting "ins and outs" to it. For example, during the first part of the day when I was working with the sweethearts who had been suspended or expelled into my window-less classroom, there was a fifteen minute break in the middle of the two hour period. During this time, we usually played hacky sack, which I hold to be a very good bonding game for these kinds of students and for anyone in general, really. It is one of the few games that are played as one team, with no opponent, with a mutual goal of keeping the sack in the air for as long as possible. That does not necessarily include the modified version of this game, probably invented by students like my alternative wonder-puffs, called "Hack Attack". In that game, after the sack is kicked three times, it becomes "live", which means it is then eligible to be kicked at any person in the circle, which thus eliminates the person who got hit. If the person plays the sack after it hits him, (meaning he kicks it, knees it, heads it, like in soccer), before it falls to the ground, he is still "in". It uses the same skill set but a different mentality.

That game of hack attack is actually really fun, and when my Coos Bay students wanted to play, I always mandated that we get a regular hack first, which is the goal of the original game. The "hack" is when each player touches the hacky sack at least once, which, for us, in that situation, was tricky since we usually had seven or eight people in those circles. It was funny too because that was before the Destinations students were really under my jurisdiction. So while I was in these hack circles which took place in the gym and supervising what was going on in the circle, I was also supervising my own AIMS/IPASS students in the same gym. During those days we would have gym with a few programs together and it would get pretty intense in there. I would join their hack circle and they thought it was the bees' knees. Whenever they wanted to play "Attack" I would say we have to get a hack first, and they always went along with it, which surprised me since I was really a guest in their circle. I think there may have been a time that they didn't go along with my "hack first" idea, so I left the circle; I guess besides that they wanted me to play. Maybe there are not too many teachers hacking with their students these days. Anyway hack attack rocks, but only when the kids are doing well and get the deal.

One time in the hack circle someone blew it. I forget which kid it was, I think it was someone from CE2, who didn't really get the situation, or whoever it was with an attitude, and at that point it was my hacky sack which was being used in the circle. We were in the circle playing and someone cussed, which I certainly did not allow in the circle, and it was the f-bomb too. So I told him to quit the language, and he cussed again, and asked me something along the lines of what I was going to do about it in the hack circle. I was very annoyed at the fact that the hack, which generally had a very positive effect, was the cause of negativity. I had always known it was an edgy prospect, playing hack with the kids, but this was the first case where it was clearly causing harm rather than success. So I grabbed the hack mid-air and brought it to my class and cut it up. The kids were shocked and the word spread like wildfire. Kids were coming up to me in total shock that I would do such a thing. At that point there were no other hacky sacks besides mine, and in a poor town like Coos Bay, ten dollars for a hack was sometimes hard to come by. So that was the end of hacking for a while. I figured I went through about ten hacky sacks in the three years I was there, maybe fifteen, but that was the only one I ever cut up. You might ask why I would do a silly thing like that: I could have just taken it home or something. I know myself too well, and especially with a positive thing like the hack circle, I was likely to relent and allow the playing of the game after not too long a pause. So this was a clear cut reminder to me: game over for at least a while. Was it stupid? Was it bold? I don't know. I just knew it had to be done; let time judge me and my hack.

Now to get back to Jefferson, I didn't let the first set of alternative education students at Jefferson play hack attack; they didn't have the kind of control and positivity of the later students at Coos Bay, who were in a different program. So in Jefferson we just played good old hack. It was great and an excellent motivator because the students knew if things weren't going well, we weren't going outside or playing hack for break. I really learned a lot from that job; in the beginning I was very laid back, I mean: I came from a pretty rebellious place myself; even though I succeeded in school, I was very opposed to the constraint and order imposed by the authority. I had many discussions with my own high school principal about clothing and apparel I could and couldn't wear, and caused a few incidents in my day; including the earlier "walkout" incident. The first couple of weeks of school, as mentioned earlier, I let students call me "Larry": I didn't think those boundaries necessary. Fortunately, my boss wasn't so keen on the idea and told me it would be better they call me properly by last name so I stuck with that.

There are all kinds of ways to be bold, and most of the time it involves some degree or element of risk. The third book in this series is planned to be called "How to Teach with Blue Hair", and that's letting a bit of the cat out of the bag but so be it. The inspiration for that title comes from a point in my teaching career discussed earlier, around 2003. This was the point in my career when I had successfully transitioned into the mainstream as a sixth grade teacher, along with all of my students who also went into the mainstream middle school. That was because the funds for the 21st Century Learning Grant ran out. During this time things were going very well, and I rode the wave big time. I think the pinnacle of that ride is captured in a picture someone caught of me, when we had some kind of celebration of town history at the middle school, and I found a yearbook with our secretary, with whom I always joked and kidded. The picture was from when she was in middle school, so I decided to photocopy it, and then passed it around to many key players in the school who were in the gym for the event. The picture that was snapped of me is at the moment the secretary caught me when she found out about my passing around her pictures, and that picture is of her grabbing one of the photocopied pictures out of my hand. In that picture that someone snapped, the secretary has a look of something like shock, anger, and wanting to crack up, all at once, and me with a grin of something else on my face, and with blue hair. I had gotten that hair idea in my head from somewhere, and I had talked to this one girl about dying my hair a few weeks earlier. Then one night, she and five girls went to work on my hair. They bleached it blonde and then frosted the ends blue. It was superb. Teaching like that in this small farm town could go under this chapter for sure in its freshness; it might go better in the chapter about being bold! At this point in my life, or shortly thereafter, I felt I was doing very well and doing very special things with these students, and wanted to tell the world how to teach with blue hair, and that's where the idea for this book started. I see now those were some of the boldest and bravest moments in my teaching years.

The whole Jefferson experience was very special and wild and probably unlike any other series of four years teaching that has taken place. One of the favorite moments was when my friends' band, which was then called "Om", came to play at the school. They set up in the gym and they were a pretty alternative kind of music, with no lead singer, which is foreign to middle school students, and they tried to get the kids to dance, which I think a few did. The kids thought it very cool anyway and a year or two later they had another school event/picnic celebration with a band and it went off well; I think that concept was kind of new to Jefferson. It wouldn't be too far a cry from "Footloose". The other musical performance involved yours truly and was the only time I have publicly performed in front of a large group, discounting deejay days which I don't count in the same category of performance, and that certainly ranks as one of my bravest moments in life. I know this because it was one of my most fearful, and despite that fact, I carried on through with it. That's a lesson I try to teach students and the world.

Slightly against a spirit of spite that seeks to arise against it, I have to give credit and thanks to my then-new principal who inspired a generation of original songs by yours truly, which are still evolving. I think before that point I had written one song, and since then I have written another fifteen or so, which is not great for ten years but it's enough for an album. The way it happened was that the principal asked me if I could put together a rap song about a reward trip that we had discussed in a staff meeting. The trip would be based on a set of positive actions including excellent attendance, no unexcused absences, no office referrals, no more than two citations, and only A's, B's, and C's for grades. It was a great program and it worked really well. In introducing it to the students the principal asked me to write and perform a rap song, as she knew I was into rap and that I had done a bit of rapping in my past.

So I wrote and learned "Tips for your Success", (Appendix E), and performed it in front of 400 middle school students. With all the performance I had done in my past, teaching countless classes, being deejay for countless parties, speaking to all kinds of groups publicly, and speaking to thousands, I was never so nervous. Middle school students are viciously honest and the first to point out weakness and/or truth. The words to the rap were going to be on a giant screen projected behind me so even though I was probably rapping too fast for most of them to catch any mistakes; I still didn't want to do so. I developed a chorus for the song that was student friendly. We had two drummers from the school band playing along, trying to keep up and follow the beat, which they hadn't heard before, since we had never practiced together. That's because the music teacher decided last minute he wanted to offer me accompaniment, but the drummers pulled it off pretty well. The students who were watching were also keeping the beat with a "stomp, clap" pattern that they did pretty well, which rocked. In the chorus the students were to chant, "Jefferson......Middle School, Jefferson......Middle School", which was heavily cool. They were so into it. It rocked and it was one of the coolest activities ever, the kids totally dug it, and were asking me to sign autographs afterwards, like I was suddenly going to stop teaching and go become a rap star and they would never see me again after this day and performance! Go figure.

That song became a bridge song for one of my students later on in Coos Bay. Actually this student wasn't even my student; he was a visitor from Destinations when I taught AIMS/IPASS, and he would come down to join our music program. He was a bass player, and he liked to play music with the other students, so he would come down and join, even though he wasn't in our program, on the condition that he followed our rules and stayed appropriate. It took many months before that students spoke real words to me, he was always very quiet and in the background; as a matter of fact, he was so quiet and background, I even forgot he was one of the most hardcore Dark Riders!! He blended in that well!! Well this student one day was leading a tirade against rap and I got into a discussion with him about the possibility of where the line blurred that there might be a rap song he liked, and that inspired me to created chords and a melody for "Tips for Your Success". I went ahead and did that, and to this day I perform with the chords and it is so much cooler, though I don't think I have performed for anyone other than my brother and his family. I believe it has been heard by a total of three people, while Bennie, my faithful dog till he passed, heard it so many times that he could probably have hummed along. Maybe I'm not so brave after all. If I was braver, I would have gone to the coffee shop by now to perform in front of real live audiences. I mean to; it has been on my goal list the past two summers.

I don't mean to brag or boast and I hope I'm not taken that way for this chapter, but it is really difficult to teach someone how to be brave and the only way I can think of is by illustrating stories. I'm sure other people could do better with my life if given the chance but these are some of the decisions I made and I hope they shed some light on the subject. These days, when I tell people I'm a public school teacher, the most common question I get is asking how students and the school react to my being Jewish, not so much because I am Jewish, but because I look Jewish and wear a Yarmulke in school. That's usually the first question, if I actually wear a yarmulke in school, (which I mentioned that I do). In general it's been very good and there have only been a couple incidents. And by the way this is still pretty fresh for me; I've only been wearing one in school for about four years. The most poignant incident took place when I was on lunch duty, and at that time the hot spot for the cafeteria, (the most active, likely to cause trouble table), was directly in front of me, three tables back. I watched about 250 students daily, on my side of the cafeteria, who were really not my own students; I barely knew any names, and I had to keep students from wearing hats, hoods, and headphones, and I had to make sure that they were behaving in a generally civilized manner, which is not as easy as it might sound.

This one table was always popping off, as we say, and one of these days, I had been over to the table a couple times in a row to correct them on one thing or another, all related to head coverings. A smart trick to trip the system from their side is to have someone put on a hat; then I have to come over and tell them to take it off. Then after that someone different from that table puts on a hat, and I have to come over to tell them to take it off, so the same person is not a repeat offender but they might think they're bothering me by making me walk back and forth. It's a question. So this happened with this table on this day, and after the second time when I told one of the kids to take his hat off, I heard one of the kids mumble something back to me, but I wasn't sure who it was, and I wasn't sure what he said, though I had a guess at the effect of the comment. The next time I came back to that table to correct a kid on a hood on that same day, as I turned around to leave, one of them said loud enough for me to hear, "Take off yours". He was referring to my yarmulke, and so I turned around and strongly said, "It's not a hood". I kept walking back to my position, and fortunately, that was the end of it. I was glad for that because it could have gotten nasty, maybe getting into religious and personal freedoms.

I guess ultimately they could take it up with the principal if that was the route they wanted to go; then I would sit with them and explain it to them but it gets tricky and I really don't wish to get involved like that, especially with students who aren't my own. They never raised another question about that issue and I guess they got the point. Another day I had a kid from one of those tables trying to convince me, and this was a smart kid who was in the top classes, but who was also "down" with the regular kids too: he was begging me to let him wear a hat, because he had gotten a bad haircut, and I almost made him show the haircut to me, but decided to let it go for a few days. Then finally one day after this, he had pulled a fake on me, and he kept on the hat when he wasn't supposed to, (after I told him to take it off). So I told security, and he actually had the nerve to get upset in the manner like, what did I have to bring it to security for? He unbelievably got upset at me for going above when he wouldn't listen. That kid had a mom who was an elementary school teacher in our district where he went to school, and he still acted like a fool to teachers. We wondered if he wanted students to treat his own mother that way in her position and classroom, but whatever. He bothered me more than most students in the cafeteria. That's because he was smart enough to know better and had better things to do with his mind, and other avenues in which he could take pride, rather than wasting his energy on little fights and little battles, without respect. That could be slightly understandable for a student who has nowhere else to vest himself, his pride, and confidence. It's not alright for a smart kid; it irks me; he's got other success.

That cafeteria duty was pretty funny. In the beginning of that period I would sometimes remind myself, and concentrate on the thought, "The only thing I fear is G-d". Those were truly brave moments. It was THAT intense for me, especially as I was on my side alone, with the rest of security and the teachers on duty stacked up on the other side of the cafeteria for some reason. I never knew when the lid was going to blow off, which really means I would have to confront someone I didn't know, and make them do something they didn't want to do. So for that reason, about midway through the year, I came up with a backup plan, which I ended up using once. The reality on the ground there is that if a kid wants to run off, or hide, or escape, when I don't know their name, they have options; for starters they can give a fake name since I don't have a computer right there. They can wise off to my face or refuse to own up later on. My backup plan was always to catch the kid off guard. If they were acting up to me, and I thought they were going to try one of these outs, like just taking off, where I couldn't get their name or bring them to security, or bring security to them, I would say something like, "Check it out" pointing behind them, which they wouldn't realize for a very short instant, was towards the camera. Then when they turned around, they, I would follow up with the fact that I was going to find out who they were, by marking exactly the time of day, and going to security. If they wanted to do things the smooth way they would best cooperate. Bravery doesn't necessarily mean brashness. It also involves careful thought.

It reminds me of a date I had not too long ago. It started off when I met her for lunch at the restaurant down in Deal, New Jersey, and her mom dropped her off at the restaurant which was weird as far as I had seen in my orthodox dating experience. The weirder part was that when we came out of the restaurant her mom was gone and, after driving around for a little since we were down the shore, I realized I was to be taking her home, which was located another 40 minutes south of where we were. I asked her address to put in the GPS and I realized she didn't want to give me her address, so I drove to the city center. Also by this point I realized she had some mental or psychological issues, and I was honestly a little nervous. I realized I better use the element of surprise if I wanted us both to get home safe. When she realized we were heading to her house and not going out for more activities, which was what she was hoping, she got upset and said so. It was a generally uncomfortable ride home from that point; it was very quiet and awkward, plus I had to go to the bathroom. When we were within a few miles of her house she still hadn't given me the address, so I was relying on her giving me directions to her house; but she kept spacing out, and we kept getting lost. Finally I caught her off-guard using the deer-in-headlights strategy; I said suddenly, "What street do you live on?" She answered before she knew what she was saying; then I asked her what number house it was and she told me. She got out of the car before we even got to her house, on some street at a stop sign. I hope she is doing better now.

I don't advocate this surprise technique except in rare circumstances when you fairly need the truth. Sometimes it's like that with kids: you have to catch them off guard to get some honesty out of them in this state, because they're so used to having so many defenses up, and really these defenses often inhibit learning. Not to mention the negative environment created by all the negativity and falsehood. Doubt, mistrust, and self-esteem issues all get in the way of being a normal happy kid, thriving in school and life, doing well, learning, achieving, being a good person. People need to be more straight-up, just like Paula Abdul said. It's a fine line between being on your toes and keeping kids positive, and having a positive mix of both of those together with a great attitude helps a person be brave when necessary.

Towards the end of that first school year in West Orange, things started getting pretty rowdy, especially in the cafeteria. A new hotspot table developed almost overnight. The former hotspot had disintegrated and there was only one hotspot in the place, and that was this one boy's table which was dead center of the cafeteria, which held about 100 round tables. I called this boy the Dancer. He would just dance in the cafeteria sometimes. I'm not sure if there was music on at his table, or someone was rapping or if he was dancing to music in his head, he had great rhythm. Once he finally called me to come over to his table: he wanted to know if it was true that hot dogs had pigs' butts inside and I told him they could; that they had all the leftover parts of animals in them, and the kids thought it was the grossest most interesting thing ever. Another time he wanted my support for some argument with a girl at his table about something; another time he liked me so much he put his arm around my shoulder; I should have distinguished my boundaries better right then. But he got the point at some point when I corrected him about his language or something. His table grew and grew; he was charismatic, exciting, loud, and energetic. It was center of the whole cafeteria, and his seat was pretty much dead center of the whole place and I'm sure he knew that. He was charged. Lots of girls came to that table. One girl would come over, walk around the table, and hug all the boys at the table. It was kind of gross and sad.

I thought that was the end all hotspot for the year but then this other table popped up, with this one kid who tipped the table halfway up in the air one day, and it was messy correcting him on that and a couple other things. The next day or a couple days later, a girl got up on the table, (yes, on the table), and danced on it. The interesting thing about that was, as things had heated up towards the end of the year, administration would be in that cafeteria more and more. It was the senior cafeteria, which made it all the more exciting, and on that day, there was actually an administrator on the same side of the cafeteria as me in view of this whole interesting incident. The weird part of it all is that, believe it or not, I was the one to go over and say something to the administrator about it. I don't know how he missed it unless he was trying to ignore it. I don't know how to comment on that situation; it's too easy and hard.

One day when I was leaving my lunch duty, I thought a kid threw gang signs at me. I was walking back from the cafeteria, in the hallway, and two kids approached me and one of them put up a sign to me, like his index finger and thumb, in an "o" and the other three fingers up and he looked at me through the "o". It was weird and it was only after I walked by I was like, "What on earth was that?" Then I got all paranoid and started looking up all gang signs to see if he was saying something to me and I couldn't find that sign. I went to security and asked them if they could look for it on the video; there was a video right by the spot where it happened, but I don't think they ever followed up with it; so finally I let it go. I hadn't recognized the kid so there was really nothing I could do about it in a school of 2100 students.

Then one day I was in the cafeteria on duty, and I saw that kid pop his head into the cafeteria, and I did a fast walk to catch him, (I don't like the kids to see me run unless it's an emergency), but I wasn't about to let him go a second time. So I caught up to him right at one of the security guards, and I asked him what the sign means, he said something like that it represents the sun or something, and I said, "So you made this sign to me because I'm the sun in your world because I'm so bright and shed light for you?" or something like that. I think he laughed and gave an affirmative. I just wanted to clarify to him that I knew who he was, and I wanted to point this out to another adult, and after that we got into a conversation about his plans for college and life. Fear cannot get in the way of rational thought.

Kids around the school in West Orange weren't as cut-throat as I would have thought, which made things cool. The only real case of kids selling each other out was in the cafeteria, with a kid who complained about a girl who had been wearing a scarf for a few days in a row, and he wanted to know why she could do that when they couldn't wear hats. I had to explain to him that if the scarves were the place where the girls got to slide on the rules, then the boys more than made up for it with their sagging pants, which I almost never corrected them on. The truth is that rule of sagging pants is a hard rule to judge, because if a kid is wearing shorts (with underwear underneath), under his pants, (which I have been known to do at my house), who can say that's not allowed? After all his underwear might not be showing; it would only be shorts, so it's the act of sagging that's not allowed; but that's just a style. If we allow that, how are we to decide or judge what qualifies as underwear and what qualifies as shorts? I'm won't tell the kids that, though; I raised enough ruckuses in my day. I wonder if they'll read this.

That was mainly the life in the West Orange High School senior cafeteria. At the end of the year when my boss was talking about my classes for the following year I asked her if she knew if I would have the same cafeteria duty next year. She asked me if I did a good job, to which I replied in the affirmative and she said then they would probably stick me with that duty again. My co-teacher said something along those lines once, when he went to administer one of the standardized tests we occasionally had to proctor. He said he would butcher the job so they would never give it to him again, but in the end, he ended up doing a good job. Sometimes bravery means doing what's right even if it's hard or annoying.

I teach Hebrew School two days a week in South Orange, NJ, at a conservative synagogue. It's a nice job with good pay. I taught fifth graders my first two years and this year I teach sixth graders. The first two years, my job was to teach the students Hebrew and prayer. To enhance the class they give me a madrich, which is an assistant, and I really had two assistants: a different one for Wednesday than for Sunday. My Sunday madrich was an eighth grade boy who is a superstar and I hope he goes into teaching one day; he always gave me ideas, and I let him implement and run whichever ones he felt and seemed able to; he has a positive attitude and is just a great all-around kid and helper. The second was my Wednesday madricha who was a high school sophomore at the time, (I think), and was super helpful and positive and a great influence on the class. This story gets a little complicated as do all games of Jewish Geography so try and follow along. Around the middle of the year, like January or so, she went away to Israel for a semester, which is normal for many types of teenage Jewish girls and boys.

Around the same time, there was an incident at school. I learned about it only after it happened; then I apparently took over the damage control, roughly speaking. There are two other orthodox Jewish teachers in the High School; both are women, and I have eaten over both of their houses for

Shabbat. They are really wonderful people with wonderful families, and I am fortunate to have such cool positive co-workers who I can relate to through a different arena that's an important part of my life. One day after school the younger teacher, who teaches art classes two doors down from me, told me about the incident which I now relate. It's a bit charged and you may have opinions so be prepared. This teacher had been walking down the hallway a few days earlier at the end of school, and had seen these posters up on the walls advertising a debate which read, "Is peace in the middle east possible while Israel exists?" She was obviously furious, so she tore down a poster and brought it to the principal's office. It's hard to decide how far into this story to get, so I'll try to keep it brief. Basically he allowed her to take down the posters, and he asked one of the vice principals who happened to be there about it all.

A week or so later, we had a delayed opening for snow. I got to pray at the local Chabad, which is my main synagogue, and as I was leaving, my Rabbi asked me about the possibility of his getting into the high school to connect with some kids about Judaism. He had asked me once before, but this time I was clear in saying that I couldn't do that in my first year as a teacher in the school, as it was just too risky in blurring the boundaries between religion and state. Interestingly, later that same day, as I was walking out of the high school main office, I bumped into the Superintendent, who I hadn't spoken to personally since he hired me earlier that year. He asked me how things were going with the students, and my classes, and my year in general, and then he told me he had a favor to ask of me, which never happened with a superintendent and me before. He wanted me to "broker a meeting" for him with the leaders of the community, meaning the leaders of the Jewish community, which I thought pretty funny considering my Rabbi's request earlier that very day. For those that are interested in the question, yes, that Rabbi did get to speak to a class of students as a result of that meeting, (or was it the result of his request?).

The relevant part of the story here is the information that came out of the meeting. Organizing a meeting of the leading Rabbis of an observant Jewish community is not easy; it's difficult even deciding who to invite, especially since I had only lived in town for less than a year at that point. In the end I had the six rabbis who I wanted there, and there was only one who I would have liked to come who couldn't attend. When we all sat down to the meeting in February we, (meaning the Rabbis and I), weren't exactly sure what the meeting was about, but we were pretty sure it was about the posters that had gone up; this, however, was not the official agenda. The superintendent started off by pointing out that we had similar meetings before this and he wanted to continue the dialogue we had initiated since we share the same community, and have the same children in mind, and interests, and it was important to build and strengthen bonds. When he asked if anyone wanted to go on or if he should continue, the lead Rabbi of the big synagogue in town, seated next to me said, "No, let's cut to the chase. We want to talk about the Israel debate." It was a classic line, it was bold, and I wish I had a recording of it: true ace.

The superintendent apparently did not know about the debate or the posters. I know this because the room looked at and to me to explain the situation to them, which I did, without inserting my own opinion, except to say that the students who had been in the "debate" advocating for Israel's right to exist, should be re-encouraged, because it sounded like they had been shocked and squashed. I only learned in the meeting right then that the debate had even taken place, (I had naively supposed it had gone out the window when the posters were torn down). Apparently the other side came very well prepared, with PowerPoint's and posters showing what they considered to be their new state, which showed all of Israel erased from the map. They had all kinds of preparation; while the lone girl representing the Israeli side had been asked that day if she wanted to be in a debate, so she was totally unprepared. The debate was a slaughter as the side against Israel's existence had probably prepared for weeks. That was the part that to me, sounded like it most needed correcting, and immediately.

So the long end of this winding story is this: I was teaching Hebrew school, and on Wednesdays, for the second half of the day, students had elective, which meant that teachers had to choose electives to teach. For that second half of the year my elective was to create a movie in which we taught about the Ten Commandments. One of my students in that elective was a seventh grade boy with a certain "berg" last name that was like my madricha's name and I remember learning that they were brother and sister, which I thought to be funny. Now when the article came out in the school newspaper about this whole debate, and it mentioned the name of the girl representing the Israel side, it got her last name wrong, but the first name is a kind of unique name, and I thought, there's no way this could be the case.

When I went to Hebrew school that day, I asked that student if his sister, (my madricha, who at the time was in Israel), was in some kind of Israel debate at school, and he said she was, and that it was all one-sided, and they had given her no time to prepare, and what-not. That was how I found out that it was my own madricha who had been the beaten-up side in the Israel debate which I had been fighting my school district over for weeks; I'm still shocked to this day. We don't believe in coincidence. I am still impressed by her that she had the strength and courage to go through that and continue, not knowing what she was up against, and even afterwards to continue to persevere fearlessly. She epitomizes the title of this chapter: Be bold; be brave; I wrote it an extra time out of admiration and respect to her. If there is one story which sums up this entire chapter, that's it. She rocks. I still barely got to talk to her about the whole thing, because she came back from Israel so late in the year, and it had been such a big situation, I didn't want to bother her any more about it, especially since she was feeling so great about her Israel trip. I hope she reads this book and knows this story is about her; I should give her a copy.

One girl I had my first year in West Orange High School demonstrated aptly the title of this chapter as well, and it seems some of the best examples of it come from students; but teaching students to be bold and brave is not easy either. It's hard to teach them to be these things, in the right way, without having them go all the way across the line into stupidity. This girl, who was one of the smartest students in my class, was clever but reserved to an extent. She would only speak up at appropriate times and would always wait to give the answer till she saw everyone else wasn't trying, out of respect for them; she was definitely cool. She had long brown hair; you'll see why that's relevant shortly. One day she came into class, and her hair was completely chopped off. Of course I was curious to ask what inspired this, but I almost never asked those kinds of questions, because of exactly the kind of answer I ended up getting in this situation. It was actually a very cool, hip style she had trimmed her hair to, and I thought it was neat, to use an out-of-date term. My students, however, did not possess the same restraint as I, or at least one of the students didn't possess that restraint. Most of the students didn't say anything, though we knew all of us were burning with curiosity; finally one boy came in, who didn't have much in the way of couth, and said, relatively thoughtlessly, something along the lines of, "What happed to your hair?" or "Why'd you cut your hair?" Her answer even stunned me, and I've heard and seen a lot in my years.

This girl told us all that her mom had been telling her that the only thing that was good about her was her hair, so she decided to cut it. I was blown away. I think that is one of the most courageous things for a sixteen year old to do, that I have come across. Really I think it's one of the bravest things I have heard. The whole class was impressed; I was the first to figure and say, "Wait, you cut that yourself?!" or something along those lines, because it looked like a very expensive haircut! She said she had, and I think I told her if she ever wanted a second career she could always go in hairstyling, because she did a fantastic job. Then I said something I had never said before, something along the lines of, "Wow, this is difficult, because, as a teacher, I'm not supposed to tell you that your parents are wrong, but in this case...."; and I think one of the students finished it off for me saying how could her mom say that, and didn't she know she was the smartest kid in the class; it was all very supportive and very positive.

On a lighter note, when I first got my job at the Union County Educational Services Commission, I had no idea what part of Union County I would be in and I held a vague hope that of all the religious schools they serviced, I would end up in a Jewish one. The way it works in that program is that due to disabilities laws, all students with disabilities, regardless of what kind of schools they attend, are entitled to special needs assistance. When I phone interviewed for this position on my drive moving home from Oregon on Tuesday, July 22, 2008, the interviewers told me they had all different types of religious schools. So I had my hopes; I was most concerned with getting a job at this point; mind you, I had two moving destinations: my possessions were "theoretically" on their way to a house I had scouted out with my brother in Ithaca, where he lived. I figured that if I didn't find a teaching job, it would be easier to be jobless in Ithaca than in New Jersey, because New Jersey was much more expensive and seemingly cold (in an indifferent way). My car, along with my dog Bennie and I with it, was on the way to Ithaca, (before I found out about this interview). But then after the interview and the call the following day inviting me to an in-person interview the following Tuesday, I changed my final destination, so that I would stay with my Dad and stepmother in Monroe, New Jersey. When I finally landed the job, the following Tuesday after my in-person interview, I had to reroute my luggage from Ithaca to Monroe for my new "digs" there; I was not sure where the location of my job would actually be, though I knew somewhere in Union County, NJ; I still hoped it would somehow be one of the elusive Jewish schools.

Alas, this was not to be the case. I ended up at Roselle Catholic High School in Roselle, NJ, which was a pretty nice place, and I had an advantage over the other Supplemental Instructors, (as my position was called), in that I went to the same school every day. Some of the other teachers went to different schools throughout the week and some even had to go to multiple schools within the same day. Roselle Catholic High School was a nice place to work, and the people were friendly. Back then, I wasn't wearing a yarmulke so I don't know that anyone realized that I was Jewish until I started eating in the staff room. The lighter side of the note I was trying to get to in this story is that, due to laws restricting interaction or dependence of church and state, the program to which I had been assigned took place in a trailer outside of the school, in the school's parking lot. When I first walked in and was setting up, I thought it was kind of dark, dingy, and lonely or something. That all changed, though, after my first visit or two into the school. That was when I realized all the people I would have to talk to, and recalled all the chaos and business of a high school, and administrators, and other teachers, and the list goes on. So when I walked into my trailer, I was pretty excited to get into my new classroom. It was quite a change from the last position I had in which I had taken over the Destinations Academy and had free run of pretty much an entire building, and my classroom was huge, and I had extra classrooms to work in to boot. I'm adaptable, though, and like I said, that's a skill in the classroom, even if your classroom is in a trailer down by the river, which is the joke I was trying to get to, for all of those who might remember the Chris Farley skits when he's a motivational speaker, "living in a van down by the river!" A long way to go to make a joke about a trailer by river, but worth it, I hope; I was close to being in that Farley skit for sure!

The heavier end of that story initiated a major phase in my "coming out" as a Jew. A few months after the school year started, after I had connected with the administration and many of the teachers in the school, they had decided that they liked me. So the principal of the school, he should rest in peace, approached me as I was on my way out of the building to return to my peaceful little trailer by the river, and he asked me if I would like to move my classroom into the school. He told me that he had spoken with others in the school and they all agreed that they liked me and would be happy if I would join them in the school. I thanked him and said I had to check it with the commission, but I let him know there could be no "perpendicular sticks" hanging on my wall, (though I didn't put it that way). As long as that wasn't a problem for them, I'd be happy to move my class inside. I didn't really want to move, as by this point I had already minimized my time in the school building in that, nice as the people were, it still felt weird being in a religious place that wasn't my own religion, and having to look at these symbols on the wall all day which weren't my own; but what was I to say? There was no way to say "no" to the offer without completely offending them. I shortly thereafter moved into the smallest classroom I ever had, which still had a loudspeaker meant for a full size classroom, so that when announcements came over it sounded like the front seats in front of the speakers at a concert; but the room had a charm to it.

That was one phase of my "coming out" as a Jew, by which I mean displaying noticeable signs of Judaism to the general public, and started wearing a yarmulke. The first real phase came earlier, when I was in Coos

Bay, and I remember distinctly walking around town early on when I was first wearing my tzis-tzis out so others could see them, (this is a four cornered fringed garment worn by observant Jews). The fringes were actually outside of my clothes, so that it could be noticed easily that I was different. While I was used to looking different growing up based on the way I dressed, this was different for some reason. One reason I guess it was different is that back in the day, I dressed differently based on whatever I felt like wearing, and so it was really my own doing and creation and much easier to defend if questioned. Another reason was that I knew there were people I was walking by who would hate me for who I was, and hated Jews. True, back then people may have disliked my taste in alternative clothes, (before I knew what "alternative" in that sense meant), or they may have laughed at the weird way in which I dressed. But they I think they weren't planning to attack me for it, and that was something I was slightly concerned about in Podunk Coos Bay, Oregon. Thank G-d no one attacked me (or hated that much).

In any case, back to the main yarmulke story, the second phase of this "coming out" was in Roselle, towards the end of the school year, when one of my co-workers, who was sweet and curious and forever asking me questions on Judaism, asked a question. She was cool and we had a good friendship; she taught me how to make pasta sauce from scratch Italian style and I still use that recipe. She asked me if the way I dressed in school was the way I dressed when I was out of school, (I'm guessing she or someone else saw me outside of school strolling the streets or such). I told her in reply that when I was outside of school I wore a yarmulke and tzis-tzis. She asked me why I didn't wear the yarmulke in school; she thought it would be good for the students to be exposed to different cultures and said something along the lines of that I should be the person I truly was, which was hard to argue with. She said I should don the yarmulke. This idea had been brewing in my mind for some time anyway so I turned to the principal, who had earlier in the year invited me to move my classroom into the school and said, "Whaddya think?" He kind of shrugged and mumbled something that was a politically correct "thumbs up", without a formal consent, which is the proper thing to do, I suppose, and the following year, I started wearing a yarmulke in school. The only questionable thing I ever heard in my year wearing the yarmulke at that high school was from a student who I overheard say, "doesn't he know this is a catholic school?" as I was walking down the hallway, but that was pretty harmless and I was glad that was the only thing that I was privileged to hear.

The following year, there came a certain point when I had to stop eating in the staff room. I figured out at some point that the topics of conversation in that staff room were generally of two forms. It was either restaurants or religion, with an occasional splash of pets or intimacy. I was one for four in this arena, being that I don't eat at any of the restaurants they do; the problem with religion talks for me was that while, they generally started with seeming harmless curiosity about my religion, practices, rituals, etc., they inevitably led to other people telling me about their religions. That was fine and good and all, and it wasn't that I was going to cut them off about that topic, but as soon as the right pause in the conversation took place, I was out the door. I don't remember exactly what the final straw was, but it had to do with a movie about a couple of men and a mountain. The point was, I was out of there, and ate my lunch in my classroom and made excuses if asked and would visit occasionally. I think I limited it to once every two weeks or a month, just to show my face and to show that I didn't dislike people. People asked me once, I believe, if they had offended me, but I was still relatively fresh out of Oregon and trying not to make waves, and I wasn't about to teach people about conversation in the work place.

Bravery, on the other hand, unfortunately, is not so easily acquired or demonstrated, and often goes unknown and unnoticed. To me, the bravest moments are the ones when you are at the greatest vulnerability, and you face up to the challenge, despite the fact that the odds are overwhelmingly against you. The case that speaks to this the most is when I had my seniors of doom as I lovingly refer to them, in my first year at West Orange High School, and we were having a bad day already. My calm response in asking them if the girls would be fighting when they asked me who would win in a fight between all of them and me, belied a slight nervousness inside of me. And this is the art of bravery, not showing fear, and more importantly, not acting on fear, or letting it get in the way when there is a job to be done. Others will have other opinions on this matter and I'm fine with that; this is one teacher's thoughts. In this case it had the winning result of these students cracking up. I think that was the moment I won them as a class. It was a use of humor to defray anger, seizing the moment, and staying calm and focused, and it worked. You could never teach somebody how to come up with a comment that does all those things, but like I said, I think the most important quality above all, which will win the day in the end, get a person to learn all the things he wants to know, and get him to where he wants to be, is positivity. The Chassidic saying that sums all that up in a simple statement is this: "Joy breaks through all boundaries." That positivity will give you the bravery you need to succeed.

There are simpler forms of bravery as well, and in my mind, bravery is connected to trying to answer questions, especially in the classroom, when you are unsure if you are right. You are taking a risk in showing yourself to be wrong and possibly laughed at. That takes courage. Somewhere through these students' education some lost the confidence to guess. Probably along the line they offered an answer to a question in class and got swatted down by a teacher with an attitude who never realized how devastating it could be to embarrass someone in front of a class. All it takes is one time, too, and a student might never speak again voluntarily in front of class, and remain petrified to speak his true mind in front of others in general. This is probably the main root of the fear of public speaking; most people are more afraid of public speaking than death and it probably stems from seeing someone get reamed in class for making a mistake, giving a wrong answer, or guessing. Or maybe he was the person who got reamed and he decides it's just not worth the risk to be embarrassed like that, and for the rest of his life he will fear speaking in front of others. People talk about public speaking like it's always a big group, but if you've got a fear of speaking in front of a big group, you're probably not too comfortable speaking to a group of people even at a party, and that could just be five or four people. So really this is a major social skill that is being damaged from these teachers who are really just lashing back from when the same thing happened to them when they were younger; fortunately, there are rescues from this seemingly endless cycle. I lay no claim to psychology, though my statements may seem to display otherwise.

One of the ways for getting people over their fear of guessing is the Math Jeopardy or any kind of Jeopardy like game I was discussing before. The key to all of it, and getting them over this fear, is making learning fun, and creating a positive, safe learning environment. In doing that, it means you are going to make sure as the leader of the class that when people give answers, they will not be put down for it, and that requires a bunch of skills discussed throughout the book, the quickest of which is a tuned ear and a sharp eye. Then people won't be mocked or put down when they give wrong answers. This is not to say that a teacher can't say a student is wrong, but really it's better to say the answer is not so correct, really we don't want to say the STUDENT is wrong. You can say something like the answer is interesting but it's not the direction we're looking for or that's an interesting perspective. Another option is just a "ehhhhh" slowly dragged out as if you're still contemplating it while saying like it, like it might be possibly right but your reply is not so short and devastating and conversation-ending. In my experience the way you put it is a lot more important than what you actually say in terms of supporting student self-confidence. Some people don't say the word "bad"; they say "not good". How's that for positivity?

This bravery is the root of one of the pillars of personality which is self-confidence, and without it, people are nearly sheep. Why is self-confidence so important? I mean, I know there are facts that need to be learned, and truths that need to be taught as a teacher and especially a math teacher. But for most of these alternative students, they won't be able to do that kind of learning until they allow their minds to flex back and forth, because that's what happens when you absorb a new concept into your understanding; that is learning. The learning will only happen if the student is willing to try on a new outfit, a new style, so to speak, or a new idea. They have to have self-confidence to learn, and that's a fact that's more important than all the facts that they're going to be assessed on these standardized tests. If you wear the same collared type shirts every day and never try another style, you never know that something else might be more comfortable or looks better. The only way to know is to try it on.

It means nothing looking at the shirt while it's on the rack, it's not until you put on the shirt you that you can decide if it's right for you; only then can you truly conceive of it, it becomes real. And so it is with learning, not until you try on an idea is it that you can really consider it, understand it, and decide if it fits into your mental picture. You have to be bold enough to allow something new into your mind, and for that you need self-confidence and bravery, to be open to try something new. Fortunately, since most of what we're teaching, (and maybe all of what we are teaching, if we are bold) is logical, real, and useful, the students will find that these concepts and ideas do fit into their mental picture, and it is something they can use and would really like to incorporate into their mentality and mindset. The really neat thing about all of this is that it is a cumulative and exponential process, so that once they get comfortable trying on new ideas and seeing them work, they try on other new ideas and see they work too; suddenly you don't even realize these students have turned into completely different people who are happy and smiling and confident and willing to learn and grow. This is the nut meat of education.

13
USE HUMOR WHEN POSSIBLE

Using humor is an important tool, and it's best to use it when possible once you have the proper rapport with your students. In other words, you don't want a class full of comedians making nonstop jokes and trying to make fun of each other and you all the time. But you do want a positive atmosphere in class where people can laugh at the right things at the right time like they do in the real world, or at least in the ideal real world. I heard of a teacher who never cracked a smile till January and that's not a bad idea; I was pretty close to that with my first year in West Orange, New Jersey. That was when the kids were tougher than most of those who I had dealt with. In the beginning of the year they might think you're a jerk, but that's fine, eventually they will figure out the truth, (unless you really are a jerk, and then maybe there are some other books you need to read as well). The kind of humor I'm talking about has to be connected with positivity, because if it's not, it might have a detrimental effect. If it is caustic, while making the speaker feel better in the short run, in the long run, it eats away at everyone.

One of these humorous opportunities came from a student who was one of the more Pillsbury like students I had when I was in Coos Bay; he was just like the Pillsbury Doughboy: really gentle, puffy, with rosy cheeks and bright blonde hair, and a really positive attitude. He was a little to the pushy side in his being positive though; I know people who are really excited which is fine, but some people can't satisfy their excitement on their own. They may need to get others involved in it, and don't necessarily get the cues when others aren't interested. I don't even remember exactly the story but it was the fullest my Coos Bay IPASS class ever got, which was the high school students: around eighteen students. All of the students in that class were boys, with the exception of one or two, so it was a pretty thick class, and it was crowded. We had a lot going on one day, and in that classroom, I sat behind the students, and they faced forward toward the chalk board, so I could see what they were doing all the time; that may have been my toughest class. This boy came up to me to ask me something, which was not the way we did things in my class; even if students called out, I might not be too concerned, but I had personal space and I wanted it respected.

So he was standing right next to me and I asked him something about why he was standing so close to me, I mean, he was in my space, almost touching me, like hovering over me, and one of the other boys in the class said something about this boy wanting to be close to Mr. Miller, and we all cracked up. Nowadays and in New Jersey, I think I would have been more careful about laughing, but things were a little looser in South Coast Oregon, and you could do that. For the record the boy laughed too; it was an honest laugh and he wasn't ostracized at all; he was, like I said, extremely positive, funny, and sweet and you have to know each student and the humor they have and give.

The next story could easily fall in the category of setting boundaries, though it would more likely fall in the category of breaking down boundaries, which is not a topic for this work; it will have to suffice to stay in the category of humor, since it was pretty funny. One of the toughest kids I had in my entire career was a student who I actually had for a couple of years in my IPASS class, and he had manic depression and/or bipolar disorder. Thankfully, whatever issues he had he eventually worked out, it seemed, and the last I saw him, he had a job working for a contractor doing construction and I hope that worked out for him. This boy was tough, he had huge arms, really long, he was strong, and the reader will just have to accept my word on how difficult a student he was without me going into all the details. I will say this; it's an adage and a truth that the worst students have the best attendance, and this boy almost never missed a day. I think he missed one day the entire time I had him as a student, and while he would constantly give me a hard time about whatever rules I imposed on him, I think he actually liked and respected the authority and structure I imposed, due to a lack of structure he had growing up.

Towards the end of my second year in IPASS, which was the last year I had this boy, I loosened up a little bit, as I had gained a good measure of control in the class and felt like I pretty much knew what I was doing. I was looking forward to a third year there in that program, as I had the routine down and had respect from students and I was making the class work well. I would therefore take the students outside on nice days, and we would play games on the field for physical education credit, and I think one day we were playing kickball or something, and the students kept challenging each other to wrestling matches. Then some of them started challenging me, and I don't remember if they knew I was a high school wrestler, but if they did I'm sure they didn't really believe it. I pinned the first student or two who challenged me, (remember this is South Coast Oregon, much more is allowed there). Then this boy who's the center of this story challenged me, right after I had just wrestled another kid and I was pretty worn, but I didn't really see another option other than accepting the challenge. He was pretty good, but it wasn't long before I had him pinned on his back, and then all the other students, like ten of them, came over and piled on, yelling, "Pile on!" At first he was yelling to get off, and then he finally gave in and realized there was nothing he could do, and I heard him laughing under that dog pile. When we finally got off of him we all had a big laugh, including the boy, who apparently really needed a big hug!

Another classic quote, which shows the other side of humor, as in knowing when it's appropriate not to chastise a student for humor, was in the same class, with the one girl that was in the class at the time. I don't remember what had happened, but the students were working on the far side of the classroom, and someone or some people did something wrong. I must have looked at the students in a pretty mean way, because the girl said, "Mr. Miller, if looks could kill, we'd all be dead right now!" I'm not sure if I laughed or not but I certainly didn't give her a hard time for it because it was a good line, the tone in which it was said was not nasty, and she wasn't disrespectful when she said it. I always wondered about how those girls managed in there; in all my alternative classes, with the exception of my current position. There was always a disproportionate ratio of boys to girls, with very few, if any, girls in the classroom. Even in West Orange there are more boys than girls, about three to one, but that doesn't compare to my earlier alternative classes. My only explanation for this disproportion is that girls are better behaved, and nicer, and are therefore not thrown out of class and suspended at the same rate as boys are, and that seems to be the truth. But don't let the police of politically correct language hear it.

I would say one of the funniest things I did in my teaching career didn't necessarily involve the students. Toward the end of my last year in Oregon, in 2008, when I knew I wouldn't be seeing these people who I had developed strong ties with for a long time, I decided to attempt to memorialize the time and people there through video. I came up with a list of funny questions to ask people in the school, which included what their fake name would be for the video, so I knew how to address them, (my video name was Mr. Chucklehead). I also asked random questions like who their favorite superhero was and what their favorite color was. If you want to access those videos, type the following on www.youtube.com, or on www.google.com, without quotes: "thisoneaintused". You can view the videos for yourself and decide if they're funny or not, but I definitely entertained myself, and the interviewees got to have a good time, and now I can always relive my time with those people if I ever feel like I miss them a lot, or just want to reconnect to that time in history. It was a pretty funny time, and I'm glad to have lived it that way.

Using humor in teaching is one of the hardest things to teach and it's really going to come only with time, unless a one happens to be a naturally funny and clever person, who's in control and takes to teaching like a fish to water. Even if a person is naturally funny, and uses humor from the start, it could backfire if he doesn't know how to handle the class in general, so it's really a better tool to use later in the game, once experience is garnered. Regardless, it really makes a class so much nicer when you get that comfortable that you can make your students laugh, and in turn, teach them how to make each other laugh appropriately. One student who was one of my stronger comedians in my first two years at West Orange High School, who was also one of my smartest seniors when he finished school, was always making jokes. I tried to get him to stop, because most of the time, the jokes were inappropriate; and when he would cross the line, it wasn't a casual crossing; it was full speed, often disgustingly so.

At one point, I suppose this also falls under the category of "choosing battles", I decided to stop trying to get him to stop making jokes, which were meant to make everybody laugh, and to start trying to get him to make me laugh. I figured and told him that if he could make me laugh, it would probably be funny enough to make everyone laugh, because he was that clever. While he didn't like sitting in the front row, this strategy succeeded in that he started learning how to make appropriate jokes which were still funny, and how to make everyone laugh, including me. That was a surprise new strategy that I figured out and it worked nicely, and I will probably use it again in the future. I thought I might get a little argument from him when I told him he should try to make me laugh, but he didn't argue the point, and I was pleasantly surprised to see him making appropriate jokes that I too could laugh at, because if he can make it to the business world, that skill will help him. You have to know your audience, and while it is easier to make crass jokes that will make crude people laugh, you have to be able to make more appropriate jokes for those operating at a higher level if you want an extra tool for real world success.

The hardest thing about using humor is that you have to be pretty relaxed in the moment. Now this is not the kind of humor which some of our worse teachers use, which means mocking the student. There are exceptions to this, like when you know your students really well and you know who can and wants to handle what, and who wants the attention in that way. However, this is a very fine point to tell, and requires years of experience and knowing your children and students. Referring to the kind of mocking humor which our "not-best" teachers use, this is a different kind; because the nasty kind of humor can be done by anyone with half a brain. It doesn't require much skill to make fun of someone and hurt them in order to get the rest of the group to laugh, and there are teachers that do this. It's mean and it goes without saying that there's no place for it in the classroom or anywhere. The following is a simple example of the proper type of humor, in using the moment and being chill in it. When I was looking for jobs in 2010, after I had been told I was not having my contract renewed for the following year, (along with all the other non-tenured teachers, and I was told three days before I was about to close on a house, which, for the record, is too late to really get out of a closing), I was getting a little nervous around June. I had gone across my desire NOT to work in inner city schools, and I had applied to a couple of schools in Newark, though they were all charter schools, so I thought they might have a higher standard. Not surprisingly, the interview process was kinked much like the schools; I was asked to teach a model lesson for observation, and it was in a middle school, and I was told I would have a Smart Board.

The students wore uniforms, so that was cool, and there were only about thirteen of them in this class I was to teach, which was also cool, but the building was pretty run down and not appealing, which was not cool. Also not cool was the fact that it wasn't a real Smart Board they had in the class I was teaching; it wasn't even a Promethean Board, which is the next best thing. It was junky, and it took a while to boot up, and they had to get their tech guy there to connect my flash drive to it, and it made things unsmooth, but I was able to handle the class well. There was one boy, who was the funny kid, and the leader, so to speak, who kept piping up about this and that, and when I asked for volunteers to give their name and tell a bit about who they were and what not, he volunteered someone else. I replied quickly that you couldn't volunteer anybody else, and that in fact, by doing so, he had just volunteered. After a slight reluctance, he was happy to tell about himself, and I then made him my lead student and had him getting the attention that he really wanted, and it worked out really well. Coming to him with humor at his first messing around was the right call and he didn't get put off by it, and really thrived on it. Like I said, it takes a lot of skill and time to figure out how to use humor, and it's not necessarily a beginner's tool but it should be employed once comfort is developed; it really adds a nice flavor to the classroom and relaxes students and lets them enjoy being there more than in a dry class.

14
BE FIRM; DRAW BOUNDARIES

Drawing boundaries is a very personal experience, and so I do not intend to dictate what your personal boundaries are or should be. I will discuss some events that shed some light on my personal boundaries, and I think you'll see an interesting part of my figuring out what my personal boundaries are and were. I figured that out, often times, when they were crossed, which technically might count as a mistake; who's counting? You should know, as you might find out G-d willing in the *Porch Stories* book, if I ever get to publish it, that my boundaries in the old days were pretty loose. I was an extremely open-minded individual. In fact, when I was growing up, my mother, (She should rest in peace), was pretty strict. When the other kids were out partying, I had to stay home, and when the other kids got their ears pierced, I couldn't get mine pierced, and when the other kids grew their hair long, I couldn't grow mine. I thought she was the strictest person ever and I always used to say that when I was a parent, I was going to be the coolest parent ever, and let my kids do whatever they wanted, and grow their hair, and all that stuff that I wanted to do and couldn't. I can say that after teaching a couple years, I flipped my position completely. It is much easier to loosen the reins than to tighten them. Not that I'm purposely mean or purposely strict, but if I make a rule, I stick to it for the long run, and that is firmness.

How and when you let students and children know what those boundaries are is up to you. I'll say it again: it's easier to loosen the reins than to tighten them. Don't let the reins out further than you want to reel them in, unless you know you have total control. No one can tell you what your boundaries are or what they should be, but the boundaries have to feel comfortable to you, and should reflect what you expect your children or students to be and become. There are many ways to enforce your boundaries, and most of those are the constructs of this book; there are countless other methods to preserve your boundaries. Of great importance is that you maintain your dignity and self-esteem, and if you're not sure what that means, there are other books you will need to read. If you don't preserve those two things, students and children will walk all over you, and they will never learn respect, and it is your job to teach that to them. I have twice in my life seen a child tell a parent, "shut up". Once when I was about nine years old and in a carpool with another family, and the child, a boy I knew, told his mother who was driving to shut up. I couldn't believe my ears and couldn't fathom how a parent would allow their child to talk to them that way. Surprisingly, I think the only other time I ever heard that again was recently in my West Orange community; only this time it was my friend who was the parent, and his son who told him to shut up. This is only a symptom of a greater problem; I have seen that in recent relationship where the child makes fun of the father disrespect him, punches him, the father telling the child to stop. I can't understand the pattern and I don't know that I want to, because there is some very wrong psychologically and in the intra-family dynamics going on there, which I am not licensed to diagnose.

I can give a couple examples which highlight when boundaries have been crossed. Unfortunately, in education as well, many times you only learn about boundaries when they are crossed, or at the moment they are about to be crossed, and as a learning teacher, it is easy to slip in that regard, as students will constantly be testing those boundaries. When I first started teaching in Coos Bay, I had no students for the first half of the day, as I mentioned earlier. When I finally got my first middle school student he seemed very calm and average, a pale skinned blond hair blue eyed seventh grader. This boy, who was from Reno, Nevada, and liked to rap, was great and easy to work with for the whole time, especially as it was just me and him. For about two weeks it was just him and I in that morning class, and everything was peachy. He pretty much did everything I wanted him to and then some, and got into all the work and really never caused a problem. Actually things were pretty fantastic and much like the arm-biter situation, I was beginning to wonder what all the fuss had been about at the middle school that this kid was kicked out in the first month of school. He maybe cussed a couple of times but always responded respectfully to my corrections and never gave me any reason to be seriously cross with him, nor any serious problem or attitude. As a matter of fact he really seemed to be enjoying himself in the class. He was very bright, a great writer, excellent at math and algebra, had a fabulous memory, and I figured maybe he's just too smart for regular class and was causing problems for that reason. However, as I had already learned from that arm-biter, I wasn't about to fall for the easy-at-first show again.

After a couple weeks with just him and me, I heard I was getting a second student and I figured things might get a little more interesting. What an underestimation that was! Our meeting for this second boy happened in the morning before school started. I was meeting with my principal, the new boy, his parents, and the principal from the middle school, which I soon learned would be the normal routine for the transfer of a student across these boundaries; things were going smoothly in the meeting. The first boy, the Reno rapper, walked into class, took a look at what was going on, and as he walked by our meeting table, which was on the left half of the class where there were no desks, launched his backpack about twenty feet towards his seat, and I heard him mutter under his breath something like, "Now this f--- is gonna be here too?!" I went over and told him that was inappropriate and I think I had him apologize to the people sitting at the table. In the bigger picture, though, I knew I was in for something special and this was the beginning of a whole new phase in my education as an alternative teacher. I had just those two students for a few weeks and that was plenty: it kept me on my toes for sure.

I remember back then they liked to try to challenge me and push my limits and see how far they could go; and even though I had taught for four years before this, I had never taught students like this before. With the second student from Southern California and the first from Nevada I realized that these were the first students of this caliber or lack thereof I was dealing with. It was a whole different breed: they were really an urban type that had been transferred into a suburban or less-than-such situation, and were running amok with their newfound freedom, power, and control with a bunch of softer kids in rural Southern Oregon where they were able to easily dominate the situation. I think I was the first wall they were to come up against that was to reshape them into functional beings. And in being that wall I was to learn what my own boundaries were and how I would need to reshape and re-designate them.

Just as a side note about the publicity of my disciplining the first boy while others were there: the point is that he had disrespected all the people their in the meeting with his behavior and he needed to correct himself and apologize to all those he had affected. In that respect, when I was growing up, I have a clear memory of my Mom, (She should rest in peace) yelling at me in the supermarket, (which was probably only disciplining me, but felt like flames of fury!) and this was pretty embarrassing. I guess before that, I thought I could get away with something in public and I found out the hard way how wrong I was. Whichever type of discipline a teacher or parent is willing to implement, they should also be implemented in public or in front of others if necessary; rules of behavior don't change just because others are around. I differ from others in many respects who always pull kids out of class to have private conversations with them when they've crossed boundaries. I'm a pretty public person in that respect and especially when the kids are publicly crossing lines they know they shouldn't; one simple reason is that the other students who saw the boundary crossed need to know that it's not alright.

I learned both boys had their issues and both had their problems but in general, to me, the first boy seemed more fun about things and was really trying to make people laugh, which I have found to be a common trait with alternative students. The second boy, on the other hand, had a mean streak in him and a nastiness in him. I hope his moving back to Southern California after his last suspension from our program finally cured him of this streak, (it was supposed to be a final suspension, which, as far as I knew, never happened before). I remember one morning, I'm not sure how the situation came to this, but the Cali kid had come to me at my desk. These, for the record, are the final points of this long winding story about boundaries. Two incidents in my learning my own boundaries involved standoffs. They also both involved the Cali kid, who, unlike the Reno rapper, who, with all his shenanigans, always seemed to have a hidden smile and a joy at seeing what might happen. It seemed that however mad Reno might appear, he was always on the verge of cracking up. This is not too unlike the role of teacher in these situations, who has to be dead serious about things that come across his path, which often happen to be the funniest things he has seen before, but he can't laugh or appear to be humored lest all sense of control disappear. The Cali kid, though, had a real mean streak to him, and as I discovered, a father who was in prison for some kind of violent crime, and this boy seemed like he might get violent.

The main incident involved the Cali kid coming up to me, and trying to get eye to eye with me and see how he could challenge me. I did not have a physical space rule at that point, written or otherwise. I don't have one posted now, but it's there, and the kids know it. So at that point in my career I didn't think it harmful to let this boy come up to me and quite literally stand up to me, because I didn't want him to think I was afraid of him. That was the case until one day he did that and had a pencil in his hand and said something about stabbing me in the eye, and I knew the line had been crossed. He had a smile when he said it, and it was the bad kind of smile. The smile seemed to say that he thought the fact that he was that close to the possibility of doing it was actually funny. I brought him to the office and I'm not sure what the consequence was but I made sure to never let myself get in that situation again.

The other situation was with the Cali kid also, on the way down to the office one day, he had gotten in trouble for something, and while we were waiting outside the office, he did in super slow motion, bringing a fist towards my face. As I write this I can't believe I'm the same person I was then. But this was a kid who got away with whatever he could, and I was a young teacher and a tough person trying to show I was unafraid. The point is, that while he was doing this, he "accidentally" very lightly touched my face. This was obviously a case of the line being crossed and it's interesting that I allowed both of these to happen. It could even be the case that they both happened the same time, the office incident being after I was bringing him up for the "stabbing threat" but really no one will ever know, unless I try and go back and dig through records, which I have no time or interest in doing. I'm embarrassed enough to write that I let this happen to me, but I never thought about that situation happening before it happened, and there was no way to imagine how I would act in it until it happened. I act differently now. I learned my lesson about extending boundaries further. In alternative education things are always different anyway, but I shouldn't have let him get that close to me. Considering what could have happened, and the fact that kids are almost invincible when it comes to the law and that if he had connected in a punch, nothing real would have happened to him, I'm glad that's all I got away with: to learn a pretty easy lesson about setting clear boundaries and making sure they're far enough away.

I think boundaries go hand in hand with personal space. In most of my classes I always had my desk set up in a way that I was able to exit my desk from either side (left or right), and go out to the rest of the class, which is great, because if a student comes to the front or a side for help, your other side is always free. Then, if other students want to come up, they can wait or, at worst, they could wait behind the other students. There would be no reason to have students at both sides of the desk, since a teacher only has one mouth with which to talk. In my position at West Orange High School, however, the setup is kind of weird, and the wiring for the computer on my desk makes it so that my desk is right next to the entrance to the class. My desk, which is an "L" shape, butts one end of the "L" against the wall, so that I can only get to my seat from the left side. This is actually kind of like it was in Destinations Academy, which has its advantages as well. When students come up, I have them come to the front of my desk, and only rarely at the side of my desk. It happened at least twice since I have been in West Orange High School, that suddenly a few students were there at the desk and surrounding me, leaving me with no exit, that I would get up and say, "excuse me", and walk to the far side of the room, and ask them all to sit down, because I don't like to be surrounded without exit, and it's not a smart position to be in for a whole host of reasons. That's one of my boundaries and sooner or later the students learn it, and I stick to it for safety's sake. Choose and enforce your boundaries wisely. I have a whole bunch of other boundaries, but it would take another book to explain them all, and I don't think it's essential to share them all; just know I make sure they're adhered to. I think you get a feel for them through the book.

On the lighter side of boundaries, and I still can't believe this story actually happened, I should have known what was coming when, in my year at Destinations Academy in Coos Bay, we decided to take on an art project involving a local artist who did murals with students and special needs children. In the interview with her, my principal, another teacher from the program, and I sat with her as she showed pictures of the work she had already done. She was definitely dressed in hippie attire, and she had her two children with her; I hadn't really been ready for that, as they were kind of playing around while we were interviewing, (I think I actually gave one of her children a coloring book with markers to work on). What I really wasn't prepared for, was when her two year old daughter, (maybe two and a half), came over to her, and the artist mom lifted up her shirt, and began nursing! I am pretty open minded, and was maybe more so back then, but the age of the girl, and the location and timing, (a school interview?) threw me for a loop. I naturally figured that was the end of her chance for the job; but we were pretty open minded in South Coast Oregon, and we had her come in to work with our students; ha!

It was a very process oriented project and we were able to get a few of our more artistic and curious students to work on this project, including most if not all of the Dark Riders, and they got some curious ideas about what they were going to do with the mural. We had to impose some boundaries along the way as they wanted to center the thing on these hallucinogenic-looking mushrooms, and I think they even managed to draw a little mushroom on there in the end, I believe. Then the next question that came to us was where they were going to hang this behemoth; it was huge, like four feet by eight feet, if I remember right, and I think the principal finally put her foot down when she said it could only be hung in the Destinations areas. She said that it would not be hung in a public forum within the building, as they included the mushroom(s), and we had younger students in the building, who we did not want to influence in that direction. I definitely respected my principal's position on this; and if they had a little artistic freedom in what was included in the picture, I'm not so concerned, since it is their expression. What more concerned me is who and how they are going to influence or not influence, with said artistic expression. There were any number of times we could have imposed boundaries; if we had nixed the nursing artist, I'm pretty sure we never would have had an art elective that year. That art project was a nice alternative elective and option for the program. On the other hand, if we had quashed the mushroom idea earlier in the project, we might have squashed the mural altogether, as I recall we had trouble in getting students even to complete it. They probably would have dropped out of the project if we imposed those boundaries too early on in the process. Choosing the location of the art was an appropriate action, because really, the students in the program that year were the main ones affected, and that is a reasonable outcome for any art project. So we limited their larger target audience.

So here's a funny situation of how I am with boundaries and how the year ended for one class. This boy, who I ended up passing finally at the end of the year, was in this class that was the joker class I was discussing earlier. They were always joking, and generally good natured, but they entertained themselves too much and couldn't get on task and fell behind and fell off. One boy in that class was good 95% of the time, but when he was bad he was like a completely different person, almost a split personality and I'm not surprised if that is truly the case. I saw this first when he took his HSPA and I happened to be the proctor in his classroom. For those standardized tests the examiner administers the tests, and the proctor assists with monitoring students and other necessary details. When I walked into the classroom the examiner was arguing with him about taking off his hat. He had already been my student for half a year by that point. For the record this is the boy who came up with the "Chill, chill, chill" phrase which became a calming technique. I went over and talked calmly to him and got him to take off his hat; then he had his headphones on and I went through the same process, but in the middle of this discussion the examiner had enough and said we need to remove him. So I went to the head of the testing process; we removed him from the test. You have to realize this is a big formal process. It's so formal that if the fire bell rings you have to make sure to collect the tests first before going. This boy was a completely different person than I had ever seen before and it was only after that event that I really saw that person come out again. Incidentally I think they let him take it again in a different environment and I honestly don't know if he passed. At the end of the next year he graduated though.

On the last day of that class, after the students had taken my final, this was the one class that couldn't handle the simple task of being chill when they were done with the final. This boy led the brigade in that failure. First he was on his phone in the class which I never allowed, and I called him on it. He argued, refused, and said it was his mother, some garbage line he was trying to give me. I think I let that slide because I was trying not to call security and my supervisor was not there at that point. Next he was actually on a laptop computer in the class, which our school does not allow. He must have had a wireless card, because he was video-chatting with someone when I walked over there! So I called security and they came down and had him turn off the computer. Security is another issue. So knowing I was going to have this boy again the following year, knowing how relaxed and refreshed I became after a summer vacation, and knowing I might lighten up and forget or forgive this incident, I wrote myself a reminder. I wrote this reminder into the opening slide of my smart-board "notebook". A "Smart Notebook" is a style of document equivalent to a PowerPoint for smart-board. I had already created the Smart Notebook with which I was going to start the following year. This way, I could walk right into school the first day and start teaching, with my preparation done. The reminder I wrote for myself was that this boy was to have a very short leash with regards to electronics. I was stricter with him, since he would take it to the limit up to the end. So I lowered my bar so his limit got lowered too; oh well.

I had a similar situation with another student in that class who I mentioned earlier as the boy who I convinced to make me laugh instead of the class. He was one of the most comedic students of that class. He and I had a couple of battles around the middle of the year and he tried to stomp out mumbling whatever garbage he was muttering, but he always came back the next day or days later with a better attitude. We had a pretty good relationship as well, but the same thing happened with him, at the end of the year he got all obnoxious and got attitude, and pushed it too far, and argued too much. Therefore, for him as well, I wrote him into the opening slide of the opening note-book the following year, not so that they could see it, but so that I would see it, and remember not to be so nice to this person. That's because I had to lower the bar for him too, so he didn't raise the limit too high. In his case, the thing I had to take away was a higher privilege. The laptop boy only lost my kindness in my not coming down on him so strictly with regard to using a cell phone in class. The front seat comedian, on the other hand, would sometimes come into the class period before his own class, and sit as a guest.

I had a couple of students that did that; amusingly, some of the students chose to come and sit in my class rather than go to the cafeteria for lunch! This is one I still cannot get through my head. My best guess is that they see the cafeteria as a place where it's too easy for them to get in trouble so thinking smartly, they choose a wise alternative. It's possible that they really didn't have lunch at that time and they were cutting class, but I think my boss would have found out about it, or their method of telling me was so calm that it seemed like they were telling the truth. I think I was always so shocked that they wanted to spend extra time in a math class that I let it go. I was always used to kids trying to get out of class and my job being to keep them in class; so when I had students that were trying to get into class, it was very hard for me to turn them away. Back to the front seat comedian's story and the end to his year, I wrote into the slide on the Smart Notebook for the beginning of the following school year, that he was not to be a guest in another class the following year after he had ended the year by being a jerk. He had probably assumed, like the other boy, that since it was the end of the year, he could do whatever he wanted, because teachers forget over the summer or something. The funny thing is, I don't remember how long I wrote the sentence of judgment for, but whatever it was, I kept it for the whole year. I took the privilege away, and did not allow him to be a guest in any of my other classes.

A relatively new phenomenon for me the past couple years was the taking of cell phones. I'm not sure why it wasn't such an issue in the past; I guess the times were different and the kids didn't have so many phones, especially in the South Coast of Oregon. In my second year at West Orange that was the big new issue for me. With most students it went alright: I would tell them to put the phone away and they would do so, and on the second time I would take it; because this is a clear school rule and there's no gray area in this situation. There was only a few times when it became a difficulty. The one that stands out was this girl who sat in the back corner and had a tremendous attitude when she wanted to, which basically meant whenever she was made to do something she didn't want to do. I guess her attitude also cropped up when she felt the boy in the back was bothering her, but that wasn't the same attitude, and didn't have the same magnitude. I think that's because the boy would acquiesce and back off out of fear of her anger, whereas I would not. That may sound mean, but in one case, when I told her repeatedly to put away her phone, she took issue with that, and refused to give it over. When I got my supervisor, she took the phone, and that was that. Years of relationship trust helped greatly in that.

The thing I find interesting along these lines is what happened when I lost my school ID. We have electronic ID's that scan us to get into the bathroom, and into the building, as do the students. Actually some of the teacher bathrooms use a standard key, but our ID's will open student bathrooms as well. One day I noticed my ID was missing, and I looked and looked and couldn't find it. Finally I had to give in and bought a new ID, I think it was five dollars, from the office, not a big loss, more a loss in terms of embarrassment and annoyance in having to ask the office to replace mine and their recognizing that I made a mistake, which I don't like. A few days later, during another class, my student who I played guitar with later in the year, came into my class and apologized, and gave me back my ID. I had lent him my ID to go to the bathroom, and he forgot to give it back. At that point, I lent my ID regularly to students who needed to go to the bathroom but had lost their ID. When they would come back from the bathroom, and go to return my ID to me, I was usually in the throes of teaching and might forget to ask it back of him. For a few days, I refused to give any students my ID to go to the bathroom. That was fine and then I think it was a student that suggested I take some kind of collateral in exchange for the ID and from that point on, I would require a phone, keys, or something of importance that a student would not forget for too long. That system worked, and is still in place. These days I have expanded that system to include borrowing pens or pencils, as I never used to get them back. Now I get them back.

Taking phones away in the cafeteria was a little trickier. I generally didn't have a problem with students talking on the phone in the cafeteria, though it barely happened and when it did they were smart and discreet about it. I suppose they had no need for it since they were freely able to talk to their friends however they wanted for that half hour and there was no reason to talk to people who weren't there. The problem came when students put the phone on speaker and played music out loud, if you can believe it. It happened three times that I caught it. Actually, those three times were all on the other side of the cafeteria, and even when I went over there, and even when I told the other teacher, he still couldn't hear it. Nice guy he is; but he told me he has hearing problems, which makes for a funny question of his being on cafeteria duty. In general, they more regularly texted in the cafeteria and that I didn't really mind at all, even though it was technically against the school rules; I could deal with that.

The first time I caught someone playing music out loud on their phone in the cafeteria, I went over to the table on the far end of the other side of the cafeteria. As I got to the table I was able to pinpoint where the sound was coming from, and when I realized who it was, the boy tried to pass the phone around the table. When security came over the table wouldn't give up the phone. That was fine because I knew who had the phone when I went over to the table, and that kid got in trouble. H got defiant anyway, even with security, so that was that. The second time it happened I think was at the dancer table. I think he was dancing even to the music playing and I went over and told them it would have to be off or I would have to confiscate it and I don't think I had to take that phone, which was fine.

The third time it happened was at this table in the middle front of the cafeteria. They were smooth at causing problems and not getting caught. Their main trick was a few minutes before the end of lunch, someone would mimic the sound of the bell and the whole cafeteria would fall for it, whether they really believed it or not. It was very difficult to catch the "bell-ringer" at that table, because they weren't consistent with it; they didn't do it that often. Also, when they did "ring the bell", everyone was getting up at the same time, and you couldn't see who was where, not to mention that it was a one-time sound from fifty feet away which I could not pinpoint. They also had some close calls with throwing things and hats at or to each other, but it was always on the edge. One day they crossed over and had the music playing and I wasn't sure which table it was. At the time there was a janitor talking to me. He would talk to me almost every day. He was developmentally disabled in a noticeable way; he would come over and tell me about his neighbors, the kids he would pick up, and the cars he wanted to wash. He told me the same stories and had the same questions every day. He would ask me if it was OK to do x, y, or z; if I told him it was not OK, he would listen, but then the next day more often than not he would tell me he had done what I told him not to do. One day he came in and told me that he had dropped a kid he was bouncing or holding; I got a little upset at him and talked to him in strong words to try to get the point across that he should not be picking up other people's kids, even if he knew them and all, for this very reason. I felt bad later because I spoke to him so strongly; I corrected myself by telling him I did that in order to assure he didn't get in trouble or hurt anyone. He listened and understood well.

While this janitor was talking to me that day, I suddenly heard the music coming from the general vicinity of that table. But I knew that if I went over, it would most definitely shut off and I wouldn't be able to catch them. This was one rare thing in my teaching experience I hadn't been able to catch. And this was one of those violations that really bugged me: it was a flagrant violation of the boundaries and an obvious disregard for and disrespect of all of the teachers in the cafeteria, (along with other students who may not have liked their music selection). True, they were in fact on the other teachers' side of the cafeteria; regardless, I was on duty too; I took it to be in my realm. So I sent a spy: I told this janitor to go over there and find out where the music was, and tell me when he found it; I knew they wouldn't suspect him of such activity, nor me of trusting him, nor of some new newfangled idea like this. It worked perfectly: he went over, and came back to me, and told me which kid it was, and I went right over there quickly, before they had time to do anything about it, and told the kid to give it to me or to security, and that was the end of that. It was a smooth move. You have to keep them on their toes.

The other one that was like that in the cafeteria, with respect to obvious boundary crossing, was some girl that was throwing food at someone else and the boy threw it back or something. I already knew the boy well; he had once informed me that there was something shady going on in the boy's bathroom that I should check out. That was actually very cool because I had never really spoken to him, except in being nice and greeting him, because he always seemed friendly and never caused any problem. I went in the bathroom that day and it looked like the boys were about to do something; I have no idea what, but I don't think it was drugs, vandalism, or violence, and I think it was involving a camera, if I remember right. Anyway on this day, where the girl and the boy had exchanged airborne food, I went over to the pair, and I asked this boy to clean up the spilled milk. He said that she spilled it first, which he was right about, so I went to get that girl. She was busy trying to escape hastily through the horde and mass of students that formed at the end of every lunch period as all the students got up to leave at once, and the traffic would come to a standstill as it did then; she had nowhere to go. I told her she needed to pick up the thing she threw; she tried throwing some attitude at me saying something about whatever. I told her that was fine, I would just look at it on video camera and I knew her now anyway. She huffed and puffed and went back and cleaned up the mess, and as she walked back, and I was talking to the other teacher, she said, "Are you happy now? You feel better about yourself?" Whether I responded affirmatively or if I just ignored her is another question; it wasn't worth too much time. I was happier that she cleaned it up but not so happy that she had to do it with an attitude. That's no fun for anybody.

There was one thing I would sometimes tell myself on cafeteria duty; I wrote this briefly earlier but I think it's worth more detail; I get a little religious in this paragraph. It was not an easy job, especially in the beginning of the year: I had no idea what would come up, and how I would handle it, and how students would respond: I had some adverse reactions in the past. It was a bit of an intimidating situation, and the kids always have less than me to lose: that's one of the advantages of being a kid, that they're almost invincible like I mentioned; anything they do, say, or get arrested for doesn't really go on their record or lead to jail time unless it's serious; they can get away with a lot. Sometimes, when things looked bleak in there, and they seemed like they might get rowdy, or I was having this thing like fear try to creep up on me, I would concentrate in my mind on the thought that the only thing I have to fear is G-d. I would think about the fact that he is the only one who can do anything to me, and that the entire cafeteria of what seemed like tough, noisy, rowdy students was not even a pin drop compared to the awesomeness, power, and dominion of Him. It's the truth and it got me through some of the thicker scarier situations, and I think it would help a lot of people to have a similar set of thoughts in their mind when things seem difficult, tough, or thick, so to speak. Boundary strengthening requires courage.

There was another kid in the lunch room who I connected with like that other boy from the cafeteria I mentioned before, in a positive way. This boy always seemed to be in a good mood, never caused problems, never wearing a hat, and carried himself in a positive upright manner; also you could tell he was a cool, hip kid. This was a new kind of move for me, that one day, as he was walking out of the cafeteria, I just complimented him on the aforementioned qualities, and introduced myself, and he did the same. From then on he was always waving to me, and coming up to talk to me and tell me about his situation and life. I could tell even at the moment that I said that compliment to him, that I was affecting him. It was nice to have such a positive effect, especially since it was completely unnecessary and above the call of duty, him being student in the cafeteria who I had little connection to. We developed a nice camaraderie and I suppose that lasted through the year; he kept telling me about his college plans and aspirations, and it's nice to have a positive connection like that. Once, however, he donned a hat in the lunch room, and I had to correct him; my guess is some of his friends were giving him guff about a friendship with a teacher, and he had to prove them wrong. He responded well to my directive, but I was still disappointed that he would do such a thing; it was not cool in my book; it took a while before I even really started looking his direction when he would pass by so as to greet him, because for the time being, I didn't really have much to say to him. Like I said I was disappointed.

The other students from the cafeteria I developed an interesting camaraderie with were these two boys who also always seemed to be in a good mood, and were always positive, and I almost greeted in the same fashion a few times. Then one day, when I finally taught myself to enjoy snowboarding on the east coast again, I was riding the (relatively) new high speed gondola at Mountain Creek. There were like five other people on it, and we were talking about how long it took us to get to the mountain from our homes, and where we came from. I think they were asking me where I came from, (because I barely talk to anyone on the lift), and I told them West Orange, and they said they go to school in West Orange, and then they asked me if I was the teacher in the cafeteria and I realized who they were. I introduced myself as Larry but said it was Mr. Miller at school; they really got a kick out of that whole thing and so did I. It's weird outside of school running into students, especially when they are high school age, and the question of different boundaries or a change in boundaries occurs. In Oregon there were a couple of students who found out where I lived and they wanted to hang out with me. There was nothing to be gained on my end and everything to be lost so I had to kibosh that situation, but they took it well. This event was nice though, running into the students randomly on the mountain, especially since they were two of the nicer students I came across in school. Then when we would see each other in school: it was funny because we had hung out on the mountain riding. There were three other students who I had connections with outside of school. Two of them worked at kosher stores in the strip of stores where I would eat in town. In those situations I introduced myself the same way, especially since those were girls and I wanted to put a stronger definition of the boundaries on that situation without being a jerk.

There are so many stories about being firm with students, and it really may be the most important skill, especially with alternative students and/or difficult children. Along these lines, it seems to me there is a spectrum leading up to and including at least one diagnosed student, and sometimes more undiagnosed bipolar students, in every alternative class I have, and I hope it ends soon. In my first year in West Orange I had one such case, and I still don't know when she was diagnosed. I only know that I found out about it when she left my class for an extended period of time and I had to start supplying work to her "teacher" at the hospital/center where she was recuperating. This is a very difficult and unpredictable disease to deal with and I haven't seen any training on it in all my teaching experience. Even if there was training for teachers, it would never be enough to really deal with it, because every situation is completely different, volatile, and always surprising in new respects. When this particular student came back to our class from a couple months of being away, I first noticed she was incredibly calm, and seemed almost like a different person. She had an almost perfect peace to her, seeming to have a slight smile on her face all the time, and everything seemed peachy and fine to her, as far as I could tell. The two strange experiences I had with her were as follows. Once, one day, she came in, when she had been back for a week or so, and was asking, in the middle of class, about her grade. I think this was on a day I was giving the students a test, about which she had little understanding since she had been away for such a long time. In trying to explain to her that I would have to confer with my supervisor, she was getting upset because her "teacher" apparently told her she had done all the work and so would be earning a "B"; she was so upset because I wasn't assuring her that she would have a "B" right then.

I don't think I even gave her an answer, and apparently that upset her, because all of the sudden she was yelling and freaking out; even the students were silent. This was a rarity because if someone went off, usually at least one person in class was entertained, and came out with some comment or some support, or at least laughed. In that respect, the reason the other students would normally get entertained was that the person going off was usually doing it at least partly as a show for his or her classmates. In this situation I think the students were in shock because she was really truly angry, and it came out of nowhere, and she was obviously not doing this for entertainment value, because she herself was not looking cool in this event. Usually when the kids are going off you can tell they're still having fun with it or at least staying cool or trying to make the teacher look worse. This girl didn't care what she or I looked like in this situation and that was obvious. In response to her trying repeatedly to sway me into giving her affirmation that she would be getting a "B" like her teacher told her, I simply stayed firm with her in my answer that I would have to discuss it with my supervisor. She actually handled her exit well; she said she had to go talk to her counselor and I said, "OK", and she left. The next time she came in was like a week later, and she came in totally fine, like nothing had happened, though she seemed a little nervous at first walking into class, understandably, but to me the past was all gone, so we continued as if nothing happened; that was that. She did pretty well the rest of the year.

15
SPEAK SIMPLY

Use simple statements and explanations. That's the simple statement; the caveat is: there are times for complex discussions, and those times should be decided consciously by you, and with student buy-in, to the point and extent that you choose to have a philosophical discussion about the situation. There are different ways of speaking simply. In the second case in this chapter in which I discuss the math department, I use the longest paragraph in the entire book to make my point; this seems counter-intuitive in a chapter about speaking simply. The truth is that there was a lot to be said, and this was the simplest way to do it. I had four or five points to make in that case, and I had to have the basic points memorized so it didn't look like I was reading off a planned statement, and that's what I did. In that case, speaking simply meant ordering my points of statement so they were still clear and simple enough to be heard by a room of teachers and more importantly, by administration, and even more importantly, that they would impact the above recipients. Speaking simply is certainly an art.

On the other hand, when it comes to students, there are countless examples that can be given, and I try to make every set of words that comes out of my mouth as simple and clear to understand as possible. Even when I'm talking to a student who has a very high level of understanding and functioning, there are probably others listening to our conversation, and it's easiest and best to teach a lesson once to the whole class, instead of teaching it over and over fifteen to thirty times. When I was in Jefferson, I had a student who was one of the smartest kids I ever met. He had moved to my mainstream 5th grade class from somewhere in the mid west, and he was very personable, though he also had a way of annoying the other students, which he was really doing on purpose. He got a kick out of it. He was one of two students who ever turned me on to a band that became a band I really like, and that band is Good Charlotte; he gave me a copy of their CD and I still occasionally listen to it to this day. He was tested at genius level as I heard; his conversation, knowledge, and manipulative ability proved the test's accuracy.

The problem with this boy was that he had a cartful of issues that went along with his life, starting with the fact that his father was in prison in another state, and he did not know when he would see him again. He had not seen him enough to get a positive intelligent model to guide him in a good way. I was not necessarily that model, but I think I helped him along the way. This boy did not use his skills towards a positive end for himself too much. He spent time goofing off and setting up manipulations in class that would get others in trouble or would entertain him. He spent a lot of his time watching others work. One time I caught him watching someone else work on the computer. Mind you I like when students work together, but not watching someone else work; it is not productive. I surprised him with a little sharp call of his name or something. When I think of it now, this may not have been the coolest way to get him to stop watching others working, but I was still a pretty new teacher, and I was trying to snap him out of old habits, and surprise is sometimes the best way to do that. I made sure there was no anger in my voice when I said it, and I think it had the desired effect; if anything it caught him off guard, but didn't scare him. It's an art to surprise someone without scaring them, and a fine line for sure.

Using a strong voice is useful for preventing danger and teaching basic avoidance but keep the words simple, like "Sit down", or "Get to work", or "Quit talking." Otherwise the kids are going to try to engage you in an argument about where your words might technically be wrong, and I prefer to be right rather than getting into an "because I'm the boss" type of answer or discussion. Simple statements are the most recognizable and easy to follow. Using the word "no" or "quit doing that", (especially specifying the behavior which you are talking about), is the right way to go. That's because discussions about the morality of bad and good is philosophy, and the time for this discussion should be chosen carefully. In this case, when we are teaching it is more useful to teach the behavior. Basically, "no" or "quit it" is more useful when you are catching the person doing something in the moment, and teaching about good and bad is better after the fact, to teach the person what behavior was not acceptable and why it was not acceptable. There are many advantages to using simple words when catching in the act.

I have mentioned before and I will mention again there are obvious and major differences between teaching people and animals but there are similarities as well, and with simple language and simple statements the similarity can be seen and evidenced. With my dog, Bennie, who just passed away in the beginning of my third year at West Orange, I used the word "no" when I was catching him doing something, like if we are walking and he was trying to eat food off the ground, and "bad" when he has already gotten away with the deed, like when I come home, and he had a party. I would bring him over to the scene of the mess he made, (meaning he got into the garbage, which was really my fault for not having a proper structure set up to avoid this), and tell him he was a "bad dog" in a very stern voice. I would then place him in the bathroom for five minutes. I do not recommend this with children if you do not want to meet your local DYFS representative, but the "timeout" concept is similar to this action. With children, however, I prefer to lead them in a discussion to figuring out what they did wrong and coming up with a solution such as timeout so they have ownership of it; I never got Bennie to that level of self-directed learning. Fortunately children have the ability to learn at that level; most do anyway.

The difficulty with New Jersey is being ahead of the curve, in that it's always got to be at the forefront of education, which has its obvious advantages but disadvantages come along for the ride. Unfortunately, the new and improved education system seems to look like something out of my fraternity pledge book, which is: unity, unify, unite. We are doing away with individuality in the quest for permanent standardization; and we are on the way to computer teachers for students who want to learn and work, and road work jobs for students who don't want to work. The people at the top of the education system pyramid are obviously very smart, too, the way they bring this stuff to us and get people on board. They put it on teachers first, then implement it with students, and apparent parent approval, which I haven't figured out yet. I guess the parents that care about education and their children's success in the system want to see scores that prove that their students are keeping up with the Jones's; except it's no longer keeping up with the Jones's, but keeping up with the Jones juniors, and that's quite a different story.

One example of this came in the math department meetings over the last year, and this was the long-winded discussion I mentioned at the beginning of this chapter. I wasn't really even supposed to be in the math department. Back in the day before I got to West Orange High School, there used to be department meetings in that high school. When those would happen, Horizons would have their own department meeting, where, I suppose, students and issues and combinations of the two were discussed. My second year there, however, the Horizons Supervisor, my boss, was suddenly made to be the English Department Supervisor, (English is her specialty), and we were no longer able to have those department meetings. I still haven't figured out whether I made a good decision in going to the math meetings; they are not *so* fun because we got and get a lot to do; but the math staff is pretty cool.

The big push of the second year was to unify and improve all midterms and finals. The scores on those tests were too low according to those above us, so we were to adjust the tests, so we spent the year doing that. At one meeting, administration announced next year's push to focus on unifying our curriculums and regular chapter testing. So, for example, everyone teaching Algebra 2 would be teaching polynomial division at the same time, and using the same test for it. It also meant unified assessment weighting. The difficulty is that, as we learn in our education programs, we learn to assess through a variety of methods so different learners can demonstrate their knowledge in different ways, among other beneficial advantages to these varying types of assessments. I understand the necessity of matching school goals with state mandates I had some educational points I wanted to convey on this.

While I had a lot to say, I had to voice my thoughts quickly and simply in order to be effective. The main points of the condensed but packed presentation were that, first of all, this plan was going to make difficult our ability to differentiate our instruction, which is something we've been taught to do since time immemorial. Differentiation includes leveling assignments based on differing levels of student ability. The second point was to answer questions raised earlier: how a teacher could have two sections of the same class, (like two Geometry classes), with dissimilar assignments and tests for them. I said as classes develop their own personalities, some classes assess better from Math Jeopardy, some from testing, some from homework, and some from learning in the class and assessing on the fly. It is our jobs as teachers to figure out these differences and assess accordingly. All had to be spoken simply.

The third point was that we had just been congratulated in the previous week on our students' success on the New Jersey High School Proficiency Assessment, on which our students excelled, and as a department we had done very well. So why were we going to change all the progress we had made using our systems that obviously succeed? The fourth point I squeezed in was in response to a question about the difficulty of tracking students as they switched to different classes throughout the year. It had been possible till then to switch students to other classes at any point during the year, based on the fact that they might not work well with a certain teacher, they weren't succeeding in that classroom, or some other reason. I said we spent the whole previous year organizing, remaking, and unifying midterms and finals so that all the Algebra 2 classes were taking the exact same final, (with exception for special education and honors). So if we wanted to be careful about knowing where students were academically before they switched math classes, we could make an executive decision as follows: we would only transfer students into other classes at midterms. That way, we could use those midterm grades as indicators, especially since we did a problem analysis on the entire test, in which we listed the topic and curriculum standard number tested by every question, to assure we were covering a good sampling of the standards. That would give a good analysis of where students were academically with respect to their particular class. The final point I left off for brevity's sake but it is interesting to note. Pretty much all administration is on board with it too, but at the mercy of other forces. The point is that while assessment is important, it should not be at the cost of education; it cannot be. Speak simply.

16
MODEL

Model what you want the students and your children to do and achieve. In my opinion, students learn best from modeling. The easiest way to teach modeling is to show by doing. It is a lesson of "do". You have to model the behavior you want your students or children to follow. The easiest example is with manners. This goes back to the change from the old days of students and teachers being on completely different levels where the students had to use manners and teachers didn't. It's a different world in that respect and I'm OK with that. I always felt teachers should speak to students with manners. When someone is doing something that's not alright and way across the rules it may be a different situation; in this case manners may need to be excused to immediately correct that behavior. In normal situations dealing with manners, however, this is the easiest example of demonstrating how to model for students. Model the manners you want students to use and they will learn how to use manners themselves. Another way to show where modeling works simply is in teaching how to ask questions, in asking questions of your students, the way you want them to ask questions, they will do the same. In all these habits, in everything you want to teach, in all you want to impress on your students and children, the best way to teach them is to do it yourself. The only disadvantage this method has, although it is the most effective, is that you never really get to know when you had the effect. That is the case unless you're fortunate enough to have a student tell you how you affected them, and that doesn't necessarily happen so often. On the other hand that might be an advantage: it keeps us humble, and that's a good quality, and certainly a good quality to model; though encouraging humility borders on imposing ethics.

Along the lines of having students point out the effect you had on them, and as a slight side note, I saw one of my former students when I went to Enchanted Forest in Oregon in 2004. I think this is one of three times this happened in my life. It was when I was working in Coos Bay, and I went with the senior trip, which was supposed to be to the "Thrillville Amusement Park" on Interstate 5. This was a trip with about eight students, which was all we had in our senior class for Destinations that year, and when we got to the park, we found out, in classic *Vacation* style, that it was closed. Any who, as the park was closed we went next door to "Enchanted Forest" which is really for younger kids, but we had a good time anyway. I said one slightly clever remark to the ride attendant after the ride; she asked me if I ever taught in Jefferson; turns out she was one of my former sixth grade students. Small world! I think that was the only "run-into" student situation where the student had grown up, after I had known them as a child, not counting a child I taught as a swim instructor when I was sixteen. I found out at a speed dating event when I was about 35, sitting across from this girl that seemed oddly familiar, that she was one of the swimmers. That was weird and kind of awkward. But back to public school students, I don't think I ran into too many students in Oregon after they grew up, mainly because each time I worked at a district for three or four years, and then moved to someplace else, far away, which is easy to do in Oregon, it being a huge state. Until 2008, before I moved back to New Jersey, there was always the chance of some random "Enchanted Fores" type encounter. Now that I am back on the East Coast, the chances of running into a former student from Oregon seem slim indeed. Facebook shrinks the world.

All of which is a great way to delay the real work at hand which is to write about modeling in an alternative classroom or a regular classroom or as a parent. Boy, in certain respects, I am a slacker. With respect to that modeling, I truly make sure to save this book on the computer very well as I type, and even as I edit it, with multiple copies, on my computer, and I email it to myself at different emails so I don't lose it, which is what I always tell my students to do. I am sure I learned that once the hard way. That discounts the beginning of this novel which is gone with the wind due to poor saving. I will always wonder what I wrote. So maybe twice was all it took for me to learn the lesson and now I always save documents as soon as I start. That is why I always title the paper or document the way I want to save it, in the first line, so I save a step in the saving process: the first thing written is what Microsoft gives as the title. How's that for a syntax twister? And is it not even better at prolonging the inevitable?

Mentoring and modeling really work well with difficult students. The first real experience I had in supervising mentoring in action was in my first position as an alternative education teacher, which was in Jefferson if you're keeping track. I really lucked out with this position in that it opened up and exposed the whole world of education to me. This position entailed three jobs rolled into one as I have explained, and the mentoring position involved a link between the first part of the day at the middle school site and the second part of the day at the elementary school site. The middle school site was in a building which separate from the middle school but on its campus, in that building I mentioned which housed the shop program in years passed. Occasionally the other teacher and I would cover each other's class, and her classroom, along with my boss's office, in the same building, were the two main places I could send students when they were misbehaving. There was always a warning system and options for ways of avoiding this consequence but sometimes the students really just needed to get away from others, especially when our number got up around fifteen and there only was my assistant, (a mother of a middle school student) and myself to tend the whole flock. We ended up taking a tenth grader into the program, who I mentioned in the introduction to this book, which changed the dynamics a bit. So that is why this alternative classroom, which was my first teaching position, was officially fifth through tenth grade. So we added him to our class with the understanding that he was in a class with middle school students and he would have to follow the rules just as they did. He was actually a fantastic part of the class. He really enjoyed taking a leadership role, (which is where the whole point of this story is going, to illustrate the positive power of empowering low esteem students by making them into models for others). The kids generally liked having him in the classroom. I think there was really only one time when I was envisioning my fastest route out of the classroom if this boy, who was GIANT, decided to hurdle my desk and come after me. That was when I had to discipline him just like the other students because he was acting up like a middle school student. He did not go that route however, and so I never had to enact my escape plan. I was thankful for that. All in all he was a good model, but when you have students being models you have to be extra careful because they are affecting younger students who are more impressionable and that's a responsibility. It takes a lot of attention and care.

In that teaching position, I had to learn a lot and fast, and was introduced to the concept in education of being flexible, and what kind of work goes into offering choices and alternatives, and all that's involved in setting up mentoring and modeling programs. It is not easy. At one point in the second term of my first year, I believe, my supervisor told me we were going to be starting up a new program. Working with OPB, Oregon Public Broadcasting, this would be an ongoing program for about two months. We would partner middle school students who would have to go through an application and screening process, with low level readers from the third grade, and we would meet once a week. The screening process took place after middle school ended, on site at the middle school campus, in the high school alternative classroom, since those students who were to be the mentors were coming from the regular middle school classroom. After the screening process, we gave the mentors a brief training in working with younger students and what they might expect, and how to help their partners learn. That training also took place in that high school alternative classroom, so this process really joined a lot of programs, which is inevitable when doing any kind of mentor program, and really one of its benefits.

The program was a blast and a smashing success. OPB sponsored it and every week the mentee got to take home the book he or she read with his or her mentor. There were about fifteen pairs, and it was a total joy to watch this program take off and fly. The third graders just thought it was the coolest thing to be working with these older students, and the positive energy that connected these kids to reading was magnetic. The little tykes tried harder than ever to read with their partners, who would coach them along, and if they couldn't read, the mentors would read to them, or they would take turns, or whatever worked. It worked so well for the term, that we ran it again for the last term of the year. The responses we got on all accounts were amazing. Honestly the coolest part was watching the glow of the mentors. Without a doubt the younger partners benefited tremendously and measurably in their marked improvement in reading. My greatest joy, however, was watching the middle school students get to be pure, innocent, kind, loving, helping kids again. It's hard to hold on to that once you hit middle school.

Middle school is generally a time when things get turbulent, kids lose sight of who they are, and get lost trying to figure out who they are going to become and who they should be. They end up making so many mistakes and doing things that are probably some of the more shallow choices of their life, that it probably is the most confusing point of life for many people. The gap between child and adult, which is supposed to be a transition, seems to turn into a blend of anger, emotion, and confusion. It is a fun time for sure, but I think middle school students generally are on guard more than most people and that, more than any other time in their lives, people are confused about who they are. This leads to the building of walls and fences, and defenses, and offenses meant to be defenses, which serve to separate people from themselves. Even writing about fences it seems to do it for me in terms of confusion!

To create a time and space where these students are safe to be themselves, to be kind, loving, and nurturing, like kids really are in their natural environments; it is truly a blessing and an honor to be a part of that. The experience obviously affected me, stayed with me, and remains with me to this day. It is a successful method which works in a variety of circumstances and a host of conditions and settings. It is an amazing, wonderful way to connect students to themselves and to others, foster understanding, build self-confidence, and strengthen self-esteem. I cannot sing the praises of mentoring programs enough; and since having run this program, I have come across several other teachers at professional development events doing very similar things. Whatever the method, if you can make it happen, do it.

We were actually able to institute one similar program in Destinations and one in AIMS/IPASS as well. Both went very well and I never heard or saw a case where the older students took advantage of the younger students' inexperience. It is almost obvious that the program in Jefferson was bound for success within the setting in which it was run, with it being sponsored by OPB, where our students were all filtered and educated and pretty much hand-picked to be mentors and mentees. It is quite another thing to see the same type of program work in other scenarios where there is no funding, no reward books, and a less careful selection of students most need to be helped to be mentees and students most caring and dedicated to be mentors. In these other programs we went with students who wanted to help, and who had a relatively healthy record in recent history, and we made them into mentors, and looked for students who were willing to be helped, and made them mentees. It was a much simpler process with much less supervision, so there was more risk. That also made it more rewarding in certain respects, because the success of the program depended more on the basic goodness of the kids. There was much less preparation in these latter programs because there wasn't time or ability for co-planning. So in effect we were much more reliant on the character and honor of the mentors to be great models.

In fact I set up the Destinations mentor model program with a couple teachers, based on what I learned in attending a seminar given by Richard Curwin; ours was to be a joint venture between Destinations Academy and the AIMS program downstairs. In this informative, fun, and enlightening seminar, Mr. Curwin presented alternative methods for dealing with alternative students. He had some amazing ideas, activities, and thoughts; he is a former teacher who now runs professional development trainings, offering teaching tricks, tips, and strategies, along with a set of philosophies that differs markedly from the norm. One of his mainstays is the concept of mentoring as an alternative to punishment. One of the difficulties with his teachings was that they center on and depend on a fact I think he took for granted. He is a very funny, charismatic, cool person. Also he is older, with lots of experience, and I think it would be hard to copy his model. One of his main philosophies was not using any kind of rewards or punishments, which makes things really difficult in education, though not impossible. He was all about setting up situations where students could try the social activities and other practices they had to learn, in order to succeed. The example he kept using was with basketball, that it would make no sense to expect someone to learn how to shoot baskets, without letting him practice shooting first. So we need to give students activities that give them opportunities to practice the skills we want them to learn, by his ideas. The difficulty I had was that I think he mentioned using positive praise and that really is a form of reinforcement, but he was still excellent; I enjoyed his session greatly while I was there.

One of his suggestions that, apparently I implemented, was his "mini-mentor" program, as I now call it. In this program, when a student does something wrong which normally gets some kind of punishment, you send them to be a mentor. I tried this program while I was upstairs teaching at Destinations Academy, and I modified his program because I didn't want to force students to be mentors. I thought that could be unfair to younger students: if the mentor students, being in a bad situation, are forced to be mentors, they might head there with a really bad attitude, and then spread their bad situation to those younger than them who it's easy to pick on. The modification I made, which is based on one of the founding principles of this book, was that I would give them a choice. In this case one option was the standard consequence, which might be going to the principal's office, calling parents, or detention or something like that. The second option, which I always hoped they would pick, was that they could choose to be a mentor for some amount of time, like an hour or more. I think we only did it a few times with a few students, because there were too many logistical difficulties. The times it we did it, though, it worked well for our students; all the students who went to AIMS had a great experience. They came back raving about the feeling of accomplishment they had, how much they had helped, and even the fact that they would like to do it again, maybe for credit if possible. It was very cool to see it succeed given our limited circumstances and abilities; like I said, it was organic, based on the goodness of kids. But the difficulties from the administrative end were too large; we didn't have the proper resources to address them. We firstly had to coordinate with AIMS to find a setting and time for pairs to work together; the AIMS program was being taught by the teacher who had been the Destinations Math Teacher. This mentoring program really put the burden on him, and it turned out to be too much, since there wasn't enough supervision. He was getting an extra student to take care of, and a trouble student at that, and I completely understood his point and the difficulty with this program. A teacher has to have a very clear and specific connection to mentors where the communication can be subtle and there can be no misfiring because, as I said before, other students are at risk, and there's little room for play.

By its very nature this Harding Learning Center building, which housed Destinations, as well as all the alternative programs in Coos Bay, was really a model of modeling. There were eight different programs all going on in that one building at one time, (two floors plus a basement cafeteria/game room). One of the many things that made it so interesting was that the teachers and the students were always modeling when they were in the building. This was going on pretty much every minute of the day, and for all different ages, since we literally had babies up through 21 year olds learning in the same building. Everyone was really on stage all the time needing their best game. I think the only ages missing were kindergarten through fourth grade, so you had to realize all the time it wasn't like you were only dealing with teenagers or middle school students or any specific age group. There was every age group there, so everyone was a model for someone younger than himself or herself. I suppose the only exception might be the babies tooling around in their carriages who weren't really modeling for anyone else, except for their modeling to the rest of us how to be pure, if you want to get philosophical. There was always something exciting in that building; it was always in motion and there was a lot of connection between all the different programs; it was a special building in which to work; it was ace.

One of the programs offered in that building which I discussed earlier was and is the Teen Parent Program. This program is what the title implies, which was always a little weird to me, and I wasn't even as religious, but it was just funny with the dads leaving class to go help with their children downstairs. The weirdest thing was just seeing girls with babies walking around the building and what that taught to younger students in the building, if they thought that far, which they did. Combined with the efforts of those teen parents to finish high school; it was quite a range of emotions and politics and realities blended into a program. The most interesting thing, though, was that once, there was an article in the local newspaper, <u>The World</u>, about someone who had been keeping an alligator in their bath tub, and that the alligator had gotten loose, and was out and about on the Coos Bay Peninsula. So the funny part of the story is, it turns out, it was apparently one of our students in the Teen Parent Program. Seemingly, a baby for a teenager was not enough entertainment for that family; (it may have been her mother, father, or siblings who really owned the alligator); apparently they needed something more stimulating around a baby to help its development along, like a large predator reptile.

We had varying models of the mentoring-modeling program in Coos Bay and that worked out pretty well, and had its ups and downs. I don't think there was ever an official program, per se, but we managed it and pulled it off regardless. Going out of time sequential order, which might bother some of my readers, the first modeling program I instituted in that building was during my AIMS/IPASS instruction, (there may have been other mentor modeling programs before I got to that building). I would have AIMS middle school students before lunch and then I would have IPASS high school students after lunch. I had some high school students, who, after having been with me for a while, wanted to come in the morning and work with middle school students. I thought it a great idea: these high school students did something positive for younger students, and gained in their self-images from that experience. Younger students benefitted from having a cool older model, who helped them with work and showed them better paths to choose. This reinforced for older students these were the right paths they would need to stick to, especially if they wanted to continue being role models in other classes.

The first student to do this was the same first high school student I had in IPASS, the one who came to "interview" me. He was a good student with a great heart, and was with me from the first day of school, on board the whole time, and had nearly perfect attendance. At a certain point he asked about coming in the morning to help out: I think it was towards the end of the first year, and I checked with the principal and all systems were go, so we went ahead with it. It worked great and his attendance was excellent; the kids really liked having him there. I liked it; there was really never a time where I felt like I had an extra student to watch out for, which is a risk inherent in mentor programs: that you might have another body to take care of in class. A mentor program should make things better, smoother, and easier for a teacher, period. It generally worked well and I had no complaints. As time went on I had at least two other students that became mentors as well. One of them worked well, and was more of a quiet leader and an extra body, whereas the first boy was always involved with everything going on. He really and truly wanted to help out and very much wanted to help the kids to become their best selves, and help them make good choices. The second quieter student was more of just a presence there which was actually easier for me to maintain, but may not have had the same impact on the younger students.

The third student though, was a different story; he later became the "dark rider" who had little to believe in himself about. I could start to see those tendencies coming out when he was trying to be a mentor, and he was starting to lead younger students in the wrong direction. I had to stop him from being a mentor, and that's awkward because, when students ask to do this program they're going out of their normal boundaries a bit and reaching out to the teacher to try to be a better person. Regardless, this student just wasn't cut out for it: he was being a negative model for the students, and causing them more trouble than they already had by trying to lead them in the wrong direction. I think he had trouble keeping the lines between being a mentor and being a friend and was more concerned with them liking him and thinking he was cool, than being a positive influence on them. It probably has to do with self-image and self-esteem. While the experience might have been good for him in the long run, I could not afford to take the risk with the damage it could do to younger students, because that is not fair to them. So I had the difficult conversation with him, ended his time as a mentor, and moved on. It was not so easy to do, but without a doubt, it wouldn't stop me from doing a similar mentoring program again.

17
BE PATIENT

Patience is another of those essential skills that I give as an answer in interviews in describing my best qualities as an educator, and I think it usually comes up as my first and most important quality. Students and children need patience from their teachers and parents on so many levels and in so many ways in order to succeed. Of course there are some students who are naturally bright and brilliant, and they will understand things on their own for the most part; they may not require so much patience since they will succeed whatever circumstances may be. For the majority of the population, however, patience is your best ally, and sometimes the hardest skill to acquire, hone, and manifest. The forerunner of patience is really a sense of cool, calm, and chill, and not being in such a rush to do what you think you have to do. As teachers we have tons of deadlines, pressures, and demands that need to be met, and the list keeps growing and the chores and tasks keep getting piled on us. Ultimately, though, when you're in the classroom, especially with challenging children, they want to know you are not going to give up on them. They need to develop a sense of trust which will foster self-confidence. Self-confidence is a difficult quality to lack; if we wish to give them this most beautiful gift, we have to be patient. Patience allows them to ask questions; it allows them to be wrong; it allows them to think, to wonder, and to grow.

The easiest way to check your patience level and to develop it is in dealing with questions you pose, and in dealing with questions students and children pose. In the ideal, you want to encourage them to think and ask questions. If they are asking questions then they are curious, and they want to learn; that is really the most important skill you can teach. In my first position as a teacher, in Jefferson, I had one word written in cool bright big letters on the front of my desk: "Learn". Students need to be comfortable and confident if they are going to learn. Learning generally comes along with asking questions: whether from teacher/parent or from students/children, that's how you know what is being absorbed by students. It is the most basic unit or form of assessment: you can tell what they learned by asking them questions, and you can tell what they learned by the questions they ask. Try to get them to reach out to you and seek knowledge so they have ownership of it; knowledge is not and should not be something simply thrust upon them from above which they are meant to take in robotically.

Always use the ten second rule when you ask a question. After you ask a question, wait ten seconds and DON'T SAY ANYTHING! This works with a parent as well, if you really want to hear an answer from your child, whether it's about what they learned in school that day or any other range of topics. You could even wait for 30 seconds, and that will feel like an eternity. It is tempting to fill the void and silence with little comments, but you must resist the temptation! Let the silence happen and LET THEM THINK! You can vary it as low as ten seconds or as much as a minute or more but when you ask a question you better give them time to answer it. Otherwise, who are you really asking? If I was dictating this book I would wait ten seconds after that question. This is a rule I learned in my graduate program: when applied, it seems awkward at first, but it works like a charm. Some of the best and most creative answers will come from some of the quietest and most unsuspecting students, if you can "hold on" a little longer: give them the time they need to think and answer. This is a wonderful and simple trick.

If you're waiting for a long time, and you have counted the time in your head, and there is no answer, then at that point you might prod them a little: encourage them to take a guess, tell them there are no wrong answers. Usually, though, if you wait long enough, students will get more uncomfortable from the silence and someone will speak up and answer, if for no other reason than to break the silence. We are trying to teach the students how to think, speak, and problem solve, among other paramount skills. Most of us, in our mental pictures, confine problem solving in academics to math, but such is not the case; the skills involved in thinking and problem solving in math are not mutually exclusive from those in the other disciplines. So let them think and solve problems! They need to learn guessing and estimating and making suggestions in testing their answers. They need to be willing to be wrong in front of others. Patience allows, fosters, and encourages courage to grow. Trying is the only way to do that, and when we give them these opportunities, they strengthen this skill. Sometimes, on the other hand, they handle the silence very well, for what seems like a long time and no one speaks, and it seems like it might be too hard of a question. In that case I occasionally give students a stronger lead, or direct them by asking the question in a different way, or give them choices to choose from, ask them what they think, generally lead them down the road to the answer and the truth. I try to give them the least amount necessary to get them to think and answer more on their own. It's tempting to help them more to get them to speak, but try to keep your ideas to a minimum; they need to have ownership of it to digest it.

18
CHOOSE YOUR BATTLES

It's hard for me not to choose to battle. The best advice I got on this was from my supervisor in West Orange High School, who told me to choose my battles with regard to my cafeteria duty I had for the first two years. I never had cafeteria duty before I worked there and it was a bit hectic supervising 250 kids whose names I didn't know, by myself; these kids had too much time to eat, in a giant senior cafeteria which held double that amount of students. I'm of the mind that if a battle comes my way, I fight it, if it's the right thing and for the right. What I had to realize, and the main point of this lesson to realize, is that you have to have your mental health and sanity when you're in these situations, and if you don't have that, you won't be able to apply all of the other lessons I've listed here effectively. When I told her about something that happened in the cafeteria and she gave me that response, I had a surprised feeling about it at first, and then I realized that I didn't get a Master's Degree in Education to supervise 250 kids in a cafeteria who I didn't know. There was but the slightest degree of education going on there. It was large group babysitting, and the key in my situation there was letting it go, and not forcing myself to control everything going on in the entire cafeteria of 500 kids. That was a good case of choosing a battle, which really means choosing not to battle; I can do it when I put my mind to it.

Sometimes it's not worth the fight. For me it doesn't come often, but there are times to let it go. Generally, I don't like leaving things alone, and if someone starts something in the wrong direction that needs correcting, I like to finish it the right way. I like that everyone involved knows the conclusion, and figuring out who's right and wrong, and what's right and what's wrong. Then we all learn. There are all kinds of fluffy statements about peace and love and not fighting and all that stuff. Mind you, I'm all for peace, but peace needs to be present side by side with justice, or else it will not last, and it's not true peace. A brutal dictator might maintain peace among his people by instilling fear based on persecution and violence; that might keep the people peaceful, as in not revolting, but that is obviously not a real peace, and as Syria shows right now, as nearly the entire Middle East has shown in the last few years with the Spring Uprisings, this "peace" will not last. It must be just in order to be true peace.

I used to tell my students to try and catch me being wrong; at least I did that in Oregon, where the students had a pretty light sense of humor and the school and government weren't pressing down on us from every angle and with every force imaginable. Those students in Oregon could handle a task of correcting me in a *respectful* manner, and I could handle being corrected, (though inside I sometimes didn't like it, I didn't necessarily let that show). One of the other teachers even called me quietly on it once, and a couple times to the class, something to the effect of how "Mr. Miller is never wrong", and like I said, it's OK to be wrong; it's just easier as a teacher not to be! With the Jersey kids I don't tell them to try and catch me being wrong, because they're always looking with the most watchful eye anyway. They need no encouragement in this arena; plus, their method of telling a teacher he is wrong is not so kind and friendly. It is a skill they are still honing, though I saw it done well a few times in my third year at West Orange by one or two students. There is a time, a place, and a manner in which to correct, however, and I'm cool with any time and any place for a correction, as long as the manner is appropriate. This basically means that the correction be done with a level head, and respectfully, which is the thing that the New Jersey kids usually get wrong. Incidentally, this is why they miss a lot of opportunities to catch me being wrong. If they would catch me being wrong and call me on it in the right manner, I would fess up instantly. New Jersey kids, though, like I said, (understandably), are so serious about education and getting their credits and grades, that it's hard to have fun with that aspect of it. It's a tough state, and you have to go after your stuff tough, and I understand them in that respect.

Choosing battles for me sometimes involved these situations where I turned out to be wrong, much as I don't like to admit to those events taking place. So when I am wrong, I like to make a show of it, and laugh about it, so that students can see that it's alright for it to happen and that it's OK to be wrong. In the end, though, like I said, and in real life, it's just easier not to be wrong, so I work real hard at that. This generally comes easier when I pause before speaking, think to myself, and then I am less likely to make a mistake. I think that is a pretty solid rule to follow, and it really brings a much greater degree of accuracy, truth, logic, and correctness, which are great traits to have and to demonstrate as a teacher or parent. I will have to try and think of more scenarios where I chose not to battle, but I have a feeling they are few and far between. Thank G-d I still have a strong will and seek to stand strong when a discussion of right and wrong is on the table, and if something is wrong, I work hard to correct it. This was a tough chapter for me to include, and I think you can get a read on the reason for that in getting to realize the kind of person I am. I clearly remember one time though that I chose not to battle.

I was walking down by the Coos Bay Library, and there was a student there by the library who wasn't even in my class. At this point I was teaching AIMS and IPASS downstairs; it was my first or second year in Coos Bay, and I had started a music class where high school students could earn credit in music. The amount of flexibility, control, and authority I had in issuing credits while in Coos Bay is slightly staggering. Regardless, I knew I had musicians in the class, I was playing guitar more, I had an extra bass guitar, and I had bought a guitar for $2 at a garage sale, so I figured I would try hosting a music elective in the later part of the afternoon for my high school students. It went pretty well mostly, and then students started coming down from upstairs, from Destinations when they heard about this music class, they wanted in. At that time Destinations was much more unstructured, and the students pretty much did what they want when they wanted with whom they wanted, and when two or three students asked to come down and join the music class, I said it would be alright as long as they followed class rules, which, for them, basically meant they could not cuss the way they did up in Destinations. They had a much shorter leash, so to speak, than anyone else, as well, since they were guests in my class, and I wasn't about to have them influence my students in a negative way, when I was voluntarily taking extra students into my classroom. I was willing to have them if they behaved excellently. My class was full enough; I certainly wasn't about to keep them there if they added problems to the mix; who needs that?

This reminds me of a "Seinfeld" episode, where Kramer gets a job. He goes in to work every day, even though he never got hired, with a briefcase full of crackers, and sits at a desk and doesn't do any work, just to feel like he's being productive; he says he likes the structure that has been lacking in his life. In the end, the boss ends up firing him, and Kramer points out the fact that he doesn't even really work there, to which the boss replies, "That's what makes this so difficult". So when I was down at the library, one boy who was in my class for the music credit was down there; he technically wasn't in my class. I had sent him back upstairs recently due to the fact that he couldn't keep his mouth clean and wouldn't deal with that issue at all. So he saw me, while he was riding his bike, and yelled out something along the lines of "_____ you Mr. Miller!" So on one hand I thought it ironic that while cussing me out he still addressed me properly as "Mr."; on the other hand, I thought four additional things. Firstly, there's not too many positive directions a conversation like that can go when I'm not on the clock, and he doesn't have to really listen to me. Secondly, this is my "off-duty" time and I don't need to correct this kid when I'm not getting paid for it, (though I might do the deed for one of my own students). Thirdly, this is not even my student, so I don't even owe him the courtesy of a reply; fourthly, anyone who says something like that in public that doesn't earn a reply. Those were roughly my rapid thoughts, and I chose not to fight that battle. I hope you see the connection to the Kramer incident. It made things pretty awkward, especially for him, when I saw him in the hallway the rest of the year because he knew he was wrong. The following year, though, when I had him in Destinations, I gave him a fresh shot and let the past wash away. Mind you this was the dark rider I spoke of before who I almost forgot he was a dark rider. I would think he was probably nervous around me for a while, I know I would have been if I had done something like that. Then again, I wouldn't have talked to a teacher like that.

19
USE PROJECTS AND JOURNALS

This is one of the easiest concepts to define and teach, and that might be a relief for the reader, who this late in the book, has heard several times how difficult some of these methods are to teach, (though that doesn't mean they are as difficult to learn!) In the olden days, journals were just free-writing about any topic that interested the writer, which is what I did for journaling when I was in high school. In fact, it was journal writing in Mrs. Fischer's high school junior English class which got me into writing poetry; to this day that helps me in writing songs. And the poetry that I wrote which helped me through my teen angst years till my 30's, is some pretty heavy stuff which will possibly serve as the core of my fourth book, which I cannot believe I am already pondering. Journaling is probably one of the things which as much as anything, got me to enjoy writing, and brought me to the point of writing a book. But even those journals were more focused; they weren't necessarily just free writing, which, at the minimum, is still a useful skill and a great tool for allowing and encouraging students to express themselves. It was and is a useful skill, and helped me to clarify thinking and writing skills for sure. I highly recommend offering some kind of credit for students keeping an independent journal at home. I have used journals in pretty much every class I taught, though they have varied greatly in their tone, purpose, and nature. Similarly, I have had projects available and/or mandated in pretty much every class I taught. Both of these tools and skills are of the greatest importance for students and children in our quest to prepare them as successful and productive citizens of the future. The types and models of journals and projects vary greatly and I will try to give some scope and breadth to the variety of both, though the emphasis will be on projects, which are much harder to implement, because journals don't take much doing at all.

The journal which I had my students write in Coos Bay, in Destinations, was prompted. I photocopied a journal sheet every four days, and that went in orange folders which they kept with them. I used <u>Daily Starters, Journal of the Day</u>, (Appendix I). This set of journal prompts is engaging and exciting for students: elementary through high school, I have seen it work well with all. There are six subjects making up the book's journal prompts and they are science, health, history, career awareness, people/social skills, health/sports, and the arts. It is fantastic. In the beginning of the year students did not want to write at all. I mandated that they write one to two lines per day. I told them that people writing more than the minimum would get extra credit and that worked well to inspire writing for some. The second term I upped the game, and told them that they would have to write three to four lines.

In the third term I told them I was upping the bar again and they would have to fill the journal space which was five or six lines. I was always ready for the complaint of having to do more and more, and I was not sure what I was going to answer, because truly, they were doing more work for the same credit. But we don't want our students to remain stagnant: we want them to grow, strengthen, and improve, and I think they realize that. The students must have seen the fairness aspect of it as well. I doubt they knew that this was part of the concept of value added assessment, to include improvement as a component in assessment. I think they did understand, though, that the general goal in education is to strive, improve, move forward, achieve, and grow. We as teachers include improvement as a part of their grade, and maybe for this reason I never heard a complaint. It is things like this which give me continued hope for Generation X.3, a term I coined that someone else said as well, I'm sure. We were Generation X back in the 90's; these students are very different from us, with technological innovations and all; every five years I say they add another tenth to the "X"; now maybe they are Generation X.5.

Some of the best journaling I saw was in Destinations, and the kids wrote some great stuff. For our purposes I wanted to get positive social and philosophical discussion going from their thoughts on these prompts. Getting students to share journals publicly was sometimes like pulling teeth, because you couldn't necessarily reward it properly. You couldn't force students to share; they had to open up and trust. Also, there wasn't necessarily the obvious credit reward for this particular task they were used to working for; it was like a micro-version of the project-based learning in that respect. I thought this the sharing of journals to be one of the most interesting phenomena. I had to be very clever and open minded here. In the beginning, everyone shared voluntarily. Somewhere along the line a student did not want to share their journal on one particular day, and I allowed that. The goal was to get students comfortable sharing ideas, thoughts, and beliefs that were important to them. If I was too rigid in making them share, it would seem like a consequence or punishment, which was the last thing I wanted. Writing the journal, in my mind, was the easy part; though I still had to circulate and make sure students were working and not ignoring the task, which was sometimes the case. These kids were great slackers.

Then the fun system was that we would ask for a volunteer to start and whoever started we would go clockwise from that person. We always had a volunteer, even if I had to wait a little or encourage a little. Probably the first day was the trickiest but it didn't take long to get a volunteer. Students actually enjoyed sharing their journals, though they might not have freely admitted it. I came up with a good system for the one(s) who flat-out refused. This was the case with one of our new students who just said she wouldn't do it. I asked her if it would be alright for someone else to read it for her and that was OK for her. I think at first she had a friend read it for her and then I volunteered to read students' journals for them and they were more OK with that. It became a regular routine; as part of the circle of people reading, I included myself. I would read my own journal, along with several students who gave me theirs to read. When it was my turn, I read mine mixed with theirs. I remember a student telling me once they could tell mine because of the vocabulary and the like. I always tried to make my vocabulary more "kid-like" after that to fool them in not figuring which was mine. I never heard if they knew or not, which is a good thing. That solved the problem of the student(s) who didn't feel comfortable sharing. I was always extra on guard when people were sharing, to make sure that no one was talking. I think so many people are afraid of public speaking because they don't think people want to hear what they have to say, and I needed to create a safe environment for people to speak their minds. The students generally knew the parameters of what was acceptable and appropriate or not, and they respected these boundaries. Only occasionally did someone go too far, and then a teacher would correct them.

One of the best ways to empower students is through project-based learning, so in theory this discussion could go under a chapter about giving students and children choices, or any other number of topics in this book. Projects have a host of benefits and really mix in a lot of positive ingredients. Even at home, parents can have their children take on projects. To me, the most notable aspect of a project is that it takes place over a period of time, like at least a week, and usually more like a month, a few months, up to a year or longer. This helps students and children think long term and become more mature; anything around the home that requires this period of time for its completion would be good to get kids working on. Even if it's something like keeping track of weather changes, planting a series of plants and watching them grow, keeping track of song play repetition on the radio, or a child tracking their own game, computer, or social website time usage during the differing days of the week. There are limitless possibilities to what defines and makes a project. It might be helpful to do an internet search based on your or your child's particular interests or needs if you don't find inspiration from here.

This is becoming a more common mode of instruction and education in all parts of the school system but I feel it most essential in our alternative arena. There are many exciting facets in this type of learning and oodles of books on the subject, but I will just give a rough outline of what I see as the most pertinent benefits of project-based learning for alternative education students. Firstly as mentioned is the fact of ownership. Whereas most assignments are given to students in a preset format for them to insert answers or answer questions or whatever the case may be, in a project, the student decides the format, structure and presentation of the product. I will say that on the other hand the teacher has the right and option, and really has the need to establish his own guidelines for the project and means of assessment, if something real and assessable is to be created. There is a great range of flexibility in this area and it is up to the teacher to determine his own parameters. I will discuss my own parameters and what worked for me as a teacher but that is by no means a final answer. But it can hopefully serve as a rough framework to give a general picture of what this type of learning scenario looks like in practice.

Another advantage to project-based learning is the adaptability and real life experience it offers. I realize fully that I have stated previously the advantage of teaching students to "listen to the boss" in the respect of respecting boundaries, and how firm a teacher and parent needs to be. On the other hand, students entering the business world, going into business for themselves, and going into a host of other situations, will be expected to problem solve, work on projects, and think creatively to find solutions. These skills are not generally taught by standard instructional techniques. Project-based instruction hones these skills, along with the ability to work in an unpredictable environment with new and challenging endeavors and sometimes different kinds of people. These problems, unlike standard assessments which generally have a predetermined structure, format, and time period, generate their own guidelines in these aspects. Students must take the scope of the project into account and make their own estimates of how long the project will take, what type of structures they will need to utilize to make the project a reality, create a time line for its implementation, and plan and create a format for research, study, presentation, and documentation. In doing so the student becomes a responsible learner who is engaged in his education with a desire to answer questions, and accountability to meet his own guidelines, deadlines, and parameters instead of ones predetermined from above.

The most exciting part of this type of learning for me is that which wholeheartedly addresses the deepest needs of students like the Dark Riders, and all other kinds of alternative students who don't necessarily learn well in the standard structure and environment. Their needs need to be met as well. The hardest thing to do with the Dark Riders is to bring out something light, to find something good, and to get them to be enthusiastic about something constructive, because generally their excitement is towards that which is negative. Usually their responses, as I mentioned, are mostly geared as reactions to that which is established; they are anti-establishment, which is fine. But that doesn't say what they are for, only what they are against, and they are generally negative in that direction and respect. So a teacher can engage a student like this with a project, and says, "Alright, what do you want to learn about? What are you interested in?" Then all of that negativity is forced to disappear. Now one might worry about some of the topics chosen by such students, but again, the topic choice is ultimately under the direction and authority of the teacher who has every right to say "no". I found it easier, and more proper in such cases of doubt, to run through higher channels of authority, like administration.

There were really not too many projects I had to reject, and those that I wasn't sure about I told the student I would ask the principal and whatever she said, we would go by. Generally what I did, actually, in that scenario, was to have students prepare an initial proposal for her and submit it to her. The same was the case when students wanted money from school for parts of their projects, and this worked very well, even when proposals were rejected, because these channels are how things work in the real world, and students recognize and accept the validity of this. Also they enjoyed the challenge of really getting involved in their own education and going straight to the top to make something happen. I thought it important to involve my principal on such matters because I knew these projects were going to be displayed publicly, and if parents, other administrators, or regular people came in asking questions, I knew it was my principal who was going to have to answer for them. So I figured she should have jurisdiction in questionable decisions. I had a great relationship with her and we really were a team.

What I discovered with project-based learning when I tried to show other teachers how to guide students is that a teacher really needs to be open to education and learning from different subjects. Students will come up with all kinds of things they want to study, and with students like Dark Riders, the topics are generally going to be dark. Often students will want to do projects on drugs. Now I got a little strict in this area because if the project is going to be on our walls or in our halls, it needs to be school appropriate. So when I did allow students to do a project like this, I was very closely monitoring how the final output was going to be presented. I put a heavy emphasis on the fact that we had younger students in the building who were still in middle school who would be reading this information. So it would need to be presented in a manner that aimed toward dissuading people from doing the researched drug. I was always wondering if I would get strong reaction about that from students. I was always waiting for it too, something along the lines of free speech or censoring type argument, but I never got it that kind of guff. I think the students knew the boundaries here and I was always impressed that I didn't have to have the free speech discussion on this topic. It showed me that students knew, or were learning, how far they really could go with something, and how far they really should go. I mean, it is one thing for your teacher to let you do a project about a drug, and students should appreciate that; it's another thing to argue with that teacher about the parameters he imposes. I guess they knew deep down if they really wanted to address health issues I had plenty of alternatives for them I could have suggested to them, starting with a project on a connection between childhood obesity and fast food.

The Destinations students really knew they were going to have to do a project one way or another, so they might as well have picked something they would enjoy. Now how I got them to do the projects was another story all together, but it is relevant. On one hand kids love projects, they get into it, they can pick what they learn about. But on the other hand, this is a term-long or year-long ordeal with less than clear boundaries and guidelines; and this type of thing can be overwhelming. True, students enjoy this type of freedom. But the same students who mock the system that presents question/answer, true/false, and matching tests, really crave and cling to this type of education with clear and defined boundaries and expectations. But here, we break them of those chains, and set new ideals for abilities.

The idea for the first project actually completed by a student came from a suggestion from the teen parent teacher, on the history of how football teams got their names; it was an idea she got watching football over the weekend. It was the fall, hence football season, and she got to wondering where one of the teams got its name, and she put forth the idea to students as a project researching the history of how football teams got their names. One of our students got interested in the idea and ran with it. He found every team and wrote a little summary. He then made a large map of the United States on butcher paper and labeled all the teams with strings connecting them to cards describing the history of the naming. He put it on the bulletin board in our meeting room where it was seen by students every day, so no one could ever say a project couldn't be completed in one term, since he did it in much less than time than that. Once that project was done the whole system was flying, because his project was a success. He was super proud of his work, and rightfully so; he beamed from miles away about it, and from being the first one to finish a project, and the project shined. All the projects shined. I think that project still hangs in the meeting room and should until the building is demolished, as should his Great Stellated Dodecahedron, (to be discussed); or I like to dream it to be so. He was also the first to complete the Dodecahedron project; his project hung in the entrance to the Harding Learning Center.

Once this student got the ball rolling with his football project, it still took a little while for the next project to get done, but throughout the year I could certainly notice a consistent acceleration in project completion and a constant improvement in their presentation. It was just like the confidence built into students with Jeopardy; students see others guess and be wrong. They see it's OK and then they try themselves and that's how they learn and grow. In this case too, students needed to see someone doing something fun, interesting, and not perfect, and get credit, praise, and achievement for it. The kids were petrified to try a project; it seemed so big, open, and unlike the standard handed out assignments with due dates and percentage grades they were used to. No one would volunteer to start a project until this boy broke the ice. By the end of the year, though, we had a lot of projects getting done and most of my afternoons after midday meeting were spent working with students on their projects, checking their progress, signing their credits for work they had done. We really had a production house going there. The evidence still stands and will continue to stand, I believe; we have a closet full of completed project posters and completed research projects that forever serve as education decoration for the halls and wall and will hopefully continue to grow. I hope they're still there!

The more specific, defined, and targeted type of projects involved the projects we did within my science class in Destinations, which took place within the regular classroom rotation. I had at least one project per term that involved math and or science and I did this for several reasons. One was to get students more comfortable doing project type work, and to improve their skills in a more controlled environment where I could work with them daily and help them get the feeling of working on something long term and seeing it to fruition. This built their ability to sustain attention in a manner necessary to complete a project that would take an entire term or year, instead of a few weeks or a month. Being that I had control of the curriculum, I made sure to keep the project a regular weekly activity that we would revisit in a dosage that didn't seem to painful or difficult. What I found with these projects was that some students, even those who had complained about the projects upon first hearing about them, ended up enjoying these projects and even asking to do more for extra credit, which was nice to hear.

One type of project we did in science class came out of, or evolved from the Geo-kit, which was when we designed a human body with all major organs on butcher paper. Each class made their own body, and these hung in one of the classrooms till the end of the year. For this project, each student studied and completed detailed research on their chosen organ and then placed a drawing of it properly on the butcher body, so we had a really educational, team-created product. This was no elementary art body project; these were detailed and technical analyses of organs which students really put lots of work into.

Another project-based component of this science class was instituted towards the end of the year when we successfully linked up with the resource room teacher's community involvement programs. We connected mid-year with the salmon fishery project somewhat but not fully effectively. I told the resource teacher I needed to know ahead of time what the project was going to be so I could do adequate research ahead of that deadline, since I wanted to make it meaningful and relevant for the kids if they were going to do field work. In the third term that teacher gave me good preparatory time and notice for the invasive species work he would be doing with the community. We were therefore able to join as a team of classes and teachers and actively work together; we managed to do some really cool invasive species projects. We did this first as a class, in which we were researching the concept of invasive species with emphasis on the blackberry bush, which we would be working on with the resource teacher. We did this secondly with students working in smaller teams of their own choosing, in which they chose their own particular invasive species to research, study, and present a project on.

We were studying invasive species in the science class all term long. I got some exciting curriculum and activities for students to study and we worked on this regularly. This turned out to be a multi-level project. After studying the topic in depth enough that students had a thorough understanding of the material, I assigned them their own research project I mentioned last paragraph. This was a case where I allowed them to work in teams of two if they preferred, and they were to pick an invasive species, research it, and find out critical information such as where it came from originally, how and when it got to Oregon, how it could be eradicated, and how it was harmful to humans. There were ten research components in all which students were supposed to research and present findings on in a format of their choice, such as a poster, which is what most chose. This type of project turned out generally more uniform in its final production, in that most of the final formats were similar, but color and style on the posters varied great; that was fine. We got some really great information presented in neat designs.

The really fun part of this whole study was that when we finished the unit, the students went on a trip with the Resource Teacher to a community location that had been overrun by blackberries, which are one of Oregon's most invasive non-native species, (even though they taste delicious). They spent the day cutting down the plants, but with a much greater understanding of how they were really helping the community, the environment, and the state, as they especially learned from one student who chose blackberries as his research project for this study. The students truly got involved; it was easy to see them enjoying themselves and thinking of themselves as project-based learners and problem solvers. The project was amazing and students got a lot out of it, especially because they were learning both in school and out of school, and going out into the field to get rid of an invasive species, namely blackberries! This project was also inspired by www.unitedstreaming.com, which our district subscribed to, and which my current district subscribes to; if you haven't used it, I highly recommend it. It has thousands of videos on every topic and every subject, organized extremely well. Many videos come with entire teaching lessons, plans, and information. You can search easily for videos about a topic by grade, subject, field, and you can even search for videos with accompanying lesson plans and quizzes.

Like I mentioned earlier, one of the hardest things in that school with respect to projects, was getting the first one done, and in general that's always going to be the trick of getting individual projects developing. Before the first one was complete I don't think students really believed they could get credit for doing work on something they were really interested in. I spent many days reminding students to work on projects and sitting with them individually after lunch to check their progress. Surely there was a substantial amount of work that got done in the afternoons, but there was also a good bit of goofing off. That's because there was no accountability in terms of monitoring what students had to produce in what amount of time, and what they would have to show for proof of completion. Rather than work, for students it often became a social hour. The English teacher devised a neat system of students turning in evidence of what they worked on at the end of the day. It was a five day sheet he created; students would write down what work they completed in the day and what kind of research they did, and that sheet served as a model for one class project I led later in the year. It would work even better with a little modification, but it was fantastic that he saw a flaw and took the initiative to make an improvement in the situation, because a lot of project instruction is going to require creating and altering, modifying and improving. I think he got annoyed with his sheet or projects after a while; maybe it was that the students weren't working on projects as much as he hoped or expected. I think he stopped using the sheet and it petered out. The idea of afternoon monitoring was workable; it was an essential improvement for the program; it increase project productivity for sure.

The Great Stellated Dodecahedron was a perfect example of the difficulty in getting projects started, and it illustrates a few other interesting points about project-based learning. First of all, I found out that in doing this project and introducing the students to it, I made a mistake in informing, but more about that at the end of the paragraph. I made sure to do a class project at least once a term as soon as things were rolling in Destinations. For example, in the first term, we did the science project which evolved from the unit on the human body, as mentioned earlier: the butcher body. It involved art, and these alternative students enjoy art, and it is good to include art in as many activities as possible to keep them connected. And still I avoid talking about the Great Stellated Dodecahedron because I don't like to admit to mistakes. To this day I have only told maybe one person. Oh well, here goes. In the second term I decided it would be good to do a major math project. We had done a math project first term also, namely a negative space project, which was a math and art project. Actually it was more of an activity as opposed to a project, yet fun and interesting, and a good introduction and beginning to long term project work. In that case it involved construction of a picture using the concept of negative space. In this case for the second term, we needed to do a math project, and I told students they were going to make the Great Stellated Dodecahedron. I talked it up a lot, and got them excited about it, and that's a neat way to teach and catch student attention. Well, one of the interesting things with these kids is that even though they spurn and mock regular school, they at heart want to be smart and successful. So when I told them they were going to make these things that were a mandatory senior project in regular high school, (as opposed to alternative school which they were in), I saw their eyes light up with pride. I could tell that they wanted to take up the challenge I was putting forth to them, they were excited that they would be doing something that was a normal thing for everyone to do in their senior high school year; that they would be doing it as freshman, sophomores, etc., seemed huge to them; they got hyped.

The mistake which I successfully avoided admitting to for at least a half a page, I found out when I talked to my younger brother. Till this is read, the only person who knows my mistake: that it was actually sophomore or freshman year that we did this project in high school. It might have been a harder sell if it had been advertised that way, because there would not have been so much of a challenge to complete it. I may have told them it was an honors class I was in when I completed the Great Stellated Dodecahedron in high school, which it was, and that would have made the challenge that much more appealing. Regardless, it was a mistake, and I didn't tell them the newly discovered information, and it is one of those things that a teacher justifies to himself for the final goal and ends. The point is, I committed to the Great Stellated Dodecahedron, and I knew how hard it was. I spent my whole winter vacation of that year in high school at my grandparents' house doing that project; it was frustrating, yet rewarding. I knew it would be that much harder for these kids, even with a teacher coaching them.

Well it was still a hard sell: the hardest sell of the year. The Great Stellated Dodecahedron has twelve sides, and they are all pentagons, (Appendix D). From each pentagon extends a point. The goal is to make one of these behemoths from straws and string. At first I offered a choice they could do it out of paper instead, as we were offered in high school by the great Mrs. Ethel Newman, our geometry teacher. The problem with that was it was too abstract to think that way, to first decide what materials to make the thing out of. Plus I hadn't made one out of paper when I was in high school, and couldn't necessarily coach so well, so I went with the KISS mantra (Keep It Simple Stupid). This was like a repeat of the beginning of the year in this respect: the first one being completed led to other ones being completed, except in faster succession. You should have seen and heard the reactions when students actually understood what I was expecting them to do. I told them it was a mandatory project for the term and everyone was going to have to do it. That was the first time I said something like that, but they could tell I meant it. I didn't even know if anyone would be able to actually construct it, let alone the whole academy. It was a rather bold risk on my part, but I had confidence, and that works wonders.

Everyone got started on it and after a few straws they realized how hard it was, and that was when the complaining began. But a few of them persisted during the class period, and I decided not to argue for that day, because I wanted to just let them digest the fact of their having to do it and accept it. There was no use in repeating myself because I laid down the law and the facts. They knew I was for real and justified because I had been very fair, lenient, and understanding of everyone's strengths and weaknesses throughout the year. Pretty much up to that point if there was something someone really and strongly didn't want to do, I would let them out of it, provided they were on board with the class and program in everything else that was going on and that we were doing. But with this project there were no excuses, options, or outs. EVERYONE was doing this project, and I think it was a good unifying activity for the program, and certainly one of our better confidence builders. There really are some great stories that go along with the Great Stellated Dodecahedron. I will stick to the two best.

Like I said, just like the slow start with afternoon projects and how the silence was broken by one student, so it was with the Great Stellated Dodecahedron. That both streaks were broken by the same senior student affirms that this was a student with a determined and strong will, a bit of a stubborn streak, and a great sense of pride in certain things, like his own abilities. He realized off the bat I was throwing down the gauntlet in a challenge and also realized it was feasible but hard. He came back to me during the period after his class, when I had introduced the project, and said he was working on it in the other classroom, and wasn't going to stop until he was done. He insisted he would be the first one done, and his would be the best project. This boy was true to his word too. He checked in with me later that day; he had to get more straws because he ran out, and he wanted stronger straws for the points coming off the pentagons. He realized it was going to take him a few days, but he was still committed.

The funniest part was that after working on it for several hours and checking in with me we realized he hadn't tightened it at every corner and so the thing had no strength to it. The problem was that he had tied knots at every corner, so there was no undoing it and he realized he was going to have to do the thing again from scratch. He considered reworking it and I said he would spend more time reworking it than starting from scratch. I told him not to let his ego or connection to past work get in the way of logic and efficiency; he recognized that and destroyed it, and started again. He asked me around this time if he would be able to get extra credit for doing it first and the best and all that, and I said it was guaranteed. This is the main point of this story, that the pioneer deserves something special, and what I told this boy about why he deserved extra credit, is that he is bringing the whole program up with his leading effort, and showing the way. He was helping everyone else achieve, and that is a form of community service, but I did not tell him the last part. I did not even realize it is a form of community service until I wrote this. I knew he would be helping others by showing them how to do their own projects; that demonstrates high level learning on Bloom's Taxonomy, which is worthy of bonus credit.

He had a few minor set backs with the Great Stellated Dodecahedron. I think the best part of the whole thing was when one of the Teen Parent Moms hid the thing from him as a joke, he almost freaked. That cracked me up. Those teen parent girls were always pulling pranks on the boys. Well let me tell you, when this boy finished his Great Stellated Dodecahedron, it was awesome. Actually, I think someone else actually finished theirs first. That's because once this boy got into working on his project, he was able to coach others and get theirs started so that slowed him down. And most of the other kids just wanted to get the dodecahedrons done once they realized they were going to have to do them for real. This boy wanted his to be fantastic. It came out so cool. He used the regular straws we had for the inner part of the shape, the connected pentagons. But for the outer points, he used giant red straws you get from mini-marts for "slurpees". He bought a bunch of them with his own money because he wanted it to be so cool, (I think we reimbursed him, I hope!). I was proud and blown away when he finished it. It was so strong with such presence; and it was impressive: everything he said it would be.

We started hanging the completed dodecahedrons in class but we hung his right above the entrance to the building. The other ones were all taken at the end of the year down from the hallways' ceilings throughout the building where they were hung during the year. But that boy's Great Stellated Dodecahedron represents a threshold crossed for Destinations Academy. It was the first real and high academic bar set for Destinations Academy, which everyone in the program had to get over if they wanted to be part of the program. It stretched our limits as a program. Like I said, I really didn't know when I put this project on them if they would be able to do it. I took a chance. I didn't know what would happen if they said "no"; that possibility didn't enter my mind. I just went ahead with it like it was happening come what may. That's how you raise the bar, and that's how good projects get done.

The other interesting story with the Great Stellated Dodecahedron, among the countless cries, complaints, and whines I heard, only to be rewritten later as successes, was with what I consider our greatest success in the Destinations program, and that is one girl's general and complete improvement. There are many stories to be told with her success and achievement and participation but I will limit their recounting. The funny thing with this girl, or one of the funniest things, was that she was present and on time more than any other student in the program. In the beginning of the year she had the worst attitude toward math of anyone in the program, and maybe anyone I ever saw until or since then; she totally hated it and wasn't shy about telling me that. She wouldn't talk, never smiled, never got involved, and usually seemed depressed and unhappy during math class. But she always came to class, even though she would barely ever ask for help, and she always seemed to feel very awkward when I did try to help her of my own accord, like she really didn't want me there, which I could respect. I understand things could have happened for her that made a comfort issue, and I am a patient person.

When I put forth this Great Stellated Dodecahedron project, I knew the risks I was taking but, like I said, I didn't care. I knew everyone could do this project, because if they couldn't do it on their own, I would sit and work with them until they got the feel and the rhythm and the understanding for making it, until they got it going on their own. I gave the assignment in the beginning of the term and told them it was due at the end of the term, which was about three months. Students had different periods of work phases in how they would spend time on the dodecahedron. They had times they got burned out and when they would need a break, and some who just got into it and kept going until it was done. There are certain points in its construction when you recognize a pattern you can repeat, which makes it a bit easier for sure. Yet you still need pay attention to the general shape, because if you make a mistake, it means you have to take the string out of the straws and redo it, which no one wants to do at all.

The other points of transition of the project are at changing phases of construction. For example, you have the very first pentagon, five straws with a string running through all of them, tied off at the end. Then, from each of those straws extends another pentagon. Yet the two pentagons which are side by side, share a straw for a side. So for the second pentagon, you need only four new straws for its construction. For the third pentagon you need only three new straws, since it has one side from the base (first) pentagon, and one side from the second pentagon. It continues at three new straws for the fourth and fifth pentagons. There are some major pattern changes at the sixth pentagon, and at the seventh pentagon, a new pattern starts, until you get to the final pentagon, and connect it together.

That final pentagon is really just a matter of connecting the top row of five pentagons to each other, (they are the ones surrounding the top and bottom pentagons). Basically, there is a top and bottom pentagon, and two bunk-bed rows of five pentagons, sandwiched between the top and bottom pentagons. That is the Dodecahedron. I can't tell you how many students did that part of the project and thought they were done. I wish I realized early to keep a video recording of their reactions when they found out, but that wouldn't be nice (or legal). They thought I was joking when I told them there was more, that they still had to add the points to it. Most of them shockingly laughed, some got mad, but all persisted. At that stage of the process, you have to add to each corner of the pentagon a straw, which connects to the other new four straws coming from the corners of that pentagon, to a point. Then you have to run a string back down one of the straws; just do that eleven more times till you have twelve points coming off the twelve pentagons, and that is when it becomes stellated, easy-breezy.

This brings up an interesting point, because it only becomes "Great", technically, when you connect the points of the pentagons into further triangles. Until this point, I have been calling it a great stellated dodecahedron, and that's what I told the kids they were building. Apparently this was my "mistake" project, as I made not one but two of them in the course of it. The first I told already, if you can remember what it was; the second is that, in actuality, what we built was *only* a "(smaller) stellated dodecahedron". That was a mistake I made until writing this book, when I went and copied pictures of the behemoth and put them in the appendix. It is so great to me that I made such a big mistake that I need to repeat it to emphasize it. I made a big mistake, in math no less. My friend and former co-teacher from the teen parent program will get a great kick out of that one, doubtless. To reiterate, for a great stellated dodecahedron, you take your smaller stellated dodecahedron, which is what I described, and then make three sided pyramids with new straws, coming off the points of the pentagons. When we were in high school my teacher, Mrs. Newman, put the challenge out for us to complete this task, and must have teased us calling it great, and that stuck in my mind so much that I made the most public mistake in my career to date. I made two big mistakes on one project. Who said I was perfect?

The reason I have told you all these difficult details about the construction of this project, is so you can perhaps see the variety and plethora of places where a student could get confused, frustrated, and weary in dealing with a stellated dodecahedron of any sort. It also gives a good insight into how flexible a teacher has to be in accommodating for the differing skills, abilities, and patience levels of students in running project-based learning. Project-based learning is not easy but it's cool and rewards students greatly, but requires lots of monitoring, attention, and awareness. In this case I had to be very aware of where different students were with respect to the phases of this monster project, in order to keep them on track and keep them positive. The original point in this long winding tale was telling of this girl's improvement and success, in case you lost track. One of the interesting things with her was that she is an artist, and likes making jewelry. Many of the patterns and physical actions involved in making the Great Stellated Dodecahedron are similar to making jewelry, and I know this because I used to make many of the same kinds of necklaces and jewelry that she made, in my younger hippie days.

The jewelry comes out faster, though, once you know how to do it, and you can wear it and most people think it looks nicer, so there's more motivation to make it. Maybe Flavor Flav of "Public Enemy" fame would wear a Stellated Dodecahedron. But he's wacked out. Anyway, on the side, sometimes getting the string through the straw can be annoying. Plus it was so obviously a math assignment, which this girl was totally averse to, that it was no surprise after a couple of pentagons she gave up for the day. What surprised me was the next day she said she wasn't going to do it. There were assignments she had not turned in, and she had a way of quiet defiance about her, as in, she would sometimes not do the work or talk subversively with friends, but never in outright defiance. She never said that she refused to do an assignment; she was generally passive aggressive, but without the aggressive. I was kind of intrigued and in certain respects relieved that she said she wasn't going to do the project, because I like for people to know the full range of themselves and their emotions, and their possible responses in a situation. I don't like to think of a person as limited or cornered, and unable to say "no" if they don't want to do something. I mean, I'm not trying to raise a bunch of rebellious, rabble-rousing rioters, but people need to know their voice and need to be able to say "no", rather than just sneakily avoiding.

So at the times when she would say that she wasn't doing it I calmly reminded her it was a mandatory project. I reminded her twice or so, and then I let her vent about how dumb she thought it was or whatever, because I knew she knew it was mandatory. I also knew she just wanted to argue about it, and it is an art to know when someone wants to complain and argue about something, and when they have a genuine need for understanding, and this was a case of the former. I was curious whether I was going to be able to get her to do this thing, and I waited a while. It was a few weeks later, most of the other students had their stellated dodecahedrons done, and I knew by that point that she liked to be successful in what she did, she liked being a good student, and she liked positive praise. To that end, my compliments were effusive when students finished the projects, I sang their praises and meant it with true joy and zeal, because I knew how much effort, sweat, concentration, dedication, persistence, and most essentially heart, students had put into completion of that project. I praised them heartily for it.

Well, one day this girl asked me a question about the dodecahedron project, which showed she had interest again, and I saw my window for connecting to her in doing it. That was overcoming a major hurdle which I had not known if I would ever get to see. I sat with her, and another student helped her as well, and we just sat with her while she worked on it. I remember I would be sitting there right with her, not saying anything, just there in case she needed help and for support, and she would make a mistake and get so frustrated, and I would ask her if I could please help her, or if I could please put that string through that one straw; but you could tell she just wanted to do it herself and do the whole thing on her own; but everyone can use a hand from time to time. It was an amazing feeling to watch someone accepting help for the first time. It's kind of like opening up a channel to connection and to another person, and as I am writing this, I this skill of accepting help is one I should be willing to better in my life, if it is something that I see as such a good skill in others. Let's see if I really put that into effect.

Now this girl persisted, right through the end. And even in the points she had difficulty, she stayed with it and got it done and it came out great, and it was probably the accomplishment that stands out most in that year for me. For some reason, even compared to being the major force behind restructuring the entire academy, this stands out as a greater achievement; maybe this even stands as the premier evidence or pinnacle moment of the success of that program, or maybe because it was such an accomplishment of persistence, hard work, and education. I really think it was a major threshold crossed, and this girl is one of those people that had such a major impact on the program as a whole, and as our most consistently attending student, affected all others considerably. After giving her the award for

Student of the Year, I asked how she would handle being the lead senior girl next year; it was obvious that she would be in that position. She smiled; but that's not even the main point of this story.

The main point of the story comes shortly, be patient. We started hanging the Stellated Dodecahedrons in my classroom in a line near the bookshelf, and those first "shorties", which were smaller than the full size ones which took longer to make, and which were like the one I made, (to check my remembrance of construction, and to model for the students) mostly stayed in the class, while the larger ones were down in the hallways of the Harding Learning Center. For efficiency and speed's sake, in making mine, I cut the straws in half and used that as the length of the basic straw. So those came out, when done, about nine inches around. But when people started completing the full size ones, they needed a better display spot, and that's why we started hanging them downstairs, from the fluorescent lights, in front of the office. There were so many great things about that. It wasn't too long that we had a line of about fifteen of them, the big and small versions. It displayed pride, workmanship, and academics.

It was pride for Destinations, pride for the Harding Learning Center, and pride for the District. Most important to me it was pride of all the students in the building. I was especially proud of AIMS and IPASS, and though I wasn't teaching there anymore, I still had a connection to them, in not knocking down and/or destroying someone else's obviously difficult and careful work. I am sure that temptation was very great, and I have similar pride in the other students in the building once all those temptations were hung prominently in the hallway, where they walked every day. They were up for a long time. When I put them up I told students of the risk involved in hanging them up there: that someone could have a bad day and those were great targets for anger. All the students fearlessly put them up anyway, even with their names on them; this impressed me above all. The dodecahedrons hung up there straight throughout the second term and into the third. You would walk down the hall and see them in a line and it was really cool, like a cool illusion. They would all match up and sometimes if you looked at it the right way; it looked like there was just one there. There was never a thing done to them, never any negative comments, they just hung there gently as evidence of a turned around program and successful, happy, bright, learning, energetic students. Do you sense foreshadowing? Do you feel foreboding?

Hopefully you do. It was several weeks into the third term when "tragedy" struck. The girl, who had made the biggest turnaround in mathematics I have ever seen, was in a now-rare grumpy mood. She brought out instantly in our morning meeting that someone had wrecked her dodecahedron. I was in shock, but only half-believed it. I went down to look at it and realized she was not playing a joke on me. And she wasn't lying about it looking totally destroyed. If you understand the making of these things you understand that they are dependent on the whole structure for their stability. At least a third of the straws had been broken and the entire structure was flimsy. I studied it for a while, analyzing it, trying to come up with ways to cure it and/or fix it, and could not think of one and disheartened, returned to class. I promptly told the class what had happened, and offered up "super-credit" to anyone who could fix, and/or help to fix the project. I really wasn't sure how this would play out and had varying hopes.

The class responded empathetically, and offered sympathy, but we all knew we would need time to figure out what to do, if there was any solution at all. It was really one of the first difficulties in the program for which I had not a solution, and that's not easy for me to handle. I like to be able to fix anything, deal with anything, and solve problems. Anyone reading this story can catch a glimpse of how much work, heart, love, and hope had been put in this project. This girl's completing the Stellated Dodecahedron was honestly probably the biggest reach and effort and accomplishment of any student I had seen, in terms of surpassing her own expectations, which sounds funny considering the kinds of hurdles overcome and successes I have seen achieved, but this is the truth of the matter nonetheless.

We were determined, however, and we did not let these things get us down, and we moved on; I speak for teachers and students on this. I kept the project on the table and did not bring it up again, and let it linger, knowing the power of the team, the group, Destinations Academy, and the force of cohesion that had developed throughout the year. I maintained my hope and belief that something would work out somehow, and if not, well there would be time to worry about that later. To quote Kenny Rogers from *The Gambler*, "There'll be time enough for counting, when the dealing's done." We continued for a couple weeks; the girl was sad for a few days, and I paid extra attention to her, but not so much as to make it obvious or forced; she recovered and persisted with her work. I was impressed with her resilience, without a doubt. She must have garnered that from other students in the program. It was great to see that improvement: the girl I knew in the beginning of the year wouldn't respond so well.

She got her second boost and support from the same student who gave her support the first time she started this project. This boy was an interesting character all around, and perhaps he will have his dream house, complete with alligator-filled moat filled, and property guarded by lions, to keep the cops out, as he puts it. I detour to talk about this boy since he's so interesting; this may be a bit of a story. He is so laid back, that he's probably the most laid back person I have come across. He is funny: some people carry themselves in a way, that the world could fall over and it would not matter: he would keep trucking and doing his thing. He is positive, upbeat, bright, and moves at his pace no matter the case.

The only time I ever saw this boy trying to hustle (as in move quickly) was the night he was in for conferences, and his dad who owned the local head shop, was with him and sitting at the table with us. His dad was talking serious politics and more serious fishing with one of the other teachers in the program, and the boy just could not wait to get out of there; he seemed like he wanted to jump out of his skin. He kept hinting strongly to his dad and then saying, "Alright, dad, we get the point", anything to get his dad moving. To me, that was irony of ironies, this boy, who was so laid back and moving at his own pace despite what anyone said, trying to move someone else to do something. It was priceless. But to gaze at this boy's chill state in a different way, using an analogy I wrote earlier in the book, here goes: this country may be the most laid back country in the world, Oregon might be the most laid back chill place in this country, Coos Bay might be the most laid back place in Oregon, and Harding Learning Center is the most cooled out school in town. Destinations Academy is obviously the coolest program in the building. This boy was the most laid back person of the program, possibly ever to go through it. Picture a puffy kid grown up to high school age and size, but who's very fun to hang out with, and who still has rosy cheeks and a kid's bright, totally hopeful and optimistic attitude, who's friends with everyone and just wants to have fun. That's him: he's a person people really like to be around.

I needed to take that slight detour to describe him, but that is how it is with him. It is just that way. If you do not get it maybe someday you will, but if you don't get it you're probably moving too fast and didn't get this far in the book anyway. Remember the trail of this story? So this boy says to me one day in Math class, while the girl who's dodecahedron was destroyed is there also, (they had the same math class together), "Mr. Miller, how much credit did you say fixing her project would be worth?" I told him he could earn a quarter of a credit for fixing it. Even though the project itself was only worth a little less than a quarter of a credit, I knew it might take as long or longer to do it. Also, there was no set pattern or method for solving this problem, as there had been for making the dodecahedron from scratch, where I could direct students and aid them, and guide them offering tips, suggestions, ideas, and I always knew the direction the project needed to go. See, I thought about fixing her project myself, and did not see an easy way, but knew that my fixing it would not have the same value as a student fixing it. Even though the person might be helping based on the credit he would be earning, it was still real problem solving, and the kind of problem solving students generally were avoiding, especially where there were no rules, guidelines, instructions, or right and wrong. Also, it would show that someone cared about her enough to help her, and that would mean a lot to her. If I fixed it, on the other hand, it would have been because I had to fix it, it was my job; though had enough time gone by, I probably would have fixed it; regardless, it would not have had the same effect. Fortunately a solution came.

Slowly and deliberately in his particular way, that boy said to me, "I'm going to try and fix that thing, Mr. Miller. I don't know how I'm going to do it, and I don't know how long it's going to take, but I'm going to do it." I said, "That is so cool. Let me know whatever help you need but you'll get it." He was not proud of his math skills in the beginning of the year and halfway through the year, he pointed out to me that he noticed his skills improving and he noticed himself being able to solve problems faster than before. And here he was taking on one of the more challenging, definitely most real problem we had. You may think this task seems quite small to be considered such a big problem, and I assure you there were other technically larger problems in the program, but this was really the first one I could not find an easy way to solve. My solution was hoping that a student would take on this project for the right reasons. But that solution was completely out of my hands and I had to just wait and hope for it to happen.

That boy attacked the thing with a vengeance. He was busy taping up straws, restringing straws, running paper clips through straws, and it was exciting because he was telling me about it as he was going through with it. When he first started the project, he realized how hard it was going to be, and he told me so, but assured me he was committed to fixing it. While there had not been a whole lot he committed to during the year, the things he did commit to, fixed my confidence in him. One day a few weeks earlier, out of the total sky blue he asked me about abstract art, and launched into a project where he studied abstract artists and then went about creating his own abstract drawing, and was very difficult for him to even conceive of abstraction. For him to go and to try to create, in a subconscious style and influence, art like this, when he had never even drawn before, was an excellent challenge. For the drawing he worked on, he colored with pencils and he put about fifty hours into it, logging his time and writing an essay on it. I never thought he had it in him till he did it. It rocked and impressed me.

So there was no doubt in my mind that he was sticking through to the end with this girl's project and his project of fixing it. And now that we had a student start it, I could totally help out, join in, and do whatever was needed. I wanted someone else to have the motivation to help a student in need; I wanted a student who would inspire. I wonder if you can understand the reason I could jump in and help, but not be the person to initiate the repair. I am not even sure of the exact psychology myself, I only know the repair, and hence the dodecahedron would have nowhere near the same value if I did it as if another student did or at least started it. And this boy did not even need my help. He didn't even work on anything else for the next day or two. I think he even asked the English Teacher's permission to get out of his class to work on this thing, which I supported, especially given the social aspect of the project he was undertaking. If only I had a camera on the girl when Matt finished the project, then that would have ruled. Even when he started building support for the dodecahedron to stand on its own, she perked up and got curious. Even when he said he was going to do the project, I noticed her happiness, and she wasn't usually an overtly happy person. But when he finished that project for her, it may have been one of my proudest teaching moments ever. I think it was a wonderful undertaking.

Her smile and happiness were priceless: it was the precursor to the "priceless" Visa commercials before they happened. The rest of the year and the rest of her life she gained a sense of pride, confidence, and trust, which, I think had gone missing for some reason. I could tell how hard it was for her to say "thank you" to the boy. It was again like when "the Fonz" goes to apologize and cannot materialize the words; he keeps trying and you know he wants to say the words, and you want him to, but they just won't come out. That was what it was like for this girl; she said it quietly but clearly, and I think my heart melted one grade that day. Those kinds of things, my goodness: what someone might pay to have that feeling, be part of that, watch it, even know people have those kinds of moments, and kids no less. We are blessed. So you can see so many of the benefits that came from this one project. What was super cool was when the kids would finish their projects, back before the tragedy struck. It was fun watching for me, and I think for the students as well: every few days someone else would finish it and would come into class to show me. (They worked on this project on their own in other classrooms once they got the hang of it, which was a skill set I was trying to build). They would come in beaming with the completed project and I could tell it was a happiness and pride they hadn't experienced too recently because a part of their expression was surprise at completing it! Other students would then ask questions like how long it took, and how they did it, and usually the answer was something involving a long time and a lot of patience.

So in that Destinations program, morning was supposed to be class time and afternoons were set aside for project work. The way the projects started was like this. Originally I created a "Project Framework Sheet", which is not included in here for two reasons. First of all I can't find it, which is surprising but not too annoying to me. But a better reason, really, is that I think it was too much. You'll hear how grand it was shortly. Just know that its replacement, in Appendix F, the "Individual Project" sheet, is simpler, fresher, and hot off the press. It's much more user friendly and efficient both for teacher/parent and student/child. It can be started and used very easily, and used in the exact same respect the other sheet was. If there are other things you want to add to the sheet, or take away, feel free. I'm not too attached to it. Back when I was using the old project sheet, I went through the entire sheet, or as much as I could, with every student upon their entrance to Destinations. With some of the students who were already bright, positive, and had interests of their own, even before coming into the program, we were able to start this process during their interview. One of the questions we asked students in the interviews was what outside interests and/or hobbies they might have. I brought the old "Project Framework" sheet to the interview of students who started in Destinations after the first term ended. (We took no new students until the second term, and then tried, succeeding pretty well, to take students only between terms, and not during them, so students could start the rotation of classes together and learn curriculum in line with each other). For those students who had interests they brought out in the meeting, I would discuss with them projects they might be interested in, and note it.

For the rest of the students, in the beginning of the year it was hectic. I had to get through 40 students in two days, sitting with each student for about 20 minutes to try and figure out what each was interested in learning about, how she was going to find information, how she was going to present to the program, and too many other categories which governed the self-starting of a project. The main point was to get the student on a track she could start the project, and check in with a teacher periodically to monitor progress, give guiding ideas, and make suggestions. That was because I knew that once the year started, it would be harder to get the one-on-one time necessary to monitor student progress on projects. After our post-lunch meeting, we went to Individual credit time. During this time students could be working on one of three things, though there were other intermittent activities and classes that took place during this time, like a health class, yoga class, and occasional Physical Education.

I should mention as a side note, this is one of the things I cut from the year before in Destinations, when I went up. Even worse for them, I think, than removing the couch and the TV which served as their video game console, was that I removed the afternoon PE at the beginning of the year. They used to go down to the gym every day around 2:00 and have a free for all; there were footballs flying everywhere and basketballs launching: 80,000 games going on at once with hacky sack in the middle. Somehow no one ever really got hurt; seriously this is one of the most chaotic environments I have witnessed. I know this because many days I was in there with them; I would bring in my IPASS students and we would play together, and I was usually in the hack circle in the middle, playing with the kids, learning the lowdown on everything going on, and that was before I was in Destinations, so I really got to know the kids well.

So anyway during that afternoon time, all the kids were working on their individual project, which was always my first choice for them, or their individual credits, or working with a teacher on projects. Some students also liked getting help on material learned from the morning, (this was more with the English Teacher; I preferred to keep these times separate and distinct). Their individual credits meant the textbooks that they were working out of at the 300 page rate. I always recommended and preferred the project for them to work on, but I knew it required more self-motivation, which is not necessarily easy to come by, especially with high school students. So this was the time I got to meet with students and work with them one on one on their projects. This meant I would check their progress, and see what they might need help with, what resources they might need help getting, or where they might be stuck. The students rarely came to me of their own accord. They would much prefer to leave it on the back burner and forget about it and hope the same forgetfulness would happen with me, as I'm sure they had established a clear pattern of success strolling down this avenue of planned forgetfulness, and finding gold. Clearly this was not going to be the case on my street. There were a few who occasionally came voluntarily and told me how they were doing, and this was such a fantastic feeling and sight: to see students who got it on their own and ran with it, the greater reality was that in the meeting after lunch, which I believe we called appropriately "lunch meeting", I would, among other announcements, say I was checking in with Mike, John, and Mark today on projects; then I would sit with them and discuss.

Also, the initial meeting was always the most fun. That was where the student got to decide what in the world they wanted to learn about. There were a few particular meetings with certain students, where the meetings were kind of like pulling teeth, and they had no idea what they were interested in. In those cases, every question of, "Do you like photography?" or "Do you have any hobbies?" resulted in a negative answer. I always found, though, that with persistent prying and questioning I could find something of interest to the student that would start the process. At that point the spark was always hot, looking like it would fan into a flame, but, as I learned throughout the year, we needed more teachers intimately involved in the students' projects to keep accurate tabs and accounts of who was working on what, when, and getting which time line goals accomplished; it's a lot of work.

It would have helped if each teacher had a plan of how they wanted to monitor projects, because I had too much authority and control in that arena. Then there would be more modification, updating, and innovation going on, advancing the whole process. It would have been better if I sat with all the teachers and discussed the sheet and what we were looking for from the students; but there was never the time for that and I came up with the sheet pretty late in the game, again because there was so little time to do so much. I am not sure it would have worked for everyone anyway. The sheet mirrors my thinking style which was rarely linear then. In terms of what would have been best and ideal, in the perfect education world, it would have been if students felt good going to any teacher. That would have gotten more projects off the ground quicker, especially in the beginning of the year. Such is the way of learning to fix an academy; it's all good. In the ideal situation, it would be all teachers should sit with every student and be involved as initial planners for their projects. If that is not possible, which is highly probable, the next ideal would be if all teachers could share information about all the different student projects going on, with each other, so that any teacher would be more able to help any student with his or her project. It would give students better access and guidance and would quickly improve teacher guidance in project advisory. It would also be that much harder for students to slip under the radar in terms of project progress because there would be many pairs of eyes on them instead of only one pair.

So about this project framework sheet, aka the "project skeleton" or "project outline sheet", more clarification is required, if for no other reason than I put so much work into it. But really it's good to get an idea of the organization, monitoring, and planning that should be involved when doing projects with students or children. The sheet in its original spreadsheet form was quite a work of art, in a manner of speaking. I enjoyed that complicated project sheet from an organizer's point of view, but it was a bit overwhelming. This sheet included all possible parts of what I could imagine a project would need. I planned out every detail what they would undertake as their project through the sheet. This was useful in helping students first and foremost choose something they were most interested in and commit to it. A definite percentage of the frameworks they created were never used; students often went in other directions from what they originally intended, but it had other benefits regardless. First, it clarified interests. In getting student to commit to a course of study for their individual project, it is one thing to say it in the interview when a person might agree to anything to get into a program in which they want to enroll. It is another thing altogether to get to the project and make it happen. This sheet gave them a sense of recognition of the direction they would be heading with their project and the specifics they would be studying for it; it focused them, and reminded them this was a goal they aimed to achieve.

It also served as a major beam in the support structure of the program. To me it is important that students always have work they can do, and something they should be working on at any time of the day, especially in an alternative program which varies in its structure from a standard program. I did not ever want a student to say she had nothing to work on, and this sheet was one of the eternal answers to that statement. So one of the things I told the students in the meeting when we planned their projects during their initial days in the program, was that they should check in with me regularly every two weeks or so about their projects. Since I taught classes in the morning, my afternoon was devoted to project coaching. Students rarely sought me out in the beginning of the year, so I set up a schedule of sitting with two or three per day. That was a good system to get all the students regularly and it worked well.

There are many points to reach on the project framework sheet. It is not really possible to get through the whole thing in the twenty minutes you might be allotted to meet with a student in the first days of school, which makes the new sheet so much more effective in this respect. If you add many things to this sheet, as in more than what's on it already, then when you meet with your students or children, I suggest looking over the project sheet and choosing several points you want to go over with them. I would say no matter what, include as mandatory for them a follow-meeting date and time. That way you won't have to rush through the whole thing like I did, sometimes leaving the student not even knowing what he was going to work on for his project, as he leaves that first meeting. This is one of the most important points I noticed to include in the meeting: exactly what three things the students would do on the project when they left that meeting. When you meet the student next it is easy to check in and see if they completed the tasks they took on. Of course, write that information for them and you.

I also felt it essential to discuss in the first meeting, source types students would be using for the project, because that is usually the first step in the process, and often the most daunting for students. One of the hardest things for me, in working with the majority of the students, was getting them to pick out reading materials to use for the process, independent of the internet. They have become obviously dependent on the internet and that is understandable to an extent considering the times. For my projects I assign to students, though, I generally want to commit to including non-internet sources. It's useful for students to be able to harmonize those different types of sources into one coherent product, but the resistance from students is difficult. They need to be able to read and use printed materials.

The other part of the skeleton which I thought was good for student confidence was discussing a time line, because a project can seem so large and inexact. I found, after discussing with them for a bit, that I could comfortably ask students what they thought was a reasonable amount of time to complete the project, and rarely did a student ever say the whole year. At the same time, this simple question and opportunity empowers them, giving them ownership over this creation and study they are undertaking. It also makes it easier to check in with them, to find out if they are keeping up with what has become their time line. Most projects can be completed in one term with proper study, planning, and attention. It is usually only long-term projects that will need to go longer than that. They can be planned that way.

I do not think we had any projects that went through the whole year. Well I guess technically the yearbook project went the whole year, but it was to go even two years because it never got completed or off the ground. The trick with that project was finding out where and how we were going to bind the books, because taking pictures was relatively easy. Two students went about surveying everyone to find out "Best Dressed" categories and so on. But it never came to fruition because they never figured out how to actually make the book, which was what I told them from the beginning, had to happen first! It was a valiant attempt and hopefully the first yearbook could be a two multi year book and include pictures from various years. Oh well, you win some and lose some, and not all projects succeed.

In looking at large projects especially, it is not easy to implement, while the projects are not already rolling. That can be understood from the previous examples of getting projects off the ground. But another part that's possibly most difficult for a teacher, and most confusing for students, is how to assign the credit properly. To really have student buy-in on the project, you have to convince the students that it's worth their time credit-wise, or else why would any student voluntarily take on a project of epic caliber? Of course we want to answer that it's for sake of knowledge and learning. But it's a lot harder, and they work in many different arenas than they're used to. You are forcing them to learn about themselves, to monitor their own work, impose their own guidelines and parameters of success, and take responsibility for their education. Why would they take that option, when they could just fill in some blanks and match some answers? In our case in Destinations it worked because I told them that was part of the program they were applying for, and they would be responsible for at least one project during the year, which they would have to complete on their own, under the supervision of a teacher. And that was that. I had seen the success these types of projects could build in low self-esteemed students and I also knew the initial and continual resistance that was often given in the process, but the benefits were too great and too well-proven for me not to use this fantastic tool with these students. I knew that if I wasn't strict with it, and mandate it as part of their entrance to the program, either they or the other teachers would let this essential building block of a great alternative education program slip away, and there would be little foundation left for individual self development.

Of course the program would manage without this component and students would learn curriculum, but the individual project is a place where students can learn so much about themselves. And for students like these who haven't figured themselves out yet, haven't found themselves, and haven't found something about themselves they think is great, special, wonderful, worth sharing with the world, or at least being positive about, it is absolutely necessary to find that special thing or quality they have within them. Then we can bring it into the light so that the student can feel good about himself. They feel good because of the quality and interest that has been fostered, nurtured, and developed, and for the pride of achievement that comes from accomplishing a goal, and specifically a goal or set of goals set by the person himself, planned out in an organized and functional manner, and followed out through its fruition to the completion of a solid, well created and researched project. That's what projects can do.

There is so much to talk about with project-based learning, that's probably why this is such a long chapter. The individual projects that students created in Destinations Academy were fantastic. Pretty much every student did a project, (a few surprisingly escaped my piercing and hawkish administration of this obligation). To describe the thirty projects that got completed would be a fifth book unto itself. So maybe I can give a taste of a couple different types of completed projects to give an idea of the diversity and range available to learning in this format. And please remember, parents, that all of can easily be administered at home as well; it just takes discipline and focus, which is what teachers use. There is no monopoly on these skills; they are free for the taking and usage. One of the last projects to be completed in my time at Destinations was also one from the boy who completed the first project on football team names. I don't know that we would have seen a project like this in too many other states, and most certainly not in New Jersey. I was able to give some slack in this area because as mentioned, he had already completed his obligatory project for the year so this was icing on his cake, so to speak.

For his final project, this boy presented a project on the process of tanning an elk hide, and he actually brought in the elk hide during various stages of the process while he was tanning it, as it takes days or weeks to do. Of course he brought it in as well at its completion, which was very cool to see. It was wild to learn the process from a student and to see the hide's transition. He also did a project on a career as a "Spligetty" professional, which involved telephone and cable installation. He was a project super star, in reality, and was a total project model for the whole class. I hope he reads this. Another student did a project on "The Fibonnaci Sequence", which is a series of numbers, which, when translated to paper, form a perfect spiral, and this pattern is found repeatedly in nature. One student did a project on elephants, and she presented the final information in the form of a desk-size paper machete elephant. It was wild, and one of the more fun presentation styles. Other students did PowerPoint presentations, and one that especially stood out was from a bright student who researched other inhabitable planets.

There were other projects we did during the year, but much more discussion on it would get this sounding too much like a letter of application for a teaching position. The point is: project-based learning works, and it brings out something special in almost every student which they usually didn't know was there before. It is a fantastic process to watch and to be a part of. The teacher or parent needs to be a part of the process throughout, and in so doing gets to know students and children in different ways from any kind of typical environment. Children benefit in ways I never imagined. I really got to do this with so much freedom only one year. In my years prior to Destinations, when I worked downstairs in AIMS/IPASS, I first really got a taste of project-based learning, I was able to do some neat project work with my classes. We had a couple exciting studies, and some fun experiments, but those classes were smaller and less driven. I got super cool projects done there with those conditions.

The first project students did in IPASS was pretty exciting. It was part of a country wide contest, where we entered to win a prize. It was the "Let's Get Real" competition and I believe it is still in existence. The way it worked was that companies would submit challenges to Let's Get Real, with incentive prizes for the best proposal. When we began our entry, there were about five different companies offering challenges. Most of them were very high tech and complicated, and above my level of understanding, which made it way above my students' abilities. These contests were open to students across the country with great prizes including cash and computers and an inclusive trip across the country to the company site. The contest we entered was sponsored by Hershey, and would have won us a trip to Pennsylvania which would have been the furthest these students had ever traveled by far. They were excited and motivated; at the time we entered, we had only two kids enrolled in class so it was easy to make it happen. It was my first high school level guided project so I was really learning a lot too.

The task presented which we were to propose solutions to, was how to save Hershey energy at a low cost in their general productions. We had to submit a professional-like proposal. One of the biggest helps was using one of Microsoft's templates to guide us through the process. The business proposal template turned out to be the most useful for us, and we pretty much just went through all the slides, and did our best to obtain the necessary information. We hit roadblocks along the way, which is always fun and interesting, the funniest of which was that when we called Hershey to get information about their systems. We informed them of why we were seeking the information but they wouldn't give it to us; this seemed like a limiting factor considering we were trying to help them in our entry. The other most limiting factor was that as class size grew it got to be more difficult doing the project together. I didn't have the means, knowledge, or skills to have a bunch of independent projects going on at that time, so it was pretty much all of us working on the one entry. I have a good memory of six or seven high school boys crowded around my computer, (this was my first year of teaching there, when I didn't yet have other computers in my classroom), and trying to keep everyone's attention on this one project.

The other funny part of the whole endeavor was in our solution. We independently and originally came up with the idea for putting floating buoys in the ocean that would use magnets to generate energy, and this was back in 2005. That was our main solution for generating cheap energy and we proposed possibilities for similar use in rivers. It was a really cool idea that could actually work. The next year I read an article how they were doing just such a thing in Sweden, I believe it was. Then the following year there got to be a great debate in Oregon because they were thinking of putting these same types of energy buoys out in the ocean, and the debate was whether the buoys would interfere with commercial fishing and other water activities. I'm sure they were already doing the research and experimentation on these energy buoys when we were researching but it was cool that we came up with the idea on our own! The students thought that was great, but they were definitely wondering about, asking about, and waiting for their cut in this "cutting edge" technology, figuring they earned it with their original idea!

The student, for the record, who was one of the main two students working on that project, was my first high school student to graduate from high school. He was also the first person to ever graduate high school from his family. He had a massive attendance problem. He would be there regularly and then be gone for days and days. We had to create a contract, I mean the principal, the boy, his family, and I, about what kind of attendance he was going to have if we were going to keep him in the program. He was the nicest kid in the world, but he would just miss so much school it was hard to validate his being enrolled. I never knew the official reason for his absences but I have strong ideas. I remember hearing a lot that he had many dentist appointments. This made sense later in the year when he had to have one of his top front teeth removed as it had been rotted away. That was a tough time I think before he got the cap. He never complained, but I always felt and wondered if he had any feelings of things he could have changed to prevent that. But other than the first day I saw him sans tooth, it didn't seem the case. I must say though when he graduated, at the end of my second year in Coos Bay, it was one of the proudest moments I have felt in my life. I was given the honor of presenting him his diploma which meant that I would also get to speak on his behalf to the audience. It's hard to argue the case for a more praised student: I showered it on him. I still have a picture he gave me of him in his cap and gown and me at the podium singing his qualities. As an aside, that year I was also given the honor of being the guest speaker. I spoke of optimism and positivity, and on possibilities and opportunities for students.

One other thing about projects that I need to mention is something that this Let's Get Real project illustrated well, and that is the fact that students can earn credits in multiple subjects at the same time. Sometimes, since they are doing so much leg work and what not, they can earn credits faster than standard seat work. Seat work involves answering questions prepared for a person, so when the student prepares all the work themselves they are justifiably earning more credits per hour than if they were just completing work that was already prepared and presented. It is a higher level on Bloom's Taxonomy where really students are doing at or above college level work. The proof of this is really the resistance offered by students in doing this work even when they knew they would get more credit per hour. That's because it is much easier to do work that's presented, knowing when they completed a certain number of pages they would get a certain number of credits. It involves less thought too.

My first projects that I did as a public school teacher were in Jefferson, and most involved bringing in outside specialists to guide the students. Allow me first tell the story of the first art project that *did* work with alternative education students. This, for the record, is the reason I was so positive and enthused later about the opportunity to do a mural project in Coos Bay, (which led to the "Mushroom Mural" which might still be hidden in the caverns of Harding Learning Center). In the first two years of my teaching experience at Jefferson School District, while living in Corvallis, I brought in some interesting guest speakers/teachers. I brought in a politician, a violinist, a photographer, a beekeeper, a rock band, and an artist. These were all friends or acquaintances of mine; I met a lot of people. I thought it good for students to be exposed to different cultural aspects from what they were used to, especially growing up in an isolated farm town. The sessions went very well. The artist unit was a series of classes that culminated in the design, creation, and painting of a mural. The artist put together a proposal for my boss who was the Director of our program, and this included a budget, a schedule of classes, a time line, an expected completion date, and an idea of what the completed work would entail.

The first few classes with this artist, which happened once a week, were about painting techniques and color work, and laying some foundations for ideas for the mural. The students drew things they thought they would like to include in the mural. Then the artist, Willow, synthesized these pictures into one coherent mural and submitted it to the students for approval and/or editing, and they liked it. She drew the outline of this picture on a wood board, and the students painted the entire board, which was about three feet by four feet. It came out great: there was a basketball and hoop on it, the year, name of the class, and some cool designs. As best as I know, it still hangs outside the cafeteria at Jefferson Middle School. It was planned, run, and supervised well; it was a great model of smooth project-based learning.

Now for a few more details about the earlier project I mentioned which I wrote about under the "Boundaries" chapter; this was with the artist who decided to nurse during her interview. The artist in question who came in to Destinations was a friend of one of the teachers, as I understand it. She came into the meeting with a portfolio of previous work she had done, most of which had been with very low-level students, much lower than anyone we were equipped to deal with, as in severely disabled. I understood from that meeting that students would be writing about their lives, feelings, and needs, among other aspects of social thought, and incorporating those writings into a three dimensional art project. The interesting thing about this project, and probably the reason it would have been hard to reject at any rate, was that it was free. Some agency was providing this artist with a stipend for supplies and pay for her time, so there seemed to be little way to lose. Still to this day I believe the project had good merit, but it got murky along the way. I am sure I have suppressed some of the memories of that project. In the beginning it was hard to get student volunteers for this; they had no idea what was involved, and how much credit was offered. We figured out along with the credits would be a lot, as they would spend a couple of days a week, a couple hours at a shot, for a term (our planned time frame). They used art, social studies, and writing so we could give them credit in all of those subjects, and we hoped for about three credits per student out of this thing. It was a risky endeavor and on their parts too; this turned out to be one of the cementing and recruiting grounds for the Dark Riders; all of them were in it; they found a bond with an artist girl who was in the program, who was their cohort.

The project got off to a slow start. For a few weeks they were free painting and free writing it seemed, and there was nothing concrete going on; for a couple months it was really like this, with a series of small pictures being created by students. Apparently, she was introducing them to art, and trying to get them comfortable with expressing themselves. The time line was lagging way behind where it was supposed to be and the principal got involved since it seemed the students were getting nothing out of their time. The few pictures that were produced were often drug related and didn't seem appropriate for school. So this is alternative education and this is the place the lines and rules can really stretch. This is what we got cautious about and even told the artist that we didn't want to have drug related themes going into this, since it was being planned to display in our school. We hoped to have a positive theme out of it, something inspiring. In the end I know the students got a lot out of it, and that was positive. They put a lot into it, which in itself was a big accomplishment, for them to focus on one project for so long. Even the experience of negotiating the ideas and concepts they wanted into the mural and working with the authorities (us) to meet their needs and form some happy compromise, was an excellent experience in project-based learning which formed useful life skills. While there were parts of the process that were questionable or risqué, I wouldn't pass up the chance to do it again; I'm happy with the outcome. Most important we created a lasting learning experience and a positive self-affirmation which helped them express themselves and believe in their abilities, even the dark riders!

Now to bring this project situation to the present, and to, believe it or not, start to wrap up this chapter, in my first year at West Orange High School, I didn't succeed in getting anyone to do projects, but that's really not a surprise. Projects are hard, as you can see from all the explaining I had to do about them, and they require more original thought, effort, focus, and work, than standard classroom work; and since there are not such clear parameters, they can seem overwhelming. But more than anything the difficulty in the first year in West Orange was that I couldn't just give them real high school credit for projects the way I did back in Oregon; that is an interesting contrast between states. I wonder if there are schools in New Jersey, (there must be), where credits are more freely given based on projects with parameters determined by teachers. There must be such schools, but I doubt the teachers have the same freedom in awarding high school credit that I did; I had pretty much total freedom in credit determination. On the other hand my second year in West Orange saw my first ever high school student projects created completely independent of any quest for credit, by a student who already had a solid and locked "A" for the term, and just wanted to do it; that tops Oregon projects in many respects!

In integrating this into mainstream classes, it is important to have some kind of project option within the regular class curriculum. Ideally it is a project that all students must do, and there can be variability and flexibility within the guidelines of the project. There can also be extra credit projects for enrichment, but these can be a hard sell in a regular high school classroom environment. The projects should be relevant to the current instruction and interesting to students, allowing them to explore further and in depth by their skill and interest. The projects within the afternoons of the Destinations Academy were much more difficult for me to organize back in Oregon, which, as a state, is not so organized. The classroom projects were all under my jurisdiction, guidance, and assignment, so it was only I who monitored and rewarded credit for them, which made things much more easily controlled and managed. Without that flexibility it requires more organization and documenting which takes a lot of fun out of it.

Conversely, the projects in the afternoon in Destinations were technically under the supervision of all the teachers in the program, which could have numbered four depending how we counted. Teachers are not often too excited to do projects: teachers are usually organized people, and the difficulty with projects is they don't necessarily follow a specific pattern or routine. Even the most organized projects with the most specific parameters and guidelines generally require more flexibility, tolerance, patience, and understanding than a standard assignment. The result of all this is that the projects in the afternoon devolved into my jurisdiction, for the most part, with help from the other teachers. In certain respects this made things more difficult, because there wasn't enough time to meet with all the students. On the other hand it forced me into really getting to know project-based learning and so I have it as a rock as part of my teaching repertoire. I intend to always have my students doing projects, regardless of the challenges or obstacles. Hopefully more teachers will become eager to implement project-based learning, so that it become more common and standard for our students, children, classrooms, and homes; it is a challenge for sure, but the benefits will be great. Some of the biggest restraining factors for teachers are things like being afraid of assigning credit improperly, managing the project, and creating guidelines, among others. It's getting harder and harder in certain respects to do projects at the upper ages, too, since we are getting more unified, more standardized assessments, and heading toward standards that are uniform across the state and country. Projects don't fit too well into that kind of model and require a very special care, attitude, attention and effort on the teacher's part.

20
SHARPEN YOUR SENSES

Pay close attention and know everything going on all around you. It takes effort, work, and consistent dedication to sharpen senses, and you want to keep getting better. It seems difficult to teach this. Modeling is probably the way people learn, and being that most of you can't be there with me to watch me teach, (not that I'm such an expert), hopefully the colorful illustrations of my exploits in the classrooms of America can help you to glean modeled ways to implement these skills. What you really need to do, and believe me it is possible at any age (I think) to sharpen your senses, is to work a little harder in paying attention, (not that your vision will necessarily go from 20/30 to 20/20), but you can notice more. You can see more. You can hear more. You can become more aware. Even sharpen your sense of touch, which obviously doesn't affect a teacher so much in its basic sense. But if you pay more attention to your body and awareness all of the time, this will serve to heighten your general awareness. It will make you keener in the classroom or your home, and more aware of what's going on. You will catch more, and in the end, you will prevent things from happening. That's because you will see and hear things happening beforehand; you can predict them, cut them off or affect them; and you will make your classroom or home a safer and more positive place by being more alert and more conscious.

I emphasize: you must pay more attention with your hearing and seeing. I write "seeing" and "hearing" as verbs, because they are active actions; you don't want to wait to see whatever is in your field of vision or range of hearing; you have to look and listen. And one of the tips of this chapter, for the maximum educational benefit, is not to let on that you're listening or watching until you need to point out some information you garnered. That's not because we're stalking our students or children; it's because in the long run, if you can catch a problem while it's small, you can correct it and educate the person, instead of its turning into a big problem. The only way to describe this process is to tell you that you have to work harder, listen more carefully, and try to put words together you think you hear, and analyze them. You have to watch carefully what you see, and think about it;

make conjectures about what you're seeing and hearing while you're observing, until you know that you are right. I can give an example or two of how sharp senses headed off problems before they turned into problems. I don't like to let problems grow; nipping them in the bud is the best way. Some of the best examples in my memory of these types of "head-off" situations involve Dark Riders, masters of hearing and seeing.

Sometimes the only thing that can bring light to the Dark Riders is time. I believe them to be deep in the mire and entrenched in their circumstances to the point that there is no sudden easy extrication even if they desired it; and I don't think it's really desired, at least not on a conscious level. So all we can hope sometimes with these kinds of students, is that eventually the conscious self will connect with something deeper than the superficial world they think to be the true world, and that they can begin the process of healing. This is pretty philosophically deep for a paper on education, but if one is going to try to understand alternative education, it is going to involve some serious speculation on the root of the psyche of students. And while one will not always guess correctly, hopefully the percentage of accuracy improves over time. Even if the estimate was incorrect, the teacher takes a chance and learns one way or the other, information about the students that enables him to consistently improve his teaching style. This also helps parents and teachers connect with students in a meaningful way, enabling children, more importantly, to connect to parents and teachers. In this respect the teacher will serve as a bridge to the rest of the world, and that is what kids need: to connect to an educator and be inspired for a lifetime. That's because, really, most of these students have become, and especially so in the case of the Dark Riders, disconnected from, disenchanted with, and disenfranchised by, the rest of the world. We are their bridge back to it. If we fail them, they remain separate. And at this time in their lives, that seems just fine with them; they're OK to let it happen. In a certain respect, that's what they want, or what they think they want, or at least what they act like they want. These are the Dark Riders, the separate ones.

That is quite an explanation on Dark Riders veering a tad off the topic, but it's good background for the story on illustrating the ways sharp senses headed off a problem at the pass and kept things calm. Many of these students are, though not always, into drugs. During this one particular period of time when the story took place, the Dark Riders had gotten a hold of some psylocybin mushrooms and had been into them for a few days. I am not sure what days they took them or if they were on them this particular day, but I noticed a change in their personalities over a few days, to where they clustered and separated themselves even more than usual. They were whispering to each other constantly and giving odd awkward looks and expressions to teachers and avoiding us constantly. I knew something was very awry. The student who the story centers around, was a student I had for two years in AIMS/IPASS, and also the student I had to remove from the mentor program as he was not following the right path as a model. In the beginning he was into a gothic style and culture; he had always wanted to play guitar, so he started learning, and finally getting a little feel for it. His favorite joke, which I later learned was from "Family Guy", was to play the theme from *The Hulk* on guitar as someone walked away. It was funny.

So that is more background on the boy. On this particular day, coincidentally, when he was building in rage or something was very off, we were being visited by an accreditation committee from the state of Oregon. This happened every few years where several people came down from Salem, the capital, to watch a day in the life of our program. They spoke with students, teachers, and administration, to decide if we had something worth keeping, and if we were in line with state laws and regulations such that we could continue our existence. Needless to say the pressure was high; especially since our program had only that year undergone a complete renovation and change, and was still really in a state of flux. So these people were walking throughout the program which as I mentioned, consisted of several rooms. I was in the main triple room, on my side of the room, teaching math; it was the geometry project where students were cutting out geometric shapes in positive negative space, using art to show properties of negative and positive numbers. The boy was in a dark mood. The day before, our principal confronted him about some drug use issues that came up: he had passed out in our building kitchen while baking cookies with a class, seemingly from the aforementioned mushrooms.

The Dark Riders pride themselves on, if nothing else, their ability to skim under the radar; they love to fly as close as possible to the law or trouble, and not get caught. They liked to create their own world right there within the mainstream, (which in our case was already not mainstream as we were an alternative program, which to them was still mainstream). They would have little quiet discussions that they probably presumed could only be heard by them and their cohorts. They weren't aware of my sense-sharpening hobbies and pastimes. I won't go into the psychology of their discussions, someone else can read up and analyze; that will be a whole other work. In the course of my teaching, however, I have made it a prime goal to NOT let anything get by without my hearing it. A couple students asked me different times how I did this; they were amazed I could hear things that seemed impossible to hear. Sometimes it's a matter of putting together the consonants I *do* hear with pauses in speech, to recognize words and sentences. Whatever the process is, I got pretty good at it and very little gets by my ears.

I was sitting at the table with this boy and the two main other Dark Riders were at the table as well, and they were working on these negative space projects. I had a class of about fifteen kids there and I was rotating among the student tables, checking progress, and seeing how they were doing with their work, while occasionally speaking with the committee members. At this moment, while I was at the table with the Dark Riders, one of the committee members was also in my classroom, not ten feet behind me. Most likely the reason he didn't hear any of what followed in his close presence was that he did not have his hearing tuned in so carefully. Regardless, another factor purposely preventing his overhearing what followed was that I had nearly mastered, from working with these kind of students, the art of "quiet speak", where only those you intend to hear your words, hear what you are saying, and it's not whispering. I am confident that if he heard our conversation Destinations Academy have ceased being.

As a side note about hearing and seeing what goes on, and a means to delay the punch line of this story which apparently brings me great pleasure, as I continually insist on dragging the reader through sidebar after sidebar, the students in an earlier year in IPASS had, what for me, became a favorite teaching moment of all time. Occasionally I let go a little with the tongue or wit when a student was just pushing and pushing, or pushing the wrong way. See, pushing is one thing, and pushing and pushing is even fine, but let's be upfront about it, shall we? So we can get to the point and move on. Once, in this IPASS class, I said something to a student, a disciplinary sanction, rebuke, or correction of some sort. In response, the (high school) student who I spoke to, mumbled something under his breath that sounded pretty dark and angry, but he was far away from me and I couldn't hear it clearly. And (as often as an eclipse) came out of my mouth, words spoken without really thinking. I said this: "Mumble... mumble... what?!?" I was even surprised at the suddenness and the humor of it when I spoke it. My goodness, the students thought it was the bees' knees, the best thing since sliced bread. They cracked up, and they kept repeating that line to me for days, they thought it was hysterical! No one heard the boy's first remark, and it didn't matter. I want students to get their good voice and use it. These Dark Riders have been so shut down they only speak in hidden whispers, which is dangerous. Students need to learn what and when they can say and write, and when and what is appropriate in this world. I want commitment; if a student is going to say something, he should say it; not this "grumble, grumble" junk.

So there was this boy in the original story, with the state of Oregon watching us and scrutinizing us. The boy was sitting across from me and I heard his tone in what he was saying, which clued and tuned me in to listen to his words. I guess that is really the first and most important indicator of what to pay attention to: the tone, the expressions, gestures, and the body language the students are giving off; this clues you in to whether to pay extra attention or not. His tone was as dark, cold, and negative as I had heard in a while. He said, "Mrs. _____, [the principal], pretty much called me a 'tweaker', [a slang term for a methamphetamine user and/or abuser], the other day, that's so f---ed up." Without a doubt our principal was there for me 100% of the time with all these students; in fact I had seen her go to bat for this very student numerous times before, when he would have been thrown out of school otherwise. She has a heart of gold, persistence, ideals, and principles, and a love for students unparalleled in my experience. She still calls me every year for my birthday and I'm 3000 miles away! This was my boss! She went to bat countless times for me as a teacher: backing my decisions, (which were consistent, so she wasn't doing it just because I was the teacher); she backed me with parents, even when situations got tense and heated. She always did so with a clear mind and a calm tone. It was amazing and she is a role model of a great teacher and administrator. It was difficult for me to hear this, sit calmly, and to react calmly; but I did. Maybe it was good timing the committee was there right then.

Knowing how much she did for these students, it is something I would not bear well: to hear of my principal such poorly spoken words. So very calmly and (possibly to divert anger and bring it on me, and hence be able to guide that anger), I said something along the lines like, from what evidence had come about, the very case seemed so. This ignited the fury but for some reason, the boy kept his tones hushed. My best guess at why he didn't complete flip out and yell or something was that maybe he had an awareness of the program's possible jeopardy in the circumstances and, despite outward complaints about the program, he truly liked it there, and didn't want to cause its demise. Regardless of my dime store psychology analysis on the matter, he responded to me with hatred whispered to his friends in a voice and volume meant (unsuccessfully) for me not to hear. He said something like, "Now Mr. Miller is calling me a druggie; I should stab him in the eye and burn his house down". I heard it well and clearly.

That was all the evidence I needed to get him out of there; it was enough and plenty more than enough, officially over the edge of acceptable, to remove him from class for the morning. But I was not sure how this would go. So I quietly said, "You need to leave the classroom now." He said, still quietly, but with growing fury, "Why, what did I do?" I told him I knew what he said, and told him that he needed to go down to the office and I would talk with him about it later. I didn't know if he was going to completely lose it at that moment, but he got up and walked out; he tried to slam the door; but the doorstop happened to be there; this kept from his making a scene, and he went down to the office. He went home shortly after that; but not before I spoke to him in the office with the principal and we discussed emotion control and appropriate expression. Somehow the accreditation committee never got a whiff of the whole thing, and we got our accreditation. I guess really, the fact that we could handle situations like that as we did, and maintain control, makes Destinations Academy such the special place that it is.

So that's it in a nutshell. That's how to teach alternative education. That's how to be a better parent and a teacher, according to one person. There's more and so much more. Other people have great things to say. Come up with an acrostic to memorize the chapter titles. Apply some of these basic lessons to yourself. Don't settle for who you are. Become better. I plan to. Keep working on yourself and show your students and children how to do that. Strive to be the best and your best; do it humbly. Be light. Be positive. Be great. Be amazing. Don't think you can't. Believe in yourself. Believe in truth.

APPENDIX A
PHILOSOPHY OF EDUCATION

A good educator has a great variety of attributes, qualities, strategies, methods, and ideas for creating a healthy classroom atmosphere, so students are responsible, self-directed learners. Modeling is probably the most important strength of a teacher. Patience is the most vital quality a teacher can possess. Understanding is the best attribute to help a teacher connect with his students. Strategies and methods should be developed with careful attention to the success and weaknesses of the strategies with respect to different students, classes, and schools, and should be studied and revised regularly. Ideas are generated by intelligent, persistent minds and student connections which excitedly inspire original thought.

Students learn best when the teacher models what he instructs. Children have an audiovisual input model as part of the framework of their world, and are believers in what they see and hear. A teacher's best strength is to demonstrate with actions and words what it is he is trying to teach. He must show students how to act and learn. For modeling to be effective, the students must want to follow the teacher. This begins with basic respect, which a teacher must demonstrate for and towards his students. Being polite and using manners in the classroom goes a long way for students who may not see this at home. Modeling proper methods of speaking and listening, and asking and answering questions creates a safe learning space. This atmosphere must be respected and maintained to assure pride in self, team, and place. Students can then think, learn, and question comfortably, without fear. Guidelines for behavior, conversation, rules, expectations, and other aspects of classroom management must be clearly defined, and reviewed regularly, so students learn academics well, firmly, and efficiently.

Patience and understanding cannot be overemphasized in the roles of a teacher, and they are partners in achievement. A teacher cannot afford to get frustrated with students who do not understand concepts, ideas, or lessons. To keep students involved in the learning process we must give them time for that process. Questions posed by the teacher deserve wait time for answers. Questions will usually be answered in that time period, and often the quiet and slower students answer in the last moments. In trying to reach students, and really wanting them to learn, the teacher's reaching across the gap to them establishes a connection and trust which makes a safe space for students to guess, to answer, to possibly be wrong, and to learn. In reaching across, and being patient, the teacher learns to understand the gaps the student is facing, and becomes a better teacher in understanding the ways to bridge those gaps.

A teacher needs to be constantly thinking, learning, studying, and continuing his own education in order to be an exciting and dynamic teacher in touch with best practices. In so doing, he models the behavior he expects of his students: he creates new lessons and activities, and learns strategies and methods for succeeding with his students. A successful lesson may last a lifetime, but it can be reviewed and improved to make it better. A teacher must continually seek new and better means of teaching. If he chooses older methods, he must still stay current in education and keep learning fresh and exciting for students. His classroom has a charged atmosphere; it keeps the teacher and students originating ideas.

Responsibility and choice compose an important part of the class atmosphere. While academic benchmarks must and will be met, giving students options in their education fosters active learning. Students become more involved and eager to learn when they have an interest and attachment to it. They take ownership of their education and engage in it. Offering a range of activities for students to choose from encourages them to guide their own learning. They take on the quality of being lifelong learners, who are responsible and enthusiastic. They become self-directed and motivated learners and workers, hence productive members of society.

APPENDIX B
EARN REWARDS SHEET

FRONT SIDE

Name _____ Date _____

Grade 5 & 6: _____

Evaluate **A**chievement **R**eward **N**otify

Basic Skills	Score
Journaling: Sentences Written	
Daily Oral Language: Mistakes	
Word of the Day: Definition/Sentence	
Math Problems	
Total Score	

BACK SIDE

Subject x 1.5	Score Today				
Health	5	4	3	2	1
Social Studies	5	4	3	2	1
Physical Education	5	4	3	2	1
Math	5	4	3	2	1
Science	5	4	3	2	1
Reading (DEAR)	5	4	3	2	1

5 = Excellent   4 = Good   3 = OK   2 = Poor   1 = Unacceptable

My Behavior Today was a:
5   4   3   2   1   _____ (Multiply by 7)
My Score Today was a: _____
☐ I did EARN break. ☐ I did not EARN break.

APPENDIX C
SAMPLE PRIZE CARD

**Harding
Learning Center**

Drink / Snack

One time use only

Expiration Date: MM/DD/Y

APPENDIX D
DODECAHEDRA

"Smaller Stellated Dodecahedron"

"Great Stellated Dodecahedron"

APPENDIX E
TIPS FOR YOUR SUCCESS

I'm here today with things to say and trick a tongue to flip
And let you know requirements for recognition trips
So you get by you might survive with tips for your success
If grades were bees these hives would have no tribes of d's and f's
To get success you better bet you better give your best
The rest will fall in jest of life's big test of "better best"
You'll be surprised what you accomplish when you luminesce
What's more you want to score, don't be a bore, just be intent
You must attend, and we won't bend, no unexcused absence
And then behavior just might save your hide to show respect
And though it's hard to track, you better bet we have a check
So no referrals, 2 citations is the most you get
Those are the rules at JM School the tips for your success
You follow them you be OK and no one give you stress
You follow them you be OK and on one give you stress

Now you can make it, do you take it here's a trip to you
It's for the better and the best and for the rest of you
I hope you get yourself together cause there's just a few
Months in the rest of your last year and then for some of you
"What's 1 semester what's the best I can do? None, I guess."
I heard that last year when the last kid failed his final test
He gave excuses they were useless then he dropped I guess

And now he's useless and he's toothless cause he dropped again
So take a shot and make us rock, and do it with a pen
This school is cool and you're a fool if you don't give your best
It's not enough to pull a bluff, you got to pour it in
If you don't fluff I bet you stuff it, slam it, score and win
What's real is tough, and work is rough, but you call "four" and swing
You jump, you throw, you write, you read, you rule, you learn, you win.
And then remember all the roots and good from which you came
And thank above you got the love to keep you free of slips

Now why would Miller spend his thriller time to tell us this?
I'll spill the filler let these thrillers know well it's just this
I put my will to getting thrills and let me reminisce
About the skills it took to fill this world with words like this
See I worked tills and never killed a thing and still I risked
My life when I denied my parents wishes that they wished
To get the high life they reminded me would bring me bliss
But still I tried to find a fine life that would make me sing
And so I find it here surprise it's right in Jefferson
Although I might sit high I'm low enough in life to win
And try as I might my verbs turn to dynamite so give
Yourself a timeout and a second let's just do this thing
cause wire charges till it tires those who cling to it
and we make world so fair and fine, and clean it up a bit
the joy of life and way to live that makes it right for we
To learn and grow in ways we never dreamed that right would be

APPENDIX F
INDIVIDUAL PROJECT

Name _____   Date _____

Estimate of date I want to finish this: _____

Project Possibilities:
1. _____
2. _____
3. _____

The project choice I am leaning towards choosing is:

The reason I would like to learn more about this topic is:
_____
_____
_____

The ways I could learn more about this topic, besides Internet are, (e.g. people, newspapers, magazines, etc.):
_____
_____

The first three things to do for this after this meeting are:
1. _____
_____
Date I will do this by: _____
2. _____
_____
Date I will do this by: _____
3. _____
_____
Date I will do this by: _____

APPENDIX G
MATH RESEARCH PROJECT

Pick a famous mathematician like: Fibonnaci, Pythagoreas, Cramer, Aristotle, Plato, Stefan Banach, Georg Cantor, Joseph Fourier, John von Neumann, Brook Taylor, Archimedes, Euclid, Sir Isaac Newton, Blaise Pascal, Carl Gauss, Aryabhatta, Ramanujam, or any approved mathematician.

1. About the writer: life, history, interesting fun facts, math life
2. About his process of discovery in the math field
3. What his discoveries meant at the time period for the world
4. What his discoveries mean now for the world
5. Does his mathematics manifests in art? If so, demonstrate.
6. How does his mathematics manifest itself in nature, if at all?
7. Why it is interesting and why is he interesting?
8. Why did you choose this mathematician? Was it a good choice?
9. How do his mathematics discoveries affect mathematics now?
10. What branches of math are involved?
11. Include citations.
12. Choose your presentation style if not doing poster.
13. Can you explain/teach this to others, like in a class period?
14. Include questions for the audience to answer.
15. For great credit, include links to National Math Standards.
16. Chart the time you worked with parent initial.
17. Add your own thing here: _____
_____

Make a poster, attach an essay, make it nice to read for the others, include art, pictures and examples.

Date you expect to finish: _____   Date to meet me: _____

APPENDIX H
BEATS PER MINUTE LESSON PLAN

Title: Proving Tempo Counts

Length: 41 Minutes

Objectives: Student will demonstrate successful use of proportions, to prove that counting varied time tempo segments will accurately predict a song's beats per minute.

STANDARD 4.5 (Mathematical processes) All students will use mathematical processes of problem solving, communication, connections, reasoning, representations, and technology to solve problems and communicate mathematical ideas/concepts.

STANDARD 4.5 E. Representations: Create and use representations to organize, record, and communicate mathematical ideas: Symbolic representations (e.g., a formula)

Materials:

- Music player
- Music selections of varied tempos for activity
- "Beats Per Minute" spreadsheet
- Pencils
- Overhead "Infocus" Projector
- Wipe board
- Wipe board markers

Prove that if a song's tempo is counted within a smaller segment of time, it will generate an accurate count of the song's tempo.

Procedure:

1. Ask students if they remember the "counting to one million" discussion and proof that introduced our 2 column proof earlier this week.
2. Introduce topic with discussion of what deejay's do.
3. Discuss different roles and tasks of the job, specifically those using vinyl.
4. Ask how students think deejays keep track of all their records.
5. Discuss different ways of categorizing including genre, tempo.
6. Explain my method of categorizing and labeling records.
7. Discuss different ways of determining the tempo; introduce the concept of "beats per minute."
8. *What is the most logical way to figure out how many beats are in a minute of a song?*
9. Ask students if they can figure out a *faster way to find this information.*
10. Demonstrate an example on the board of counting out the beats of a song with a 30 second time sample. Set up a proportion that models the equation $5/30 = y/150$. Discuss *why this represents what we know about counting beats.*
11. Explain the transitional concept *of using a variable in a different spot in the equation* from what they've been learning.
12. Discuss possibilities of *moving the variable around* to other locations in the equation.
13. Discuss *different time samples available for counting.* Discuss positives and negatives of different length time samples, including *margin of error.*
14. Continue the process with 3 more songs, using sample periods of 20 seconds, 10 seconds, and 5 seconds.
15. Ask students which they think is the *most useable and reliable samples.*
16. Have students complete the chart using 2 more samples per song to determine, with evidence, the best time sample to use for counting beats per minute. They choose the time samples and should try each one at least once more.
17. Students should include an explanation of what time sample they would choose including available time and accuracy of measurement.
18. Students share with each other and teacher the time sample they chose and explain why they chose it.

Assessment:

1. Ask students to agree on a song they can all work on at home. Assign students to complete the chart at home, using their chosen time sample.
2. Next week, students check each other's charts before turning in to teacher and compare for accuracy of their count.
3. Completed work is turned into portfolio to be shared with parent at conferences.
4. These proportions will be added as a category into "Math Jeopardy" played monthly where learned skills are reviewed and reinforced.

Observation of Larry Miller 11/18/2010

Name _____   Date _____

#	Song Title	Time	Beats	Calculations	BPM	Accurate	Useful
1							
2							
3							
4							
5							
6							
7							
8							
9							

#	Song Title	Time	Beats	BPM	Count Error	Margin Error	Yes/No
1							
2							
3							
4							
5							
6							
7							
8							
9							

APPENDIX I
RECOMMENDED BOOKS

When Are We Ever Gonna Use This, by Hal Saunders

Thought Provokers, by Doug Rohrer and Joe Spooner

Fantasy Football and Mathematics, by Dan Flockhart

Problem of the Day, by Michael Lazar & David Hoerger

Smart PAL Guides, by Kevin Simms & Mark Baezt

61 Cooperative Learning Activities in Algebra 1, by Robert H. Jenkins

The I Hate Mathematics! Book, by Marilyn Burns

Slides, Flips, and Turns, by Louis R. Kroner

Designs in Math, by Randy L. Womack, M. Ed.

Mastering Essential Math Skills, by Richard W. Fisher

Consumer Mathematics, by Kathleen M. Harmeyer

Life Skills Math, by Donald H. Jacobs & August V. Treff

Basic Occupational Math, by David Newton

Daily Starters, Journal of the Day, by Linda Bowers

The Pocket Book of Quotations, by Henry Davidoff

The First Days of School, by Harry K. Wong & Rosemary T. Wong

Educational Psychology, by Anita E. Woolfolk

Made in the USA
Lexington, KY
13 October 2013